Saskatchewan
A traveler's guide to the
HiSToRY
fascinating facts, intriguing
ALoNG The
incidents and lively legends
HiGHWaY
of Saskatchewan

Saskatchewan
HiSToRY
ALoNG The
HiGHWaY

A traveler's guide to the fascinating facts, intriguing incidents and lively legends of Saskatchewan

Bob Weber

Red Deer College Press

The Publishers
Red Deer Press
MacKimmie Library Tower, Room 813
2500 University Drive N.W.
Calgary Alberta Canada T2N 1N4

Acknowledgments
Cover design by Kunz + Associates
Text design by Dennis Johnson
Printed and bound in Canada by Webcom Limited for Red Deer Press

Financial support provided by the Alberta Foundation for the Arts, a
beneficiary of the Lottery Fund of the Government of Alberta, and by
the Canada Council, the Department of Canadian Heritage and Red
Deer College.

ALBERTA Lotteries   The Alberta Foundation for the Arts   Alberta COMMUNITY DEVELOPMENT
COMMITTED TO THE DEVELOPMENT OF CULTURE AND THE ARTS

THE CANADA COUNCIL FOR THE ARTS SINCE 1957 | LE CONSEIL DES ARTS DU CANADA DEPUIS 1957

5 4 3 2

Author's Acknowledgments
The author acknowledges the kind assistance of staff at the Provincial Archives of Saskatchewan and the Archives of the University of Saskatchewan. The author also is grateful for the cooperation of the Historic Parks Department of the Government of Saskatchewan and to Saskatchewan government staff who provided texts to the province's network of historic signs and markers. The author also acknowledges the many people in heritage groups and staffing local museums across the province. This project owes much of its life and color to their always generous and often enthusiastic support.

Canadian Cataloguing in Publication Data
Weber, Bob, 1960–
Saskatchewan history along the highway
(History along the highway)
Includes index.
ISBN 0-88995-176-4
1. Saskatchewan—History, Local. 2. Historic sites—Saskatchewan—Guidebooks. 3. Automobile travel—Saskatchewan—Guidebooks. 4. Saskatchewan—Guidebooks. I. Title. II. Series.
FC3511.W42 1998 917.12404'3 C98-910249-1
F1071.W42 1998

Contents

Introduction

On the Trail of Saskatchewan History

Because I was alone and no friend could find,
And once in my travels was left behind,
Which struck fear and terror into me,
But still I was resolved this same Country for to see. . . .

THAT IS HOW SASKATCHEWAN'S recorded history begins, with those doggerel rhymes from the fur trader Henry Kelsey, written as he paddled upriver from Hudson Bay in 1690. The first European to see this country, Kelsey brought on two centuries of exploration, trade and settlement as Europeans spread westward across the continent. Many of those later travelers must have felt the same blend of fear and resolve that he did.

But these vast prairies and forests were not the empty wilderness the Europeans fancied. The Chipewyan, Beaver, Slavey, Cree, Blackfoot, Assiniboine and Gros Ventre had lived here for 12,000 years. This land fed them, sheltered them and, in legends told by rocks and hills, explained how they fit into creation. It was their home and as the European presence became stronger, they fought to keep their place in it.

And this is the source of most of the stories in this book—the gradual absorption of the prairie frontier into western society and what happened when that world was overlaid across an earlier one unwilling to fade. It's a remarkable canvas, full of courage, tragedy, hope, brutality, unlikely friendships, dreams and more than a few old-fashioned frontier tall tales. Its characters include cowboys and fur traders, proud Indians and rebel Métis. Socialist saints, spiritual Czars, frauds, booze kings, big-money dreamers, dilettante party boys, resolute homestead-ers—they all crowd the frame and populate these pages.

In his book *The Middle of Nowhere*, Thomas Gruending divides the history of Saskatchewan into five eras. The first, and still the longest, is the time before Europeans came, when Indians followed the buffalo freely across the plains. With the coming of Kelsey and 200 years of trade and exploration comes the time of the *Great Lone Land*—the title of a book written by a British explorer that exemplifies the idea of the West as an empty land waiting for civilization. The selling of that wilderness to thousands and thousands of eager settlers from around the world marks the stage of the Promised Land. It lasted until the Depression of the 1930s shriveled its dreams with dust and grasshoppers. Good times after World War II and Saskatchewan's long history of cooperation and social experiment brought on the New Jerusalem, a time when the province led the continent in new ideas on making society a better place.

All those ideas of Saskatchewan are represented in this book. So is one not part of Gruending's scheme, an idea that began long ago and still sustains the province today. Call it, as many already have, Next Year Country—a stubborn faith that next year the harvest will bring 40 bushels an acre (.4 ha), the government will behave itself and the province's beloved football team, the Saskatchewan Roughriders, will win the Grey Cup. That faith ensures that Saskatchewan will keep making history.

This book can best be considered an introduction to that history. Dividing the province into its main tourist zones, it fol-lows the major highways, making detours when drawn by some-thing interesting, telling stories along the way. A Saskatchewan highway can indeed be long and flat; the tales it tells are any-thing but. If this volume keeps you entertained while pointing out a bit of history and encouraging you to dream a little about the landscape darting past your windows, it will have done its job.

Chapter 1

The Horseshoe Region

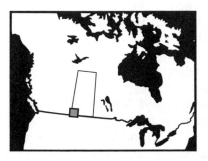

Cowboys
and Indians

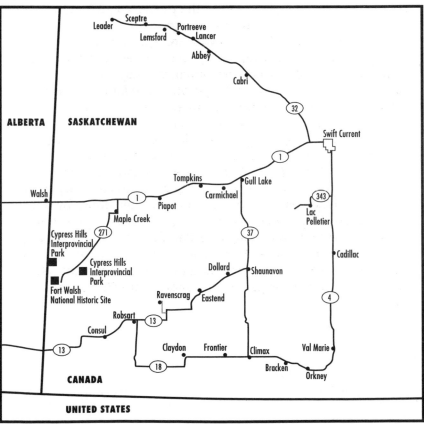

IF SASKATCHEWAN EVER PLAYED cowboys and Indians, this was where. Heroic Mounties, hard-riding range hands, cattle barons with big dreams and free-roaming, buffalo-hunting native bands have all left their stories in this southwest corner of the province.

For generations this was the home of the Assiniboine, Blackfoot, Cree and Saulteaux nations. They hunted widely over the region's shortgrass plains—usually for buffalo, sometimes for each other. But no matter how fierce their rivalry, the cool, forested oasis of the Cypress Hills, the highest point in Canada between the Rocky Mountains and Labrador, was widely considered a zone of peace for all the tribes.

Because the Cypress Hills so far south of the North Saskatchewan River, which was the West's main fur trade and exploration highway, Europeans came late to this area. It was still open buffalo range in 1860, just about the last left in what was to become Canada. But as Indians began to share the range with Métis buffalo hunters and more and more traders from both the Hudson's Bay Company and the United States, the Horseshoe Region became part of what was known as Whoop-Up Country, a lawless region that lived on the trade in whiskey, rifles and buffalo hides.

The Cypress Hills Massacre in 1873 finally convinced the government in Ottawa that the old ways were no longer relevant. They created the North-West Mounted Police (now known the world over as the Mounties) to bring law and order to the West. Here began some of the force's first posts and some of its greatest legends. The police oversaw the peaceful transition from prairie wilderness to productive range and farmland.

It was a big new country that attracted men with big new ideas for making a buck from cattle and wheat. But the prairie was not easily tamed. It's a land that at least one explorer called a desert: hot in summer, cold in winter and dry all year round. Learning how to farm here took generations and broke the heart and bankbook of many a homesteader. The crushing drought and depression known as the Dirty Thirties almost broke the entire region, but prairie grit and a lot of science taught farmers how to stay on the land.

That's the landscape you see today as you drive its highways: healthy herds of cattle, prosperous farms and the small towns that serve them through good years and bad. But the stories are still there, if you know where to look.

ALONG HIGHWAY 32

Horseshoe Smith Thinks Big, Builds Bigger

Grid 741 at junction of highways 32 and 21, 4 miles (6.4 km) west of Leader. Drive north for 5 miles (8 km). Open year round.

Nobody ever accused William T. "Horseshoe" Smith of thinking small. Even when he was a kid back in Kentucky, he always pushed things as far as they could go—like the time he decided to raise rabbits and wound up with so many of them that his neighbors rebelled.

Naturally, the expansive Smith was right at home with the bold, can-do spirit Saskatchewan enjoyed after the turn of the century. He built up a 10,000-acre (4047-ha) ranch with 2,000 acres (810 ha) under irrigation. He grew corn, alfalfa and even experimented with peanuts. He had up to 10,000 sheep, 2,000 hogs and 3,600 horses and mules—branded, of course, with a horseshoe. He was a big man in a big country during big times, and he made sure everybody knew it. And if they hadn't figured it out by 1914, they sure would have after Horseshoe Smith built his amazing barn. That barn was 400' (122 m) long, 128' (39 m) wide and 60' (18 m) high, the biggest one in North America, big enough for a regulation football field and tall enough to kick field goals in. It took 32 carloads of lumber and cost $32,000 to build, money Smith withdrew from the bank in cash, stuffed in a gunnysack and hauled home in the back of a wagon. Gawkers at the construction site clogged the roads as 100 men labored on the project for five solid months. Finally, Horseshoe Smith had it painted white and, for the grand opening, invited hundreds of his friends and neighbors to what may have been the biggest barn dance in history. Two cooks worked for days to prepare food for the throng, and two orchestras played long into the night. A 100-yard (90-m) dash was held inside on the top floor.

Maybe the barn was too big. Holes had to be cut in the roof to keep the hay from rotting, and many of the 1,200 cattle that spent their first winter there died in the damp, drafty stalls. Smith himself later said, "That barn killed me. I wish I'd never built it. It just broke me completely." But the magnificent edifice outlived Horseshoe Smith, who died in 1918 at 73. And when it

William T. "Horseshoe" Smith's amazing barn.

was finally torn down in 1921, settlers were able to salvage 875,000 board feet of lumber.

Today, the foundation is all that remains.

Town Named Out of a Hat
Highway 32, 88 miles (142 km) northwest of Swift Current at Portreeve

---

Perhaps there should have been a few more poets included in all those railway crews that crisscrossed Saskatchewan with ribbons of steel. Along with laying the track that gave many prairie towns their reason for being, the railway men also named many of them. And the task of dubbing settlements that included usually no more than a station and a stretch of siding seems to have strained their powers of verbal invention.

Many towns were named for railway employees or their families. Tompkins, a little south of here, was named for Canadian Pacific Railway man Thomas Tompkins of Brockville, Ontario. Others were named for prominent events or figures of the time: Shackleton, a little farther east on Highway 32, was named for the Antarctic explorer Ernest Shackleton, an officer with the 1901 Scott expedition, and its streets bear the names of polar explorers such as Perry, Amundsen and Franklin. Some names were historically inspired. Lancer, the next town, is named for the men who led the charge of the Light Brigade in the Crimean War. Others, such as neighboring Abbey, named in honor of an Irish village, hearken back to the old country. A long-time settler could supply the town's name, as a pioneer North-West Mounted Police constable and homesteader did for Lemsford.

But sometimes, the railway men couldn't think of a thing and just chose a name from a hat. And that, quite literally, is how the Canadian Pacific Railway named Portreeve.

Big-Time Gusher Saskatchewan's First
Highway 332, 19 miles (30 km) west of highways 32 and 332 junction; turn north at sign on gravel road for about 1 mile (2 km), then turn west for about .6 miles (1 km)

Almost as soon as it had settlers, Saskatchewan had oilmen poking holes in the ground, hoping something other than wheat and sagebrush would come out of the soil. There were wildcatters as far back as 1888 drilling the Belle Plaine area near Regina, only to come up dry. Other dry holes followed in 1906 near Saskatoon. Gas and heavy oil (oil with a high sulfur content) were found near Lloydminster in 1934. But it wasn't until January 4, 1952, in a field just south of here, that anyone struck a genuine hats-in-the-air, big-time gusher.

Norman Elphinstone, geologist on the site, remembers that the first test at about .6 miles (1 km) underground that morning didn't go well. He decided to warm up in the trailer with a cup of coffee. Then, "In a few minutes the . . . driller came up with a smirk on his face and a thick black substance on the side of his hand and said, 'We're in the oil!'"

So they were, and word spread like fire on an oil slick. That evening, Fosterton, Saskatchewan, was in newscasts across the country and in the United States. The next morning, the first of thousands of curious onlookers visited the site, beating the fresh snow down to ice. Hundreds of cars drove by. A plane buzzed overhead. Radio and newspaper reporters crowded around. One newshawk got a grinning rig worker, whose clothes had been soaked by oil when the well blew, to fill a beer bottle with black gold from the surging well. The share price of well owner

Socony-Vacuum Exploration, the forerunner of Mobil Oil, rose nearly $4 overnight. Back in Swift Current, excited folks were confidently predicting the town would be the size of Houston or Dallas before long.

The find was so new that that there was no pipeline and the oil had to be pumped into trucks and driven to Saskatoon. As well, the oil had too much sulfur for conventional refineries. But by 1956, a new pipeline was shipping the oil to a new refinery in St. Paul, Minnesota.

Fosterton No. 1 touched off an oil boom in Saskatchewan. Within 20 years of the first strike, this corner of the province had 1,029 oil wells and 373 gas wells. The energy industry continues to play a major role in the province's economic life.

Fosterton No. 1 turned out to be as good a well as any drilled in the province. It produced continually from February 1952 to November 1996. Over that time, it yielded 4,839,602 barrels of oil.

ALONG HIGHWAY 1: THE TRANS-CANADA

Cemetery Marks Early North-West Mounted Police Headquarters

Highway 271, exit west out of Maple Creek, drive approximately 300 yards (274 m), turn left on gravel road and drive about 1.8 miles (3 km) to cemetery

This cemetery, whose plots are the resting place of some of the North-West Mounted Police's earliest members, is all that remains of the force's A Division headquarters, which stood here from 1883 to 1919. One of the men resting here is Louis Lavallie, one of the guides and interpreters who helped the original members of the force on their 1874 trek west.

Railway construction camps pushing the Canadian Pacific Railway west created the need for the first police detachment here in 1882. When Fort Walsh to the south was dismantled the next year, the new headquarters was built near this site and completed in 1884. Maple Creek came under Depot Division in Regina in 1919.

This cemetery is now on private land.

Fort Walsh Brings Law to the West

Highway 271, 34 miles (55 km) south of Maple Creek; can also
access from Cypress Hills Interprovincial Park via "Gap Road"
(rough road, impassable when wet); site open May 18–October 14

Law came to the Canadian West in the form of Fort Walsh. Erected in the heart of what was then called Whoop-Up Country—a busy, brawling region crisscrossed by Cree, Blackfoot, Assiniboine and Saulteaux Indians as well as Métis hunters and freighters, and white frontiersmen—the fort's log palisades stood at the center of a volatile economy of buffalo robes, wolf skins, guns and whiskey. Only a short walk from Fort Walsh, 30 Assiniboine had been slaughtered two years before by drunken white wolfers in a dispute over stolen horses. That so-called Cypress Hills Massacre was one of the events that spurred the federal government to create the North-West Mounted Police.

It was May 1875 when the newly established force's B Company rode east from Fort MacLeod to arrive in this valley along Battle Creek. Indians gathered to watch the 102 constables and officers hoist logs in the summer heat, and soon after the fort was ringed with trading stores, a log billiard hall, a hotel, a restaurant and a barber shop. Many Indians set up lodges nearby.

Following the practice of the time, Fort Walsh was named for its first commanding officer, Inspector (and self-styled Major) James Morrow Walsh. A leader whose courage, fairness and flamboyance could have come right out of a Mountie movie, Walsh showed his stuff in 1876 when thousands of Sioux Indians fled across the United States border into southwest Saskatchewan. It fell to Walsh, then 33, to keep the peace. Clad in a black slouch hat, a trail-stained, fringed buckskin jacket and knee-high cavalry boots, Walsh led an escort of 12 men and 2 scouts into the heart of the 4,000-strong Sioux camp. They trotted past hundreds of angry warriors, some of whom were fresh from wiping out Custer and his Seventh Cavalry at the Battle of the Little Bighorn and were still drying American scalps. Impressed with the Redcoat's daring, Sioux chief Sitting Bull listened while Walsh explained how his people must live in Canada: no fighting, no horse stealing, no raiding or smuggling across the American border. Despite the increasing poverty and desperation of Sitting Bull's people, that law was largely kept,

Fort Walsh in 1878, three years after it was built.

helped, no doubt, by Walsh's determination to enforce it equally with both natives and whites. Handsome, tough-minded, unquestioningly self-confident, the lushly mustachioed Walsh was loved by his men and trusted by the Sioux. He and Sitting Bull developed a deep regard for each other, and Walsh often pled the case of the Sioux with his superiors in Ottawa.

For eight years, Fort Walsh was the headquarters of the North-West Mounted Police. From here the Mounties chased horse thieves and booze runners, administered treaties (sometimes sharing their own rations with hungry natives) and patrolled hundreds of miles of border. To amuse themselves the men played cricket, tennis and football. The local Métis settlement offered regular dances, and the men staged theatricals in their mess hall. Some made pets of the local wildlife. Constable Hardy's Canada Goose was known to accompany him on parade and sentry duty, during which the goose was prone to honk loudly at delinquent policemen trying to sneak quietly past the guardhouse late at night.

Some of those men are here still, in the graveyard up the hill from the fort. Typhoid filled most of these coffins; two men drowned in Battle Creek. Constable Marmaduke Graeburn, shot and killed in an ambush, was the only one to die violently.

After the Sioux were forced back to the United States in 1881, the fort was abandoned. It was dismantled by 1883 and moved

Noncommissioned officers of the NWMP at Fort Walsh, 1878.

north to Maple Creek to be nearer the Canadian Pacific rail line, which had just been built across the prairie.

James Walsh left the force to establish the Dominion Coke, Coal and Transportation Company in Winnipeg. But the lure of the frontier called him back one more time. With the coming of the Klondike Gold Rush, he returned to the force as superintendent and was appointed commissioner of the Yukon District from 1897 to 1898. He retired to Ontario and died in Brockville in 1905.

In 1942 the force turned the Fort Walsh site into a ranch to raise its horses. It was turned over to Parks Canada in 1968.

Trading Post Becomes Site of Drunken Massacre
Highway 271, 34 miles (55 km) west of Maple Creek, near Fort Walsh National Historic Site

---

Abe Farwell, who operated this trading post in the early 1870s, surely didn't intend for it to become associated with one of the most notorious episodes in the Canadian West. Farwell no doubt would have preferred to simply trade supplies and whiskey for buffalo robes and other skins on behalf of the T.C. Power Company out of Fort Benton, Montana. That's not how it worked out.

In late spring 1873, a group of wolfers operating out of Fort Benton had their horses stolen. Suspecting a band of Assiniboine lead by Chief Little Soldier, 13 wolfers including several Canadians rode north to the Cypress Hills to track down what they thought would be their horses. When they met up with Little Soldier's band, camped near Abe Farwell's post, they found neither their horses nor any evidence suggesting the Assiniboine had stolen them. The wolfers, resigned, repaired to the trading post to console themselves with Farwell's whiskey.

That's where it might have ended, with nothing worse than a camp full of nasty hangovers, but for the appearance of George Hammond. Hammond, who worked for another nearby trader, had recently had his horse stolen; just to keep the peace, he had paid an Indian a bottle of whiskey to get it back. Now it had been stolen again. Furious and none too sober, Hammond grabbed a rifle and headed off from this spot to Little Soldier's camp. The well-armed and well-lubricated wolfers followed, spoiling for a fight. Farwell tried to mediate, but didn't speak Assiniboine well enough to defuse things. Some of the Assiniboine also had been drinking and finally someone (some say Hammond himself) fired the first shot.

At the sound of gunfire, the wolfers galloped at top speed to a nearby cutbank. Three times the Assiniboine attacked. But they were armed with only old fur trade muskets, and the wolfers, crack shots all, carried the latest repeating Henry rifles. About 30 Indians were killed and twice that many wounded. One wolfer died. Farwell later said the wolfers celebrated by guzzling back more whiskey and looting and raping their way through the Assiniboine camp. Others said Farwell had a lurid imagination.

The wolfers buried their dead companion under the floor of a nearby post, set it alight, then headed off to look for their horses among the Blood Indians. Eventually, they returned home without the horses. The American government refused to extradite them, partly because of Farwell's befuddled testimony at the hearing. That decision touched off a huge celebration in Fort Benton, and the wolfers, considered honest frontiersmen defending themselves and their property, were the heroes of a torchlight parade.

Meanwhile, Canadian newspapers such as the *Ottawa Daily Citizen* roared headlines like "Wholesale Slaughter of the Indians" and "Another Outrage on Canadian Soil," suggesting that the nationality of the wolfers was at least as big a concern as the massacred Assiniboine. After all, it hadn't been so long ago that the Fenians were raiding into southern Ontario from the United States.

Three months after the killings, the federal government formed the North-West Mounted Police. The force rode west the next summer, and the days of whiskey posts like Abe Farewell's were over.

Not that Farwell would have been around for them. He moved out soon after, too late to escape his link with what came to be called forever after the Cypress Hills Massacre.

Explorer Thought Today's Wheat Belt was a Desert
Along Highway 1, between Maple Creek and Gull Lake

Prairie folk could be forgiven for thinking of the explorer John Palliser as just another Eastern expert who came west and got it wrong. After all, back in the late 1850s, this well-born Irishman wrote off these productive farm and ranchlands as an arid wasteland, a northern extension of the Great American Desert that came to be known as Palliser's Triangle. But tempting as it may be to dismiss Palliser, that would be unfair to this cultured, adventurous man and the knowledge his expeditions collected. Besides, a dry year can still make his original assessment seem pretty close to the truth.

John Palliser was born in 1817 in Dublin, Ireland, to a wealthy, landed family. As befitted a young man of his class, he attended Trinity College, Dublin, and joined the militia. Cheerful, sociable, handsome, fluent in French, Italian, German and Spanish, Palliser was well equipped for high society. He loved music and once in New Orleans sang both the bass and tenor parts in Handel's oratorio *David.* A life of managing the family estates and shooting pheasants might have been his pleasant lot but for a book he read about travels on the Missouri plains.

His sense of adventure fired, Palliser packed up and headed west in 1847 to join the American Fur Trade Company. He returned to Ireland the following year, bringing with him two buffalo calves. He wrote his own travel book, *Solitary Rambles and Adventures of a Hunter in the Prairies,* which sold well.

Captain John Palliser, around 1860.

But Palliser longed to be on the frontier, not just writing about it. Finally, his opportunity came in 1857. He convinced Britain's Royal Geographical Society to sponsor an expedition to the lands south of the North Saskatchewan River to describe its features, study the native soil and plants, look for resources such as coal, assess the land for agriculture and finally, far to the west, look for passes through the Rockies. That tall order was to take him and his party three years of roaming. During those years there wasn't much on the plains that they didn't see.

They spent time at the old fur and pemmican trade posts of Fort Ellice and Fort Carlton. With guides such as the Métis James McKay and the Cree chief Maskepetoon, the men camped in the parklands along the North Saskatchewan and tramped over prairie so treeless they had to carry firewood with them or burn dried buffalo chips. They saw grizzly bear, elk, wolves, antelope and deer. From a vista near Qu'Appelle, Palliser wrote, "The whole region, as far as the eye could reach, was covered with buffalo, in bands ranging from hundreds to thousands." They crossed six passes in the southern Rockies.

His party included botanists, geographers, a geologist, engineers and astronomers as well as locals who knew the country. Palliser's own skills as a diplomat must have been considerable, for he had few problems with the much-feared Blackfoot. He simply explained to any band that asked that he traveled light because he trusted the good judgment of the Blackfoot, while warning them of the powerful weapons of his own people.

Palliser concluded that while the land around the North Saskatchewan was eminently fertile, the land to the south was arid and sterile, except the Cypress Hills, which he called "a perfect oasis in the desert we have travelled." That "desert" has become known as Palliser's Triangle, a dryland belt that stretches from Emerson, Manitoba, to the foothills of the Rockies to a point long the Alberta–Saskatchewan boundary about 205 miles (330 km) north of the border. What Palliser didn't know was that 1857–60 was particularly dry. Properly farmed, with normal precipitation, parts of Palliser's Triangle are now highly productive. Nevertheless, Palliser's reports were the first systematic description of the lands from the southern plains all the way to British Columbia's Okanagan Valley.

As well, Palliser recommended that land be set aside for the Indians, that whites be stopped from buying them out and that liquor laws be enforced. He also said the area needed a police force.

Palliser returned to England, but he couldn't sit still for long. By 1862 his militia contacts had involved him in a secret, semi-official mission. In a schooner called the *Rosalind,* Palliser sailed from the West Indies to Charleston, South Carolina, in direct violation of the Union naval blockade of the Confederacy. A few years later he joined his brother Frederick to explore the Karal Sea in the Arctic, getting in a little walrus and polar bear hunting at the same time.

Eventually, Palliser retired to manage the family home in County Waterford, Ireland. His exploring days were over but not forgotten, and in 1877 he wrote a friend, "How I should enjoy going out again and seeing a few of those old wilds. . . ." He passed his time running his lands, playing the music of Bach and walking the hills. On August 18, 1887, after one of those walks, James Palliser died.

Powerful Cree Chief Fails to Turn Back Railway
Highway 1, Piapot

Chief Piapot was aptly named. Born during a lightning storm, he was called Payipwat, which means "Flash-In-the-Sky-Boy," and his time as one of the most powerful Cree leaders on the plains came as relations between his people and the encroaching whites were indeed reaching a flash point.

Piapot grew up familiar with conflict. As a boy he was captured by a Sioux raiding party and taken to live with them in the Dakotas. Cree raiders recaptured him when he was 14 and brought him back to his own people. But conflict with the encroaching whites was to become Piapot's greatest challenge when he became chief. When Treaty No 4 was negotiated in 1874 at Fort Qu'Appelle, Piapot refused to sign and continued to roam the prairie with his band. He signed later, mistakenly believing the treaty had been revised.

Piapot was suspicious of the coming of the railway in 1883, feeling, quite rightly, that it would only bring more settlers and increase the pressure on his band to surrender its way of life. When railway crews came to the Maple Creek area, Piapot erected his lodge in the middle of the right-of-way and refused to move while the young men of his band raced around on their ponies and fired their guns in the air. But the chief was no more able to stop the railway than he had been to win more concessions in his treaty. A North-West Mounted Police constable came out and gave Piapot 15 minutes to strike his tent and move. When 15 minutes had passed and Piapot was still there, the Mountie got off his horse, strode into the middle of the tent and kicked out the center pole.

He turned to the dumfounded chief and his warriors, and said, "Now move and move quickly." They did.

Piapot lived until 1908.

Cattle Baron, Sheep King Eventually Deposed
Highway 1, 2.5 miles (4 km) east of Piapot turnoff

For thousands of years the biggest herds on the prairies were buffalo. Scientists estimate that in 1800 up to 60 million of them thundered over the rolling plains in herds that stretched as far as the eye could see. But by 1885 they had been hunted almost to extinction, leaving the grasslands empty. Some men envisioned cattle and sheep in those spaces where the buffalo had roamed, and one of them was the dynamic, imaginative and ambitious Sir John Pepys Lister-Kaye.

A baronet from Yorkshire, Lister-Kaye had the bearing of a nobleman and the mind of a penny-stock promoter. He loved to play the part of a full-fledged range baron and was always good for a colorful quote for local reporters. As one newsman of the time had it, Lister-Kaye was "a tall, blond, blue-eyed young Englishman with a deliberate easy manner, a fine, sandy mustache and a shapely head full of schemes."

Lister-Kaye was already a veteran of one successful venture in the North-West—a 7,000-acre (2833-ha) farm at Balgonie— when he grew interested in the Swift Current area. In 1886, he and his wife, Natica, traveled along the Canadian Pacific Railway through to Calgary in their private railway car. The next year he bought 10 well-watered blocks of land close to the tracks, each 10,000 acres (4047 ha), to raise cattle and grain "upon the principle of an English estate," as he said. After selling the whole package to investors in England for a tidy little fortune, he returned to manage the enterprise.

Sir John, then 35, sprung into action. With two million board feet of lumber on order, he had fences surveyed and building sites selected. He bought an entire herd of cattle—5,800 head—from a Fort MacLeod–based ranch company. It was from the brand those cattle bore, the number 76, that the ranch took its name.

From the United States, Lister-Kaye brought up thousands

of Merino sheep and shipped in 300 pedigreed rams from England, which were eventually strung out in 15 camps between Swift Current and Gull Lake. They were watched over by shepherds who worked for $30 a year and two bottles of Hudson's Bay Company whiskey. Each of the 10 farms was to have about 65 horses, a Clydesdale stallion, polled Angus and Galloway bulls, and enough hogs to establish 11 herds of about 90 pigs each. To run the ranch, about 110 young Englishmen responded to Lister-Kaye's advertisements offering free passage. A similar number came out from eastern Canada.

Lister-Kaye opened butcher shops and abattoirs in Dunmore and Medicine Hat, and built a packing plant in Calgary. He would try anything, even a scheme to turn Swift Current into the dairy capital of Canada by trying to milk the half-wild range cows, much to the horror of his cowboys. His frenetic schemes and big-scale projects made him, along with the Canadian Pacific Railway, the area's biggest employer and source of investment. His was also some of the first high-quality stock in the region.

Business was good at first. Crops were acceptable and the packing plant was profitable. But things began to fall apart. Dryland farming was not well understood back then, which led to repeated crop failures from hail and drought. Brutal winters thinned the herds. Finally, Lister-Kaye's financial backers grew alarmed and forced him to resign as ranch manager in 1890. The cattle king was deposed.

The 76 Ranch rallied and carried on for over a decade under new management. Despite prairie fires, disease, wolves and harsh winters, the 76 saw some good years and eventually exported about 25,000 sheep back to England. But by the turn of the century, the old open range was being broken up and settlers were moving in. The cruel, killing winter of 1906, which devastated the ranching industry across the West, dealt the final blow, and the ranch was bought up by a meat packing firm. It was permanently broken up in 1921.

Trader Follows Indian Trail West
Highway 1, 5 miles (8 km) east of Gull Lake at picnic site

Developed by Indians and Métis, the Swift Current–Maple Creek Trail was probably already generations old when Hudson's

Bay Company trader Isaac Cowie followed it out from Fort Qu'Appelle in 1868. One of the first Baymen in the area and perhaps the first European to see these plains, Cowie eventually set up shop in Chimney Coulee near the present town of Eastend. After one profitable season, Cowie's post was burned down by a band of Blackfoot. Cowie, who was away from the post at the time, got the message and moved his trade elsewhere.

The North-West Mounted Police often traveled this trail after they came west in 1875. It became an important link between divisional headquarters in Maple Creek and the Swift Current detachment.

Eventually, the Canadian Pacific Railway came to follow its route quite closely.

Rough and Ready Hotels Serve Pioneer Travelers Along Busy Route
Highway 4, Central Avenue, Swift Current

The day the railway reached Swift Current, this little town became an important place—the major shipping point between the outside world and the Saskatchewan frontier. Between 1883 and 1890, if you wanted it in Battleford, the quickest way to get it there was to put it on the train to Swift Current, then ship it overland. Here began the Swift Current–Battleford Trail.

On a busy day, this trail head would see police buckboards, hunting parties, hopeful settlers and Métis freighters with their carts in summer and sleighs in winter. Perhaps the stagecoach, carrying mail, freight and passengers, would be readying for its regular run. The air would be full of dust, shouts, the smell of horses and the shrieking of Red River carts, which were never lubricated because the grease just clogged up with prairie grit.

The trail was a great improvement over the days when everything had to be freighted from Winnipeg. That trip took 49 days one way, while the 199-mile (320-km) journey from Swift Current took only 16 days with cargo and as few as three with fast horses and a light buggy. Still, that was long enough and a number of stopping houses sprang up along the way to ease the journey. The first was Russell House (later Goodwin House) on the south bank of the South Saskatchewan River. It's now a historic site.

In a manuscript now in the provincial archives, one old-timer recalled the lodgings past Goodwin's. The first was a place called Devil's Gulch, a dugout in a ravine with a wood roof and four bunks built against the wall. If those beds weren't enough, the overflow slept on the floor. "This place was warm, being well-sheltered from the wind; one objection that some fastidious people complained of was the large population of mice that cavorted over you when you had retired to rest," that old pioneer wrote.

Another day's journey might end at Eagle Creek, a shack of rough lumber on a hillside. August Meyer, known as Charlie the Swede, was the innkeeper. Charlie was recalled as a great story-teller who loved to haggle out a bargain, especially over horses. "He was very entertaining, a great talker, and it was amusing to listen to him telling in his broken English of his adventures and his experiences with the various passengers passing to and fro."

Sixty Mile Bush, south of present-day Rosetown, was another station. Run by an elderly Quebecois named Bernier, this house was a cut above the others and offered the nicety of curtains to separate the ladies' sleeping quarters from the men's.

So popular was the Swift Current–Battleford Trail that it saw almost 4,409,000 pounds (2 million kg) of freight between spring and fall of 1886. Even John A. Macdonald, Canada's first prime minister, visited the freighters and horsemen at the trail head when he stopped in Swift Current on his one trip west. But Swift Current didn't remain the jumping-off point for long. In 1890, construction of the Regina–Prince Albert line made Saskatoon's the closest tracks to Battleford. The old Swift Current–Battleford Trail and its eccentric chain of hotels gradually fell into disuse— although rut marks from the innumerable cart trains that used it can still be seen carved into the prairie sod.

Scientists Keep Hope Alive During Dirty Thirties
1 Airport Road, off Highway 1 at southeast corner, Swift Current

---

The grasshoppers came so thick and ravenous that they ate the handles off pitchforks and the armpits out of shirts. The skies were so pitilessly dry that they say some children reached school age before they knew what rain was. So hot and hard

Dunes of wind-eroded topsoil during the Depression.

blew the wind that farmers joked it wasn't a real dust storm unless a gopher thrown into the air started trying to dig a tunnel. And when a few bushels of wheat were harvested from the hard-pan earth, the price was often a fraction of what was needed to survive.

From 1929 to 1937, it would have been easy to give up on farming here, to admit that the explorer James Palliser had been right and that southwest Saskatchewan was an arid, unfarmable desert. But Gordon Taggart, the first director of the Swift Current Experimental Farm, never surrendered. Partly through the work of his scientists at this station, farmers learned to fight back against the drought and to persevere until the rains returned.

Taggart came out in 1922 when the station was first opened to study the problems of dryland farming. Although he couldn't offer even the brightest young scientist much more than $100 a month (and some started at $.35 an hour), Taggart was able to recruit the best young crop of science graduates from the western universities and give them freedom to think and experiment widely.

Their work grew increasingly urgent as the prairies fell into the grip of what would become nearly a decade of drought and depression. Saskatchewan was hit doubly hard as both wheat prices and wheat crops shrank. One region of the prov-ince that had grown $90 million of wheat in 1927 could barely harvest a $3-

A giant pile of tumbleweeds blown up against a fence during the drought-parched Depression.

million crop in 1936. Government estimates suggested a farmer needed to gross $5.30 per acre (.4 ha) to make a go of it; in 1933 farmers averaged $2.30; in 1937, a mere $.40. Despite hundreds of train carloads of aid from the rest of Canada—including boxes and boxes of salt cod, which few prairie wives knew how to cook—more and more farm tables began to feature the desperate diet of gopher stew, gopher pie and even pickled gopher. All businesses were affected; the *Shaunavon Standard* newspaper had to cut its subscription rates from $2 to four chickens a year.

Taggart's team began to look at how the land was being farmed. Summer-fallowing, the practice of leaving a plowed field unseeded for a season, had been in use for 45 to 50 years. Farmers were told to plow their fields after every rain on the theory that fine dust settling on top would seal and conserve the moisture underneath. Maybe it did, but the practice contributed greatly to wind erosion. Legend has it that those black blizzards were so bad that a baseball player who took off from home plate got lost running the bases and wasn't found for three days. At Swift Current, scientists studied wind erosion with a wind tunnel built from a propeller hooked up to an old Chevy engine mounted on a truck chassis. Eventually, experiments proved that farmers should not till their summer-fallowed fields except to control weeds. Similarly, farmers learned to plant crops in strips and to leave some stubble on their fields to hold the soil.

They tinkered with equipment, too. Swift Current scientists did some of the earliest experiments with self-propelled combines and rubber-tired tractors. Some of the work on the Noble plow, much better designed for prairie sod, was done here. So was much of the development of crested wheat grass, the tough grass that helped reclaim thousands of acres of blown-out fields for community pasture.

By 1934, although the hard times still had a few years to run, Taggart knew the building blocks of a new dryland agriculture were emerging. He left the research station to enter provincial politics, where he became minister of agriculture at a time when the flight from the land was at its peak. The 1936 census reported 8,200 abandoned farms in Palliser's Triangle, and a later Royal Commission found that about 73,000 people left the area between 1931 and 1941. But Taggart never lost faith in Palliser's Triangle. He fought relocation programs for southern farmers, pointing out that families who moved north were often worse off than they had been.

Eventually, Taggart and his scientists were proved right. Palliser's Triangle could be farmed, and farmed prosperously. But it had to be done right and done carefully, and the Swift Current Research Station was a big part of finding out how.

Police, Pioneers Follow in Trail of Native Hunter
Highway 4, 19 miles (30 km) south of Swift Current, turn west on Highway 343 for 7 miles (12 km), follow signs to south end of Lac Pelletier Regional Park

---

First developed by native bands and followed by Métis buffalo hunters forced to follow their prey farther and farther west, the Fort Walsh–Moose Jaw Trail connected the two communities along the north end of Old Wives Lake.

North-West Mounted Police patrols from Fort Walsh used the trail to reach the Lac Pelletier area. Ranchers and homesteaders kept its tracks fresh. Norbert Pelletier, who filed the first homestead entry in the area right near here on August 14, 1886, reached his land along this pathway. Eventually, the growing railway system stilled traffic along its route.

ALONG HIGHWAYS 13, 18 AND 37

Pioneer Rancher Turns Amateur Dinosaur Hunter

Highway 13, Ravenscrag turnoff, pass through town, cross Frenchman River, then drive east on Middle Bench Road for 10.5 miles (17 km)

Harold Saunders Jones, known to his friends as Corky, came out west from the Isle of Wight in England in 1898 at the age of 18. He became one of the first ranchers in the area, but he's best remembered today as the man who first noticed that the coulees and badlands of the Eastend region were full of fossils. It's for him that the spectacular vista point of Jones Peak is named.

Corky Jones became a self-taught paleontologist. He found and excavated dinosaurs, including a triceratops skull and a ceratopsian skull and shield. He found fossils of a three-toed horse, a rhinoceros and a giant pig. When the famous dinosaur hunter Charles Sternberg came to Saskatchewan in 1921, it was Corky who guided him around Eastend country.

Corky's interest in the past was not limited to dinosaurs. He collected many stories about the Indians and Métis who inhabited the area as well as the North-West Mounted Police, ranchers and homesteaders who came to join them. Jones Peak was named in his honor in 1972. Corky died six years later at the age of 97.

Many of Corky's fossil discoveries can be seen today in the Eastend museum, and scientists are still making finds around the Frenchman River. This valley has yielded up Scotty, one of the most complete *Tyrannosaurus rex* skeletons ever found. A fossil research station in the town of Eastend offers a variety of public programs, including tours to active fossil quarries and digs that visitors can join.

Jones Peak gives a great view of the Frenchman River valley. In the valley walls on the opposite side are layers of lignite coal the early settlers used to mine to heat their homes. To the west are the White Mud pits, which have been mined for generations for their valuable pottery clay. To the east is an open stretch of flat land where about 200 lodges of Sioux came to camp in 1876 after their leader, the famous chief Crazy Horse, was fatally stabbed by an American soldier. Also to the east is Chocolate Peak, which got its name after a white-mud miner tried to make his job easier by burning out a seam of coal that lay on top of the clay he was after. The coal burned for years, staining the clay dark, or chocolate, brown and ruining the mine.

Last Great Wild Horse Drive
Claydon area, .5 miles (.8 km) north of Highway 18 at Claydon turnoff

These days you couldn't do what Claydon-area rancher Fred Williamson and 12 other cattlemen did that autumn back in 1958. The land's too broken up, too fenced off. But back then, you could drive stock across miles and miles of prairie from range to buyer and count on good native pasture all the way, and that's just what Williamson did with one of the last big wild horse herds on the southwestern plains.

Those horses, never handled and completely wild, had spent their lives roaming free on Williamson's 12-section field. But when he lost his government lease, the veteran cattleman had no place to take them. So he worked out a deal to sell them to a cannery in Swift Current—if he could get them there.

Williamson first had to knock down about a mile of fence to give the herd an exit from his land. Then he and his crew began rounding them up—stallions, mares and colts—until the herd numbered about 475. Driven by the cowboys, those horses thundered out of Williamson's range and into open country so hard that they outran a herd of antelope.

Darkness came thick and heavy after the day's drive. So did an autumn storm, complete with snow and an odd sort of lightning that created weird electrical effects on the horses.

"It was one of the oddest things I ever saw," Williamson later told Sharon Butala, the writer from whose account this story is drawn. "There were little silvery white balls of light on [the horse's] ear tips and manes and all over them. They had like a rainbow or a halo around them. Even their eyes glowed. All you could see was this ghost thing coming at you."

Spooked by the weather, the horses began milling and eventually bolted into the stormy, cold, sodden dark. It took two days to find and gather them up, and even then, only 375 horses could be found. The missing 100 head weren't rounded up until the next year.

The drive forded the Frenchman River and kept on toward Swift Current. At one point a stallion reared up his head and took off, leaping a fence and galloping across the plains so hard the cowboys didn't even try to catch him. Nobody did until a few springs later, when he was caught in a roundup and eventually became a rodeo bucking horse.

For five days the cowboys worked, ate and slept outdoors, spending days in the saddle along road allowances and grassland, riding through good weather and bad like the cowboys of old. It could almost have been 1858 instead of 1958, except for the cook's pickup truck.

When the drive reached a ranch south of Swift Current, reporters and TV crews were there to meet it. The Mounties closed traffic just south of the city so the horses could be driven to the cannery.

Williamson got a good price for the horses. And the cowboys who had just finished the last great horse drive were taken to a restaurant for a steak dinner.

Botanist Saw Beauty Where Others Saw Desert

Highway 13 east, turn left on South Fork Road, drive 7 miles (11 km) northeast of Eastend to Pine Cree Regional Park

---

John Macoun was a teacher at Albert College in Ontario when railway engineer and surveyor Sanford Fleming asked him along as botanist on his 1872 trip west. It was to become the first of five expeditions between 1872 and 1881 to the prairies and parklands of what is now Saskatchewan. The more he traveled, the more he came to disagree with the earlier assessment of Captain John Palliser, who wrote off most of the southwest corner of the province as a desert. Palliser saw the land during dry years; Macoun, visiting during years of normal to heavy rainfall, saw it for what it could be. His favorable reports on the agricultural potential of the plains were one reason the route of the Canadian Pacific Railway was moved south from the original plan to follow the North Saskatchewan River valley. Macoun went on to write a book, *History of the Great North-West,* and become Assistant Director and Naturalist to the Geological Survey of Canada.

Macoun camped near this spot in 1880. Later, he was to

write, "In all my wandering I never saw any spot to equal in beauty the central plateau of the Cypress Hills."

Mounties Ride Border Patrol
East edge of Eastend, then about 220 yards (200 m) south of rail-road bridge along Frenchman River

Here the Mounties set up shop after they closed the Chimney Coulee post in 1889. The location was convenient because a pioneer rancher named Tom Doyle had settled here a few years earlier before moving on, and the policemen were able to use Doyle's vacated log cabin as their mess hall. From the Eastend North-West Mounted Police post, Mounties rode long, lonely patrols along a considerable stretch of international border. It was also an important post for keeping the peace among the settlers, natives, railway crews, cowboys and all the other inhabitants of the pioneer days.

One of the men who commanded this post was Don Pollack, who had a colorful career before he retired to ranch in the area. He fought in the North-West Rebellion and headed the guard at Louis Riel's hanging. But he was something of a worrier, and his men came to refer to him as Old Anxiety. Anxiety Butte, the tall peak near the junction of Grid 633 and Highway 13, is named for him.

Another butte near here also is named for an employee of the force. Jumbo Butte, about 4 miles (6.5 km) east of Eastend along Highway 13, is named after a North-West Mounted Police freighter named Jumbo, who disappeared while driving between Eastend and another small post. His horse and buckboard, along with his neatly folded uniform, were found on top of the butte, but Jumbo was never seen again.

The Mounties staffed this post for 25 years. A new post was built within the present town of Eastend in 1914.

Prairie Nurtures Budding Writer
Stegner Home, 126 Tamarack Street, Eastend

Desolate? Forbidding? There never was a country that in its good moments was more beautiful. Even in drouth or dust storms or blizzard it is the reverse of monotonous, once you have submitted to it with all your senses. You don't get out of the wind, but learn to lean and squint against it. You don't escape sky and sun, but wear them in your eyeballs and on your back. You become acutely aware of yourself. The world is very large, the sky even larger, and you are very small. But also the world is flat, empty, nearly abstract, and in its flatness you are a challenging upright thing, as sudden as an exclamation mark, as enigmatic as a question mark.

It is a country to breed mystical people, egocentric people, perhaps poetic people. But not humble ones.

It was this country that the man who wrote these words had in mind, for here is where Pulitzer Prize–winning writer Wallace Stegner spent much of his early childhood. That passage comes from his 1963 classic *Wolf Willow,* his beautiful memoir and history of what he called "the Last Plains Frontier."

The Stegner family came to Eastend in 1914 and homesteaded until 1920, when they moved back to the United States. Until he wrote his memoir, Stegner never returned. But his books are haunted by the images and memories of the prairie and the town, to which he gives the name Whitemud. Besides *Wolf Willow,* Stegner dug especially deep into his prairie roots for his 1943 novel, *Big Rock Candy Mountain.*

The Stegner home was built in 1916. Although it was at one time divided into apartments, it has been restored to its original floor plan. The Eastend Arts Council owns the house and offers it as a writing retreat to authors. Although the house is not open to the public, tours can sometimes be arranged through the council.

Chimney Coulee Marked by Hunting, Trading and War
Chimney Coulee Road, 3 miles (5 km) north of Eastend; follow signs. Open year round.

Chimney Coulee was a busy place during the days of the old North-West. Blackfoot, Cree, Assiniboine and Saulteaux tribes often hunted and trapped through here in the days before the Europeans came. During the 1860s, a community of 60 Métis buffalo hunters and trappers overwintered here regularly, even building a church and a small graveyard. The ruined chimneys of their cabins give this coulee its name.

Sometimes those peaceful pursuits gave way to war. When Hudson's Bay Company trader Isaac Cowie arrived in 1871, he found a party of Cree, Saulteaux and Assiniboine gathered for a ceremony to mourn the death of about 60 Cree warriors who had been killed in a battle with the Blackfoot at this site. Cowie didn't take the hint that this was perhaps not the most peaceful of neighborhoods and went ahead and built his trading post anyway. Business was brisk that winter. He took in 750 grizzly pelts, 1,500 elk robes and hundreds of smaller skins. But when Cowie left that spring, the Blackfoot returned, burned the post to the ground and killed nine Assiniboine who were in the vicinity. Cowie never came back.

The Mounties established a presence as well. They set up a post here during the 1880s, which was moved closer to the town of Eastend in 1889.

Chimney Coulee's long history of human habitation has given archaeologists much to dig into, and excavations have taken place on the site.

American Immigrants, Not Honeymooners, Name Town
Highway 37, 14 miles (23 km) north of border

The old Saskatchewan joke about Climax being the province's honeymoon capital isn't the only one this little town has had to bear. However, the real origin of the name is anything but salacious: the community is named after Climax, North Dakota, from whence many of the area's early settlers had traveled.

Although there had been a few homesteaders before the railway, Climax didn't really go anywhere until the tracks came in 1922. Within a few years, and even though the town never grew bigger than 250, Climax had a weekly newspaper, several stores and lumberyards, a hospital, restaurants, a bank and a men's wear store. At the Silver Dollar Pool Hall, the counterman would fry up an order of steak and eggs at any hour of the day, and the poker players kept right on dealing during the occasional theatrical performance. Baseball was popular among the town's American immigrants, and the Climax Cardinals ball club was good enough to tour the southern prairies and make it pay, even during the Depression.

Métis Buffalo Hunters Break Fort Walsh–Wood Mountain Trail to Trade Robes
Highway 37, 17 miles (27 km) south of Shaunavon

Métis buffalo hunters broke the Fort Walsh–Wood Mountain Trail in the 1850s, trading buffalo robes and pemmican to the Hudson's Bay Company. The Métis, descended from French and English fur traders and native women, were expert hunters. They would first stalk a herd, then ride into its thundering center, firing their rifles on horseback with deadly accuracy as the panicked prey tried to flee at full gallop. Many Métis could bring down a half-dozen buffalo during a single run; the renowned Baptiste Parenteau once shot 16. The well-organized Métis hunts were essential to the Hudson's Bay Company's ability to feed its far-flung empire. By 1840, the company was buying 110,230 pounds (50,000 kg) of meat and pemmican a year from various groups of Métis hunters, and that amount had doubled by 1870.

The Fort Walsh–Wood Mountain Trail was also significant to the North-West Mounted Police. For them it was an important stretch in their border patrol between Manitoba and the Rocky Mountains. Although the coming of the railway pretty much ended most traffic on the old pioneer trails, ranchers and homesteaders used the Fort Walsh–Wood Mountain Trail as late as 1920.

Chapter 2

The Great Trails Region

Last Western Frontier Lingered in Great Trails Region

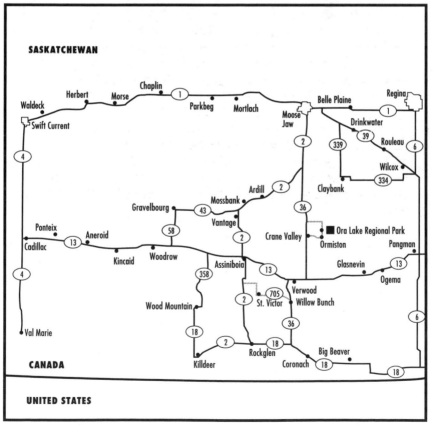

A S THE 19TH CENTURY ENDED, settlement and civilization had squeezed out the old free, wild West pretty much everywhere on the continent. Except here. This is the region where that old dream came to die.

For thousands of years, it lived here among native bands, whose occupancy stretches far back into prehistory. The traces they left—rock carvings, medicine wheels, boulder effigies—still raise as many questions as they answer about those ancient lives. But in the 1860s, the closing of another frontier brought newcomers. Métis from the Red River area in Manitoba began to move west into the Wood Mountain country as settlement began to displace them.

For a few years the buffalo remained plentiful and the old ways carried on. But the failure of Sitting Bull and the Sioux to find a permanent sanctuary in Canada after their defeat of Custer and the U.S. Seventh Cavalry at the Battle of the Little Big-horn sent a clear signal that the days of the frontier were ending. Governments on both sides of the border wanted the natives settled on reserves, and the virtual disappearance of the buffalo gave the tribes little choice. When Sitting Bull crossed back over the line in 1881, it was the end of an era.

Its echoes remained, however, and even the Mounties couldn't completely muffle them. The open ranch country drew a lot of rough-and-ready spirits, and those early lawmen had a lively time of it among the cowboys, rustlers and assorted saddle tramps. For a while, a well-established pipeline for stolen stock that reached all the way to Mexico had its northern terminus in the Big Muddy region. Even into the early years of this century, enough frontier mystique remained here to lure west a young Quebecois. Under the name and identity of Will James, Ernest Dufault was to write and paint some of the best-loved chronicles of that vanishing time.

Maybe the spirit of that dream lived on in some of the vivid personalities that have marked this region: Athol Murray, who forged a legacy of classical learning and athletic greatness in the middle of the prairie dust bowl; Tom Sukanen, who risked every-thing including his sanity to fulfill his dream of returning to his homeland in triumph; some say even the notorious gangster Al Capone.

And maybe, through the stories of this region, the dream of the open plains still lives.

ALONG HIGHWAYS I AND 39

Chaplin Takes Name from Aristocratic Hunting Party
Highway 1, 50 miles (80 km) east of Swift Current, Chaplin

Africa isn't the only place where wealthy aristocrats came on hunting safaris. During Victorian times it became almost fashionable for a sporting British noble to pack up his manservant and matched shotguns, and come out to the wild, untamed North-West for a season or two of blasting away at buffalo, deer, elk, grizzly, ducks, wolves or whatever else moved. Aristocrats roamed freely, enjoying the best hospitality the local Hudson's Bay Company post could offer and reading Shakespeare by firelight while local guides prepared supper. The sportsmen would then return home to write a book and dine out on stories of the great lone land. Nobles who hunted the North-West included James Carnegie, Earl of Southesk; Maximillian, Prince of Weid; Viscount Milton, Lord Dunsmore and Count Arrigo de Castilione Maggiore.

In 1861, one such aristocratic party, led by John Rae, hunted its way through here. Rae, of course, was much more than a great white hunter. He was the last of the Hudson's Bay Company's great explorers. Although this 1861 trip was purely for sport, by that time he had mapped nearly 1,800 miles (2,900 km) of Arctic coastline, including the eastern section of the fabled Northwest Passage. It was Rae who first confirmed the demise of the Franklin expedition, and British society never quite forgave him for relaying the news of that unhappy band's resort to cannibalism. But then, everything about Rae bothered the establishment. Instead of exploring in the style of a gentleman, with regular tea and underlings for the heavy lifting, Rae was among the first to travel Inuit-style, walking with snowshoes and sleeping in igloos, keeping a light pack and moving fast. In the winter of 1851 he covered 1,367 miles (2,200 km), averaging 26 miles (42 km) a day. He shot game for his men himself, and they sometimes returned carrying more food than they left with.

Rae left his name on Rae Strait off the Arctic coast. On this trip, however, it was to be his companions who were so honored. The party decided to call the nearby lake after Viscount Chaplin and the present-day town takes its name from that. The third member of the group lost out on geographical immortality. A nearby lake to the south, which the party named for Sir Frederick Johnstone, reverted to its original name of Old Wives Lake in 1953.

Homesteader Wins Glory at Crucial World War I Battle
Highway 1, about 9.3 miles (15 km) southeast of Mortlach off Highway 735

In April 1917, during World War I, Canada won one of her greatest military victories. A plaque here commemorates one of the thousands of reasons why.

Vimy Ridge, a rill of high ground overlooking France's Ypres flatlands, was considered key to the entire Arras front. Its defenders had withstood repeated attacks from various allied forces, but high command decided to turn it over to the Canadians to see if they could wrest it from the Germans. For the first time, all four battle-hardened divisions of the Canadian Corps were to fight together.

Private William Johnstone Milne, then 25, was a member of the 16th Battalion of the Canadian Scottish Regiment. Milne had emigrated from Glasgow in 1910 and had spent the next four years working near present-day Mortlach as a farmhand. That had been tough. This was to be tougher.

For weeks before the attack, Milne and his comrades rehearsed their roles. Quartermasters stockpiled supplies for the assault and artillerymen lobbed an unending barrage into the German positions.

On April 9, Milne was in the thick of the attack, advancing on the enemy, when he spotted a German machine-gun position firing on his fellow soldiers. He dropped to the ground, crawled through the mud, shattered land toward the gun and single-handedly took it out. His company kept moving on and again were confronted by German machine-gun fire. Again, Milne crept forward and took the position. Milne is credited with saving many Canadian lives that day, but he did not save his own. He was awarded the Victoria Cross, the highest military decoration in the Commonwealth, posthumously. That medal is now in the Canadian War Museum.

Victory at Vimy took five days, 7,004 wounded and 3,598

dead. Following the battle, the Canadian divisions got their first Canadian commander, Lieutenant-General Arthur Currie. Today, Vimy Ridge is crowned by the two great white shafts of the Canadian War Memorial. Somewhere, that's where Milne is, too. The site of his grave is unknown.

Third Meridian Invisible Backbone of Land Survey
Highway 1, 1 mile (1.6 km) east of Mortlach

Saskatchewan is the only province whose boundaries are completely artificial. No mountain ranges, rivers or ocean shores mark its borders—just a surveyor's invisible line.

The same lines that marked out the province also marked it up, and this is one of the main ones. The Third Meridian is one of two baselines from which Saskatchewan's vast checkerboard was plotted.

Saskatchewan's surveys were carried out between 1880 and 1905. During that time the teams covered more than 8 million acres (3,237,600 ha) with an unbending rectangular grid. Those rigid squares were efficient, but ignored previous systems of land ownership, such as the river lot system of the Métis. That survey came to be one of the causes of the 1885 North-West Rebellion. But the uniform, highly precise system made for easy settlement and registration of land title. The free homestead policy that brought many of the province's pioneers would have been impossible without it, and one of the two meridians still forms part of the legal description on every deed in Saskatchewan's Land Titles Office.

Those original surveys were carried out by teams who were as much frontiersmen as technicians. They lived outdoors for months at time and were among the last to range freely over a land that had yet to be chopped up and fenced off. They were themselves the advance guard of those who would do just that.

"Surveyors are not heroic figures," wrote Wallace Stegner of the survey team that set the international border in 1872. "They come later than the explorers, they douse with system what was once the incandescent excitement of danger and the unknown. They conquer nothing but ignorance. . . . *But* a young man in search of excitement in 1872 could have done worse than enlist with them."

Surveyors in Sanford Fleming's expedition of 1873.

Moose Jaw–Red Deer Forks Trail Helps Build the Railway that Replaced It
Highway 1, 10 miles (16 km) east of Mortlach at Besant campground

Ruts carved in the prairie mark the passage of hundreds of Red River carts that carried explorers, hunters, traders, freighters and missionaries from the relative civilization of Moose Jaw and Fort Qu'Appelle to the wilder country near the Red Deer River forks by the Saskatchewan–Alberta boundary. This path also joined up with the Swift Current–Battleford Trail, which was a major north–south link. It was also used by the North-West Mounted Police.

But its history goes back much further. Native bands followed it for hundreds of years, and archaeologists have found relics near here that date back to 1450 B.C. This trail likely predates even that.

Some of the last groups to travel it regularly were construction crews building the Canadian Pacific Railway main line through here in 1882. That railway, which marked the end of an era on the prairies, also marked the end of traffic on this trail.

Wood and Water Make Creek Bend Popular Trail Crossroads
7th Avenue, Moose Jaw Wild Animal Park, Moose Jaw

Today's system of roads and railways wasn't the first transportation network to lace through the plains. Native hunters, European fur traders and Métis freighters worked out a well-established web of prairie highways that was later used by policemen on patrol and homesteaders looking for their new land. These trails linked up wherever dependable water, pasture, wood and shelter made for a pleasant place to set up camp and rest for a few days. Here, the big bend in the Moose Jaw Creek was such a place.

Near here, the trail from Fort Garry (now Winnipeg) connected with trails leading to the forks of the Red Deer River and to Wood Mountain, Cypress Hills and Fort Carlton. The route from here to the Cypress Hills was a regular fur trade route from 1856, and North-West Mounted Police from Fort Walsh patrolled it regularly. Until the railway supplanted it, the Cypress Hills Trail was one of the main trails for ranchers and freighters of the southwest.

Thousands Gather for Ku Klux Klan Rally
South Hill, Moose Jaw

The night of July 7, 1927, between 8,000 and 10,000 people gathered on this hill for a huge hymn-singing, speechifying rally, supposedly to demand the cleanup of the city's red-light strip along River Street. Was it organized by the churches? A political party? Concerned citizens?

No. A huge, burning cross 22 yards (20 m) high revealed the people had gathered at the behest of the Ku Klux Klan.

The KKK, notorious for racist violence in the American south, enjoyed wide membership across Saskatchewan in the 1920s. Two forces brought it north: greed and fear.

Around 1915 the Klan began a rebirth in the United States by promoting the superiority of white Anglo-Saxons and a rigid Protestant morality and by demonizing blacks, Jews, Central and East Europeans and Catholics. Successful Klan organizers soon cast their eyes northward. Here's why: for every $10 Klan membership sold, the recruiter kept $4, a nice, quick profit on zero investment. Pat Emmons, a double-chinned former gambler,

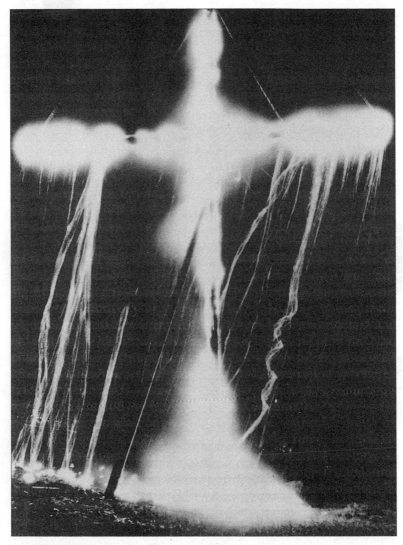

Ku Klux Klan cross burning in Regina, May 24, 1928.

saloonkeeper and evangelist who peddled the Klan throughout Saskatchewan, summed it up: "Whatever we found that people could be taught to hate and fear, we fed them. We were out to get the dollars and we got them."

Indeed. An Ontario Klan was incorporated by 1925. Alberta had more than 50 Klaverns. But the Klan's greatest success was in Saskatchewan, where it took care to separate itself from any ties to the white-robed U.S. nightriders. By 1929 there were 29,000 Klansmen in 129 locals across the province holding parades, banquets, whist drives and cross burnings. Regina had 1,000 Klansmen. In Woodrow, population 218, there were 153 in the KKK. But the Moose Jaw Klavern, with 2,000 members, was one of the largest. The Klan elected members to council, which soon passed an ordinance forbidding the employment of white girls in Chinese-run businesses. For a while a plaque on the wall of a city hospital ward read, "Confederation, Law and Order, Separation of Church and State, Freedom of Speech and Press, White Supremacy."

The Saskatchewan Klan fed on the fears and strains of a new, growing society. The Protestant, British face of the province was changing. In 1921 about 53 percent of the province was of WASP stock; by 1930, after years of immigration from Catholic East and Central Europe, they were a minority. Trade unions warned of competition from cheap immigrant labor. Voices from the Great War Veteran's Association to the Saskatchewan Grain Growers to George Lloyd, Anglican bishop of Saskatoon, called for restricted immigration. Social morality was also a concern in a young province trying to outgrow its easygoing frontier past. The Klan was more than willing to take on the boozers, gamblers and whores.

The Klan also found help from like-minded institutions. The ultra-Protestant Orange Order was also popular in Saskatchewan; it shared the KKK's abhorrence of all things French Catholic, and the two groups often shared facilities and members. Many Protestant ministers spoke against the KKK clearly and often, but at least 26 ministers from six denominations were members.

At its peak the KKK was a factor in provincial politics. Klansmen and Orangemen helped get out the Conservative vote, and Tories spoke at Klan meetings. When Liberal Premier Jimmy Gardiner's minority government fell in a nonconfidence motion after the 1929 election, the KKK burned crosses in celebration.

But the Klan's strength wasn't to last. Provincial and federal Conservative governments tightened immigration and changed school laws, taking some of the wind from KKK sails. As well, the onset of the Dirty Thirties brought a whole new set of problems that made the Klan seem irrelevant. Soon into the decade, the Klan collapsed in a welter of poor organization and infighting.

Tunnels Remnant of City's Shady, Racy Past
108 Main Street N, corner of Main and River streets, downtown, Moose Jaw

Girls, gambling and bootleg whiskey—that's what Moose Jaw's River Street was famous for back in the roaring twenties. As one journalist just after World War I wrote, "You came out of the Moose Jaw station, turned left on River Street and you could have been in New Orleans. . . . Everything in Moose Jaw was wide open. By night the streets were really filled with men roaming around, and the traffic down to the whore houses at the other end of the street was something to see."

Why Moose Jaw? That's where the Canadian Pacific Railway built its roundhouse and the Soo Line from Minneapolis had its terminus. Those crews kept a steady flow of young men with cash in their pockets in circulation. As well, Moose Jaw's law had a tolerant attitude toward River Street. As long as Main Street was safe for respectable people, Chief W.P. Johnson was prepared to wink at the roistering on River Street. Johnson, who held his position from 1905 to 1927, made many raids and arrests, but few charges stuck. Finally, return train fare from nearby Regina was only a buck, and River Street came to do double duty as the red-light district of two cities.

At its peak, River Street was home to an estimated 50 to 100 prostitutes. Poker and faro games were everywhere. Beer, whiskey and even opium were available. And after 1924, when prohibition in Saskatchewan ended, Moose Jaw became the center of a flourishing new export industry: running booze into the still-dry United States.

Given the salubrious social and legal climate and the money to be made from bootlegging, legend has it that many American gangsters rode the Soo up to Moose Jaw to hide out for a while when things got too hot at home. One story involves Al Capone checking into a River Street hotel and summoning a doctor. When told he needed his tonsils removed, Capone refused both a hospital bed and anesthetic and told the doctor to have at it right there. After the operation the doctor was sent home with large wad of cash and strict instructions to have a memory lapse.

The Capone stories may or may not be true. But one legacy of Moose Jaw's racy days is not in doubt and still exists. A decade or so earlier someone had dug a network of tunnels under the streets of Moose Jaw's downtown, connecting various buildings. Some suggest the tunnels were dug by Chinese workers as a refuge and, if necessary, an escape from harassment and discrimination. White railway workers resented the Chinese, who they felt were being used by the companies to keep wages low. By the 1920s the tunnels became mighty handy for all kinds of activities that required discretion, perhaps a little bootlegging operation or some high-stakes poker. Because of natural hot springs that flow beneath the city, a weary gangster could even get a hot mineral bath in an underground spa to wash off the road dust acquired during a quick, quiet, heavily loaded trip from Montana.

Moose Jaw today, of course, is thoroughly respectable and wouldn't dream of winking at illegal activity. But the tunnels are still there, reminding tourists of the days when this placid prairie city was known as Little Chicago.

Spiritual Home of Force Still Offers Look Back at RCMP Depot Division
Dewdney Avenue, Regina

It hasn't been the actual headquarters of the Royal Canadian Mounted Police (Canada's national police force) since 1920, but Depot Division, still the force's principal training center, remains its spiritual home. It was actually the third headquarters of the fledgling North-West Mounted Police. The first headquarters—drafty, poorly built Fort Livingstone in Swan River country near the Manitoba boundary—was abandoned without regret after a single winter. In 1875, the force moved to Fort Walsh in the Cypress Hills, then a law enforcement hot spot teeming with traders, freighters, railway crews and thousands of Cree and Assiniboine, as well as the refugee Sioux that Sitting Bull led north across the border after wiping out Custer at the Battle of the Little Bighorn. But as the Sioux slowly returned south and as the railway began to move more settlers in, it made more sense to headquarter the force here. So in 1882, they did.

That force consisted of about 500 men. They patrolled a network of posts and forts from Edmonton to Fort Macleod to Battleford to the Cypress Hills and all the way east to Red River country. A century later, that force (now the Royal Canadian

Recruits drilling in the parade square of the Regina barracks of the North-West Mounted Police in 1895.

Mounted Police) had grown to employ about 20,000 and enforced the law in all provinces except Ontario and Quebec. It maintained liaison officers in 27 foreign capitals. Its legend—largely based on the exploits of those first 500 men—has made the Mountie one of Canada's most widely recognized symbols.

Depot Division still offers a look at the force's storied past. Not only is there an extensive museum featuring uniforms, photos, weapons and memorabilia, but there's a window on the Royal Canadian Mounted Police's tradition of military spit and polish. The Sergeant Major's Parade is held daily at 1:00 P.M., weather permitting. On summer weekends, the Sunset Retreat is a colorful drill ceremony centered around the lowering of the flag.

Frustration, Rage Result in Bloody Regina Riot
1717 Osler Street, Regina

It was 1935, the Dirty Thirties, and all across the country the federal government had tried to deal with a growing army of jobless, rootless and increasingly angry young men by putting them in work camps. The military-style camps eased the situation for a while. But in April, 1,500 residents of those camps in British Columbia went on strike, protesting conditions as well as

Violence breaks out at the Regina Riot.

what they called the government's reluctance to provide real work.

By June, radical labor organizers convinced about 1,000 of them to head east and take their concerns directly to Ottawa. Riding the rails, they chugged through Calgary, marched in Moose Jaw and Swift Current, and hopped off their boxcars here on June 14. Arthur Evans was one of the leaders of the On-to-Ottawa Trekkers, as they came to be called. He'd sent out advance parties, and Regina was ready.

The men were greeted by local organizations from local unions to the Ministerial Association. They were taken to the Exhibition Grounds, fed and given straw beds as a local choir sang the socialist anthem, "The Internationale." That night, a Friday, 6,000 people attended a rally to show their support. The next day, trekkers went through town collecting donations, and on Sunday, a local committee held a picnic in their honor. Bands played, and boxing and wrestling clubs held matches.

Meanwhile, the federal government had concluded the trekkers would pick up too much strength if they passed through Winnipeg. The protest had to stop in Regina. Railway cops told the trekkers they wouldn't be allowed on trains heading eastward. Advance parties were removed from a train in Brandon.

On Monday, two federal ministers came to Regina to meet with Evans, agreeing after talks that eight marchers would go to

Ottawa to meet with Prime Minister R.B. Bennett. That night, trekkers marched eight abreast up to the Hotel Saskatchewan to cheer the news. Now, they felt, they would get their hearing.

And so they did on June 22, but only to have Bennett deny all of Evans' demands. When the news filtered back to the 2,000 trekkers now in Regina, they tried resuming their eastward march in trucks and cars. About 200 Royal Canadian Mounted Police blocked the convoy, but the trekkers refused to head to relief camps in nearby Lumsden, and both sides were in a tense standoff.

For weeks now, the citizens of Regina had fed and sheltered the trekkers. By July 1, that support had begun to flag, and that day, Evans and other leaders held a rally in Market Square to shore it up. Unknown to Evans, Bennett had ordered his arrest. When the Mounties moved into the crowd of about 300, a violent riot broke out.

The fighting started shortly after 8:00 P.M. and lasted until midnight. It tore up Market Square and spread to the 11th Avenue and Scarth Street district. Years of frustration and rage erupted, and trekkers attacked police with clubs, rocks and bottles. Dozens on both sides were injured, and one policeman was beaten to death.

Within days, most of the trekkers had been put on trains back to British Columbia. About two dozen were jailed. A national fundraising campaign for their defense was mounted, with one farmer mortgaging his land for bail money. All were released by the end of 1936.

Sitting Bull Seeks Sanctuary in Qu'Appelle Valley
Highway 6, 24 miles (39 km) south of Regina

By 1881, Sitting Bull and his 4,000 Sioux followers had been living as refugees in the Wood Mountain area for about five years. Things had gone well at first: the hunting was good, the North-West Mounted Police had treated the Sioux fairly and they were safe from attack by the American army, which might have liked nothing better than another crack at the warriors who had wiped out Custer and his Seventh Cavalry.

But when prairie fires (set, some say, by U.S. troops) kept the buffalo south of the border and the Canadian government refused to feed people it considered an American problem, times got tougher. By the winter of 1879–80, the Sioux were near starvation. Many accepted defeat and returned to the United States.

Approximately only 100 destitute lodges remained by April 1881, when Sitting Bull made one final effort to remain in Canada. He traveled from his camp in Wood Mountain along the trail to Fort Qu'Appelle, where his old North-West Mounted Police friend Major James Walsh was stationed. The great chief planned to ask for sanctuary for his remaining followers in the Qu'Appelle Valley, but Walsh had returned to Ontario on sick leave and his replacement was unsympathetic. Sitting Bull trudged home to Wood Mountain in failure. Defeated and sick at heart, he led his people back to the United States with the despairing cry, "I am thrown away."

Young Priest Founds Oasis of Learning and Athletics in Dust Bowl
Off Highway 39, Main Street, Notre Dame College, Wilcox

The young Catholic priest was probably noticed the minute he drove into town. Athol Murray was not one to shirk the limelight, and there were, after all, 15 young men crammed into his car along with him. From that moment on, Père Murray was one of Wilcox's central figures and came to found a prairie legend of sports and scholarship.

Athol Murray was born in 1892 to a wealthy family with a home in Toronto's Rosedale district and a summer residence in Quebec's eastern townships. His mother died when he was four, and his father, keen to see young Athol comfortable in both French and English, saw that he was given a traditional, classical education in Quebec. After graduating from Laval University, Murray became a reporter for the *Toronto World,* then spent a couple years studying law. But one day he walked in to a secondhand bookstore and walked out with a copy of *Confessions* by St. Augustine. The book changed his life, inspiring him to become a priest. Ordained in 1918, the fluently bilingual, energetic young cleric was assigned five years later to Saskatchewan, an English-speaking province with many French-speaking Catholics.

One of his first acts in Regina proved prophetic. When a group of young boys broke into a church to steal candy and cigarettes intended for a parish bazaar, Murray convinced the local priest not to lay charges. Instead, he talked the boys into forming an athletic club, with him at the helm, called the Regina Argonauts. The club was a great success, and it was 15 Argonauts that he brought to Wilcox with him in 1927.

Before long Murray was taking an interest in the high school in Wilcox that many of his boys were attending. He began to pass out books to them and hold long discussions on the ideas they contained, whether or not they were on the school's curriculum. By the great crash of 1930 and the onset of the Dirty Thirties, Murray was in charge and Notre Dame College was known as almost the only place where a farm boy could get an affordable education. Tuition was $18 month if you had it, negotiable in terms of chickens or meat or grain if you didn't.

His school, which received neither church nor government support at first, was based on the same classical model that Murray had benefited from. Students read authors from Socrates to Moliére and discussed their books under the direction of a teacher, a course of instruction Murray was able to get endorsed by the University of Ottawa. It was, however, a modest temple of learning. Students took over abandoned buildings and patched them with packing crates to keep the wind out, or they built their own structures with donated materials. Food was often thin. Many times the school nearly went bankrupt.

Athletics accompanied the learning. Notre Dame hockey and baseball teams, known as the Hounds, toured the prairies and often provided a source of revenue for the college. The teams were consistently good. One baseball team was able to beat the Kansas City Monarchs, a barnstorming Negro League team from the days when professional baseball was segregated, by a score of 1–0. Murray was the coach although his fiery rhetoric was better at imparting inspiration and hard work than finely honed skills. During one game away, a Hounds hockey team, sapped from the road and a strain of measles making its way through the lineup, was falling behind the Regina Pats. Murray harangued his troops after the second period, finally crying, "Goddammit, boys, if you can't beat them at least give them the measles!"

That was vintage Murray, a man one writer described as "a

Catholic priest with the soul of a saint, the mind of a Greek philosopher and the vocabulary of a dock worker." He chain-smoked, kept a bottle of Scotch in his office and in cold weather covered his thick, black hair with a World War I–vintage leather flying helmet and his short, powerful frame in an enormous buffalo-robe coat, which did double duty as a blanket for the couch in his office, where he slept. His school became a haven for "tough" kids, many of whom he turned around. He worked hard for religious tolerance and vigorously opposed the introduction of Medicare. In 1972 he became a member of Canadian Sports Hall of Fame. He was known across the province simply as Père Murray, and his life and life's work became the subject of a successful Hollywood feature called *The Hounds of Notre Dame.*

In the autumn of 1975 Murray attended an alumni dinner in his honor at the Saskatchewan Center for the Arts in Regina. A thousand former students attended at $100 a plate, and Père, the lighted sign on the building, was visible for miles. Murray entered the hospital for a gall bladder operation a few days later. On December 4 he died.

ALONG HIGHWAYS 13, 36 AND 18

Fort Walsh–Fort Qu'Appelle Trail Offers Links through Entire North-West
Junction of highways 13 and 4, 2 miles (3.2 km) north of Cadillac

---

Developed by generations of native bands, the Fort Walsh–Fort Qu'Appelle Trail became an important route for pelts, pemmican and provisions between the Cypress Hills and Fort Qu'Appelle during the 1850s and after. It's a good example of how complete the old frontier trail system was. The route offered links to Fort Ellice in the eastern part of the province as well as the Red River settlement through to Fort Garry (now Winnipeg) in what is now Manitoba. It also offered connections north and west to the Red Deer River and Fort Carlton. From there, trails led farther northwest all the way to Fort Edmonton and beyond.

The route between the Cypress Hills and Fort Qu'Appelle was a regular fur trade route from 1856 on and North-West

A group of North-West Mounted Police riding patrol out from Fort Walsh in the Cypress Hills.

Mounted Police from Fort Walsh patrolled it regularly. And until the railway supplanted it well into the 20th century, it was one of the main trails for ranchers and freighters of the southwest.

Quebec Boy Reinvents Himself as Cowboy Artist and Author
Highway 4, 5 miles (8 km) south of Val Marie at turnoff into Grasslands National Park

---

He grew up Ernest Dufault, a young Quebec boy in love with the Wild West. He died as Will James, one of the most loved cowboy authors and artists of all time. All he had to do was hide his name, his roots, his mother tongue and his family.

Born in 1892 in a village outside Montreal, Dufault was already sketching horses by the age of four. He dreamed of the open range and earned extra money by painting western landscapes on tavern mirrors. After seeing a performance of Buffalo Bill's Wild West Show in Montreal, he went west himself.

He arrived in Saskatchewan at age 15 with a bagful of biscuits and $10. For a few years he drifted from ranch to ranch with Pierre Beaupre, an old hand who took the young Quebecois under his wing. Dufault learned cowboy skills and cowboy ways, covering bunkhouse walls with his drawings. After a spell as a line rider on the famous 76 Ranch, Dufault took out a homestead in 1911 along the Frenchman River, near Val Marie in what is now Grasslands National Park. His shack and cellar are still there.

The venture didn't last. Dufault, who liked a drink, got into a barroom brawl in which a man was shot to death. The Mounties tossed Dufault in jail. He was soon released and hightailed it south to California, never to return.

He sold some drawings in San Francisco and worked in Los Angeles as an extra in some early cowboy movies. But times got lean, and in 1915 Dufault let himself be talked into rustling a few cattle in Nevada.

When he got caught he told police his name was Will James. That's the name under which he spent four months in jail, covering the walls of his cell with chalk drawings. That's the name he used when he went back to earning a living with his art. That's the name he kept for the rest of his life.

James laid out his self-invented persona in his 1930 autobiography, *Lone Cowboy*. No longer were his parents small-town Quebecois shopkeepers. His father became a West Texan and his mother a Californian. Although his real parents and siblings remained alive and well, James claimed he had been orphaned at the age of four. Ernest Dufault was gone.

The tale worked. In 1920 he married Alice Conrad, a former Miss Nevada, who encouraged him to start writing stories to accompany his paintings. The books, starting in 1924 with *Cowboys North and South,* were huge hits. From then until his death in 1942, he averaged more than a title a year. Several, including *Sand* and *Smoky and the Cow Horse,* were made into successful Hollywood movies. James—slim, curly-haired, handsome—even appeared in a few. The cowboy who once scuffled for work as an extra was now lionized by the movie elite, and James divided his time between West Coast parties and his new 8,000-acre (3238-ha) spread near Pryor, Montana.

Still, James was having problems. His drinking was getting worse. Family members recall once, during one of his on-the-quiet trips to Quebec to visit his family, James was too drunk to speak French to his mother, who didn't speak English. He also had money worries. In 1935, Alice left him. Increasingly, he seemed haunted by Ernest Dufault. He wrote to his brother:

I wish you would make everybody realize how important

it is that they don't tell anyone or have it spread that they
know me. . . . I often wish that I had not represented myself
as I did, but I couldn't dream of the success I've had and
now it's too late to change. If what you all know ever got in
the right hands it would be in the papers overnight and I
would be classed as an impostor.

Was he an impostor? He may have been Quebec born, but he paid his ranch-hand dues and his heart was true-blue western. Readers and especially cowboys still treasure his books, especially his horse stories. One of his novels won a Newberry Medal, and all are prized collector's items in their first editions. Horsemen say nobody ever drew a bucking bronc like Will, not even the great Charlie Russell. Even a small Will James sketch can fetch $20,000 today. There are songs and movies about his life. There's a Will James Society in New Mexico, a Will James High School in Montana and Will James Days in Val Marie. Maybe all that makes him real enough.

Will James died an alcoholic in 1942 of cirrhosis of the liver in a Hollywood hospital. In accordance with his wishes his ashes were spread over his ranch so they could fertilize the grass that fed his beloved horses.

Lost Tool Inspires Name
Along Highway 13, Aneroid

An aneroid barometer is a type of barometer that measures atmospheric pressure by using the flexible lid of a box that has had the air pumped out instead of using the height of a column of liquid. And yes, that's where the name of this small community comes from. It seems a Canadian Pacific Railway survey crew had been equipped with one until they lost it near this site, so they remembered the event in the place name.

Sitting Bull Flees to Canada
Highway 18, 6 miles (10 km) south of Wood Mountain, Wood
Mountain Post Historic Park

It's peaceful enough now, this pleasant country of rolling prairie and wooded coulees. But during the days of the old

The North-West Mounted Police post at Wood Mountain.

North-West, this was for five years one of the most politically volatile spots on the continent.

Wood Mountain's first settlers came in 1870, when about 35 Métis families moved here after the failure of the Red River Rebellion. Boundary Commission survey teams were through shortly after to mark out the 49th parallel. They built the cabins that in 1874 became the first Wood Mountain North-West Mounted Police post. Chasing out the whiskey traders didn't take long, and the post was closed the next year.

But in 1876 the Sioux Nation, led by Chief Sitting Bull, wiped out General George Custer and the Seventh Cavalry at the Battle of the Little Bighorn in Montana. After that, Sitting Bull knew his people would need a refuge. Wood Mountain had long been Sioux hunting grounds (Sitting Bull may have even been born here), and the U.S. Army couldn't cross the border. So it was here that Sitting Bull came with 4,000 followers to flee American guns for Canadian law.

That law was represented by North-West Mounted Police Superintendent James Walsh, commanding officer of Fort Walsh in the nearby Cypress Hills. Walsh earned Sitting Bull's respect and an undying place in Mountie lore almost right away. Walsh rode with a mere handful of constables right into the Sioux camp full of warriors bedecked with fresh Yankee scalps. He laid down the rules: no fighting, no horse stealing, no raiding or smuggling across the American border. Sitting Bull agreed, and Walsh proved he meant it when he confiscated some stolen horses on his way out of the camp.

A Wood Mountain detachment about 22 members strong was reactivated within months. Walsh had a home built for himself near the barracks soon after. When about 200 Nez Perce crossed the border later in 1877 to join the Sioux, an already tense situation became taut as a bowstring.

The Americans worried that the fierce Sioux would use Wood Mountain to stage bloody raids into Montana, a fear fueled by constant newspaper editorials. They wanted the Sioux to return to the United States in surrender or become Canadian and move farther north. Canadians feared the militant Sitting Bull would destroy peace, perhaps by warring with the Blackfoot over the diminishing buffalo herds. Or scariest of all, perhaps Sitting Bull would succeed in uniting the tribes under his leadership to drive the whites out, a fear that wasn't unfounded, especially after the Métis rebel leader Louis Riel visited in 1879.

For years the Sioux lived in limbo. They weren't forced to return to the United States, but they were denied any kind of permanent status or provisions in Canada. Both the U.S. and Canada wanted the Sioux settled safely on a reserve, preferably in the other's territory.

At first Sitting Bull liked where he was. The hunting was good. His people could sleep at night without fear of soldiers. He trusted Walsh and the North-West Mounted Police. He brandished King George III medals given his ancestors for their help in the American Revolution, trying to prove the Sioux were British. When an American delegation came to try to persuade him to return, Sitting Bull said, "You come to tell us stories, and we do not want to hear them."

For nearly three years Walsh and Sitting Bull kept a tenuous balance, dancing on the point of an arrowhead. Walsh made sure the Sioux got enough guns and ammunition to hunt, but ran off any traders who sold them enough to make war. In turn, Sitting Bull kept his hundreds of restless young warriors in line. And although the American press came to refer to Walsh as "Sitting Bull's Boss," the two men developed a deep friendship.

But by 1879, the situation began to slide. First, a series of prairie fires that some suspect were deliberately set by the U.S. army kept the remaining buffalo south of the border, off limits to the Sioux. Tensions rose. Violence almost broke out when a dispute between Walsh and Sitting Bull ended with the policeman throwing the chief out of his house with a kick in the pants. It nearly happened again when a group of increasingly impoverished Sioux, angered by a local merchant's gouging, threatened the man's infant son. Police first rescued the baby, then escorted the grasping trader out of town.

By the spring of 1880, many now destitute Sioux began to drift south, attracted by the promise of amnesty and food. Sitting Bull became increasingly isolated. Even his friend Walsh left, reassigned to Fort Qu'Appelle. At their parting the great chief gave Walsh the war bonnet he wore at Little Bighorn. Sitting Bull could see he was defeated and set out for Montana with his few hundred remaining followers on July 11, 1881. Sitting Bull's search for sanctuary in Wood Mountain was finished.

The Wood Mountain North-West Mounted Police post was closed for a couple years, but reopened in 1885 with 41 officers. They policed the border, helped round up stray cattle, rode herd on unruly cowboys and helped chase down gangs of horse thieves. It was worthy work, but the post closed down in 1918. The area's new ranchers and settlers may have already forgotten that Wood Mountain was once the focus of a continent's fearful attention, the home to thousands of the fiercest warriors on the plains, Sitting Bull and the Sioux.

Sitting Bull Finally Loses Battle to Preserve Vision
Highway 18, 6 miles (10 km) south of Wood Mountain, Wood Mountain Post Historic Park on hill near museum

---

"There was something solemn and imperious about him, a certain reserve and dignity," said one missionary who remembered the great Sioux chief Ta-tanka I-yotank, or Sitting Bull. James Walsh, the policeman who became his great friend, remembered him as "the shrewdest and most intelligent living Indian . . . brave to a fault." On the other hand, an American newspaper editor called Sitting Bull "the bloodthirsty villain who has committed more murders than any other Indian since the days of the Wyoming massacre."

This we know: Sitting Bull was a powerfully built 5'10" (178 cm) although he walked with a slight limp from an old war wound. He had a face scarred by smallpox, a hooked nose and intense, striking eyes. He was born about 1834, probably in South Dakota, but perhaps right here in Wood Mountain. Although he fought his first battle at age 16 against the Assiniboine, it was as a medicine man that he first gained influence. His gifts as a healer gave him great insight into people, and even as a young man his advice was sought. By 1868 he was war chief of the Unkpapa Sioux, so prominent that he was taken to Washington to meet president Ulysses S. Grant, who gave him an engraved rifle.

But when gold was discovered in the Black Hills of the Dakotas—land that he had helped win for the Sioux through previous battles with the whites—Sitting Bull again found himself at war. That conflict led to the Battle of the Little Bighorn, in which Sitting Bull's warriors wiped out General George Custer and his Seventh Cavalry.

Sitting Bull fled to Canada at the height of his reputation. Newspapers from New York to Fort Garry followed his every move, and his name was so feared that pioneer mothers used it to frighten unruly children. Those who called him brutal pointed to the death sentence he passed on any Sioux who told a white man about gold deposits in the Black Hills or any white who found gold. His defenders pointed to Sitting Bull's reputation for compassion to his prisoners; one, an Assiniboine named Hohay, became the chief's lifelong friend. Others mention his devotion to his family, which consisted at one time of three wives, two daughters and three sons, two of whom were twins.

A Métis who saw Sitting Bull in Wood Mountain described him in this way:

> *Though he was charged with being a very cruel man, he yet had a splendid trait of character—he always saw that his Indians were fed before he would eat, that they were clothed before he took his share of clothing. He ruled his tribe with an iron hand, yet he was kind and gentle to them.*

Sitting Bull never quit trying to find a place where the Sioux could be free to hunt and roam in the old way. He tried to limit the influence of white ways and opposed liquor. He used all his diplomatic skills to try to convince the plains tribes to unite to rid their homeland of the whites, even discussing the idea with the Métis rebel Louis Riel.

Eventually, Sitting Bull was forced back to the United States. For a while he appeared in Buffalo Bill Cody's Wild West Show. But in 1890 he had a vision while on a hunting trip. He saw his dead relatives come back to life, the plains once more rich with buffalo and a man with flowing hair in white buffalo garments. The man showed him marks in his hands and feet and told him he had returned to save the Sioux.

Sitting Bull told the other members of his band what he had seen. They rejoiced, gathering and holding dances. The local Indian agent didn't like to see the Sioux stirred up and asked Sitting Bull to renounce his vision. When the old medicine chief refused, he was arrested on a trumped-up charge. His followers tried to rescue him and shooting ensued. Although he was twice wounded, Sitting Bull grabbed a Winchester rifle and fought on until police and soldiers attacked, grabbed the rifle and broke it over his head. Sitting Bull died, fighting to save his vision.

Sitting Bull "asked for nothing but justice," wrote Walsh when he heard the news. "He loved his people and was glad to give his hand in friendship to any man who was honest with him. Bull experienced so much treachery he did not know who to trust."

Ancient Hunters Leave Mysterious Rock Carvings
Highway 2, turnoff at Provincial Road 705, 9 miles (15 km) to St. Victor, follow same road to St. Victor's Petroglyphs just south of town

---

One day hundreds of years ago, an Indian climbed this rugged sandstone outcrop that commanded a dramatic view of the plains and coulees. The Indian looked around until the spot marked with the signs of the ancestors became apparent. A chisel and hammerstone made from good, hard quartzite were produced. Perhaps there was a prayer or a ceremony before the stone chips began to fly as the Indian began to add more signs to the ones already there.

And that's about all that is known about the mysterious petroglyphs on the rock overlooking the town of St. Victor.

The carvings, some chiseled in on top of older ones, include representations of grizzly bears, turtles and the tracks of deer, antelope, elk or bison. There are human feet, hands and heads.

Nobody knows what some of the glyphs are, and some are so eroded they are unintelligible. Because there are no carvings of horses, archaeologists suggest they were made before 1750, the year the horse arrived on the northern plains.

Most petroglyphs are found on vertical rock faces, and St. Victor is the only horizontal site on the Canadian plains. But because of other similarities to better-understood sites, scientists speculate that the carvings were made by the ancestors of today's Sioux or Assiniboine people. No one knows for sure, however. Nor does anyone know why they were made. Hacking away at the sandstone couldn't have been easy work, so the reason must have been powerful. Perhaps it was part of a medicine ritual, an attempt to control the movement of buffalo, a record of a band's history or a collection of clan totems.

The best time to view these petroglyphs is toward dusk as the shadows produced by the setting sun define them more clearly. No matter how cool the evening prairie breeze, the ancient thoughts recorded at your feet are still warm.

Willow Bunch Giant the Tallest Tale of All
Willow Bunch Museum, old convent on 5th Street, Willow Bunch

Even in a province full of tall tales and larger-than-life characters, they don't come any taller or larger than Edouard Beaupre. Born in 1881 to Métis and Quebecois parents, Beaupre was a normal, healthy little boy for a few years. But starting at the age of three, he grew faster than dandelions. By the age of nine, he was nearly 6' (183 cm). At 17, he stood 7'1" (216 cm). And fully grown, he stood an amazing 8'3" (251 cm), in his stocking feet with his hair combed flat.

Beaupre's condition, known as pituitary giantism, directed his life. All he wanted was to be a cowboy (they say he was a smooth rider and a slick hand with a lasso), but his legs got so long he could no longer sit on a horse. So at the age of 17, Beaupre began to earn a living appearing at exhibitions, showing himself, wrestling local strongmen and performing feats of strength at shows from Montreal to California. He was something to see. There are stories of a teenaged Beaupre lifting an 800-pound (363-kg) horse by himself. He had a 24" (61-cm) neck, a 58" (147-cm) chest and weighed 375 pounds (170 kg). He wore

Edouard Beaupre in 1904. Also shown, left to right, Jean-Louis Legare, Prudent Lapointe and Gaspard Beaupre, Edouard's father.

size 22 shoes and slept in a 9' (2.7-m) bed. Most of the money he earned he sent home to his parents, and in 1903 that's where he returned to recover his health. Edouard was beginning to show signs of tuberculosis. But the next year Beaupre hit the road again with the famous P.T. Barnum Circus. It was to prove his last trip. Three days after leaving Willow Bunch, Beaupre died while performing at the St. Louis World's Fair.

Sadly, his travels were far from over.

His parents didn't have the money to have Beaupre shipped home. They thought their son's body had been buried in St. Louis, but Beaupre's agent had the corpse embalmed and put it on exhibit. After hearing it was being displayed in storefront windows to draw attention to promotional campaigns, the family sent a friend to St. Louis to settle Beaupre's affairs. The friend shipped the body to Montreal, where it drew huge crowds to the museum that displayed it. The ghoulish exhibit ended up in a freak show, and when the freak show went bankrupt the body was abandoned and then discovered by a group of children.

The University of Montreal claimed the body for research purposes, which didn't prevent the institution from keeping the body on public display until 1975. The Quebec rock band Beau Dommage wrote a hit song about the ghost of Edouard Beaupre roaming the halls of the university. Finally, the Quebec government banned the photographing of corpses and Edouard's public career, which lasted 54 years longer than his short life, was over.

Eventually in 1989, the university reached a deal with Edouard's surviving family in Willow Bunch to ship Beaupre back to his hometown, which he never wanted to leave in the first place. In July 1990, the Willow Bunch Giant finally received a Christian burial. His body, never again to be stared at, was cremated.

Métis Trader Plays Vital, Quiet Role in Dramatic Standoff
Highway 36, turn west on last grid road before leaving Willow Bunch, take first south road at sign, drive 1.2 miles (2 km) southwest of Willow Bunch to Louis Legare Park

---

In the great drama that unfolded between Major James Walsh of the North-West Mounted Police and Sitting Bull, chief of the Sioux, there is an often forgotten third character: the gentle, compassionate Métis trader, Jean-Louis Legare.

While Sitting Bull and the Sioux pleaded for permanent sanctuary in Canada and Walsh strove to uphold the law as his government dithered over the Indians' fate, Legare quietly befriended the great chief and ensured his people were fed. He probably did as much as anyone to keep the peace.

Until 1869, the Quebec-born Legare was a free trader based in St. Paul, Minnesota. But when the Hudson's Bay Company surrendered its lands to Canada, he moved north and set up shop on this site. The tall, bearded Métis' courteous, fair dealing soon made him popular among the Wood Mountain hunters, and his business prospered. But in 1876 Legare found his role in history when Sitting Bull brought 4,000 Sioux over the line, fleeing American wrath after wiping out Custer and the Seventh Cavalry.

It was Legare to whom Walsh, commander of the nearest Mountie detachment, entrusted the dicey job of supplying the Sioux: sell them enough ammunition to hunt but not enough to make war; give them the food they need but don't encourage them to stay through abundance. As the hunting worsened and the Sioux grew poorer, that trade got closer to charity. Sitting Bull and his people came to trust Legare. North-West Mounted Police Commissioner Acheson Irvine praised him, saying, "His disinterested and honorable course being decidedly marked, particularly when compared to other individuals."

By 1881, Legare could see no future for the Sioux in Canada, and he offered to feed, transport and plead the cause of any Sioux who wished to return to the United States—all at his own expense. Many took him up. Eventually, Legare talked Sitting Bull into returning south and escorted him there himself. Legare estimated he spent about $10,000 keeping the Sioux during those desperate years. The U.S. government reimbursed him for about half. Later, Legare turned down the Canadian government's grateful offer of a township of land.

He got that township anyway, at least in spirit, as Legare is remembered as the founder of Willow Bunch. Legare stayed in the area and died in 1918. This park was created in his memory in 1965.

Outlaws Hole Up in Big Muddy
Highway 18, area north of Coronach

Riding the outlaw trail is an old western expression referring to life on the fringes of society and the law. But once there was a real outlaw trail, a well-organized route complete with hideouts and supply depots that horse thieves, desperadoes and assorted no-accounts could follow all the way from Canada to Mexico. Here, in the buttes and badlands of the Big Muddy, was its northern terminus.

The Outlaw Trail was organized in the late 1800s, some say by the train robber Butch Cassidy himself. Running through wild country and friendly ranches, the Outlaw Trail moved north from Ciudad Juarez in Mexico, to the Wilson Ranch in New Mexico, to Robbers' Roost in Utah, to Hole In the Wall, Wyoming, to Deadwood, South Dakota, to Miles City, Montana, and then over the line to the Big Muddy. It made a great escape route for the train-robbing syndicate The Wild Bunch. And horse and cattle thieves made regular traffic on the northern end.

The major gangs operating out of the Big Muddy were the Dutch Henry and the Nelson (aka Sam Kelly) outfits. "Dutch" Henry, or Henry Yeuch, drifted to Canada after being run out of Kansas and started out cowboying at the Bonneau ranch near Willow Bunch. He was a skilled rider and cattleman but an even better horse thief. Sam Kelly, red-haired, tall and slim, was an expert marksman who neighbors said could shoot the horns off a steer at 100 yards (91 m) with his .30-30. His Jones–Nelson gang was affiliated with The Wild Bunch. During the 1890s both gangs thrived by supplying the growing demand for stock north of the border with herds stolen from ranches to the south. Brands were often unregistered, and brand inspectors and Mounties were few and far between. The canyons and gulches of the Big Muddy were ideal places to hide a hot herd, even better after the gangs dug out several good-sized caves to hide their ill-gotten merchandise. There was reliable water and the buttes offered natural lookouts for the approach of any law.

Once, the gangs herded 200 stolen horses into Canada, sold them, then stole them right back and resold them in Montana. A $1,200 reward was offered for the gang leaders after 140 cattle were stolen from the Diamond Ranch.

By 1902 the North-West Mounted Police was forced to set up a detachment on a local ranch to control the gangs that had become, in the words of Inspector J.C. Wilson, "the terror of our community." Gang members were rounded up on both sides of the line. In 1906 Dutch Henry was shot dead in a gunfight in Minnesota. Sam Kelly turned himself in to the law in

Plentywood, Montana, but he beat charges against him and returned to the area in about 1913 to take up ranching. He died, they say with his boots on, in a North Battleford hotel bed in 1954.

The Big Muddy country is now accessible only by guided tours from Coronach.

Mysterious Rock Effigies Recall Indian Past
Big Muddy, off Highway 18, Coronach

The original inhabitants of this land wrote their story not in stone cities or temples but directly on the prairie sod, leaving boulders behind them outlining where they pitched their tepees, where they hunted and perhaps where, and what, they worshipped. The plow has since erased the plains, but in some never-cultivated places that writing remains. Like in the Big Muddy.

Although they all lie on private land and can be seen only on a guided tour, this rugged valley has some of the most interesting and mysterious boulder effigies in the West. Outlined in rocks big enough to stand out but not too big to carry, most are located on high, open land that commands a view. Archaeologists believe they are between 2,000 and 3,000 years old. Some represent animals; some, humans. Some, it is thought, mark battles while others tell tribal history. Some are inexplicable.

Turtles represent wisdom and respect to the Dakota Blackfoot, and here there is a turtle effigy about 33' (10 m) long and 20' (6 m) wide, which at one time ringed a burial cairn, since destroyed. A large ceremonial circle lies nearby that at one time may have been the site of a large "meeting hall" lodge. There is a medicine wheel, which some believe was a powerful element in hunting rites. The outline of a buffalo, the animal that gave so much to the prairie Indians, may be the only such effigy left on the plains. There are numerous outlines of buffalo pounds, used to gather buffalo for slaughter.

After centuries of weather, they're almost part of the landscape. But a tepee ring sitting in the wind on high ground overlooking the open prairie can evoke as much about that ancient life as the grandest ancient monument. The Big Muddy country is now accessible only by guided tours from Coronach.

Wood Mountain–Fort Qu'Appelle Trail Links Buffalo Herds and Whoop-Up Country with Outside World

Highway 36, take Ormiston turnoff west from highway, turn north at town, then drive 3 miles (5 km) to Ora Lake Regional Park

The Wood Mountain–Fort Qu'Appelle Trail was one of the most important thoroughfares in the network of trails that once crisscrossed the plains. Its 260-mile (420-km) length linked good-sized Métis settlements at both ends and gave the North-West Mounted Police a way to get to the bustling Wood Mountain country from the force's headquarters in Regina.

This spot marks the rough midpoint of a trail that dates back to the early 1850s. Like so many other prairie trails, it was scouted out by Métis buffalo hunters. Some of the last great herds were still living in the country to the southwest, and this trail became so popular that by 1868 tiny settlements and homes had sprung up along its path. Cart trains of pelts, pemmican and provisions would normally make the trip in three weeks.

Wood Mountain marked the eastern end of Whoop-Up Country, a lawless stretch of the northwestern frontier where Indians, Métis, American and Canadian whiskey traders and hinterland riffraff mingled and circulated around the few pioneer settlers. They met to swap horses, rotgut booze, buffalo robes and sometimes gunfire. After the coming of the North-West Mounted Police in 1874, the trail became a vital link to other detachments for the busy Wood Mountain police post.

Here's an example of the kind of action the Wood Mountain officers faced, as relayed in one of their reports:

On the 17th inst., I, Corporal Hogg, was called to the hotel to quiet a disturbance. I found the room was full of cowboys and one Monoghan, or Cowboy Jack, was carrying a gun and pointed it at me against Sections 105 and 109 of the Criminal Code. We struggled. Finally, I got him handcuffed behind and put him inside. His head being in bad shape we had to engage the services of a doctor who dressed his wound and pronounced it nothing serious.

Like most other prairie trails, this path was used by settlers and ranchers into the 1920s.

ALONG HIGHWAYS 43 AND 2

Missionary Colonizers Found Gravelbourg
Highway 58, Gravelbourg

Gravelbourg band playing for St. Jean-Baptiste Day, 1927, in front of cathedral.

Although French voyageurs, French traders, French priests and French Métis gave the old North-West a strong Gallic flavor from its earliest days, by the end of the 19th century the leaders of that community feared for its future. New, English-speaking, Protestant, pro-British settlers, many not noticeably friendly to things Catholic or Francophone, were pouring in. By 1885, almost one-third of the population of the present-day Northwest Territories had been born in anglo Ontario. In Manitoba, the proportion of Catholics had fallen from about half in 1860 to 13.5 percent.

Starting in 1887, Archbishop Alexandre Tache organized the missionary colonizers: priests with specific knowledge of areas who would work with the local Bishop to bring out French settlers. Father Louis Pierre Gravel, the founder of Gravelbourg, was such a man.

Gravel's plans were ambitious. Trolling the townships of Quebec and the expatriate Quebecois communities of New

England, he hoped to populate a string of dozens of French-speaking, Catholic settlements between Weyburn and Lethbridge. But the pace of English immigration swamped his efforts, and he was forced to retrench to the spot along the Wood River where he and his five brothers and a sister had settled in 1906. Here, both French and Catholicism thrived. By 1919, the town now known as Gravelbourg had an imposing Romanesque cathedral. It was named the seat of the diocese in 1930. The town remains a center of French cultural and educational life in Saskatchewan.

Casualties of March West Pause to Recuperate at Cripple Camp
Highway 58, 1st Avenue, Gravelbourg

The fresh, young recruits of the newly formed North-West Mounted Police were hale, hearty and enthusiastic when they set off from Dufferin, Manitoba, in the summer of 1874 to bring British law and order to the West. That was soon to change. The so-called March west has since gone down in Mountie lore as the force's trial by fire (or rather, trial by prairie).

The column of 275 officers, 20 drivers, 310 horses, 140 oxen, 100 cattle, 73 wagons, 114 carts, 2 field guns and 2 mortars must have been an impressive sight as it stretched for nearly 3 miles (5 km) along the trail. But the truth was that few, if any, were experienced plainsmen. The young men from the farms and cities of Ontario may have been strong and willing, but they couldn't have known what was in store.

There were constant problems with finding fresh water. They were traveling in a drought year, and drinking from alkali ponds or streams just caused dysentery. Their animals had trouble finding pasture. Clouds of black flies and mosquitoes plagued both man and beast. One morning the men awoke to hear what they thought was rain falling on their tents only to find it was grasshoppers. Prairie fires also threatened the column.

By August 19, 8 men and 26 horses were too sick and weak to go any farther. Commissioner George French ordered them to set up camp here and rest until they recuperated. The spot came to be known as Cripple Camp. By October the "cripples" were well enough to proceed, and they saddled up to join their comrades at the force's new headquarters at Fort Livingstone on the Swan River.

Mossbank Bombing and Gunnery School Trains 1940s Top Guns
Highway 2, east edge of Mossbank, now a golf course

These days, golf balls are the only things flying through the air around here. But during World War II, these skies were full of young airmen training for battle, part of a massive plan crucial to the Allied war effort. By the late 1930s Britain's top military planners knew air power would be crucial in the next war and that the Commonwealth didn't have enough of it. Trained pilots and crews were the greatest need. Britain was no place to train the number of air crews the Allies were going to need: 29,000 pilots, navigators, gunners and radio operators a year, according to early estimates. Space for airfields was limited, the weather was unpredictable and it was dangerously close to the front. But none of that was true of the Canadian West. So on December 16, 1939, Canada and Britain signed an agreement that would bring tens of thousands of young men from throughout the Commonwealth to the prairies for air training. There were a dozen such schools in Saskatchewan alone, one in nearly every major city or town, but Mossbank's was special.

Here was the province's only bombing and gunnery school, an advanced center where the best young pilots trained to become the top guns of their war. The training was straightforward. In one exercise, a lead plane towed an unmanned drogue about 33 yards (30 m) behind, and a trainee in the rear cockpit of a following plane fired at it. Trainees achieved varying degrees of accuracy. Not surprisingly, target towing was an unpopular assignment. As one instructor wrote, "If someone didn't want to instruct, we arranged a posting to a bombing and gunnery school as a target towing pilot and after that we had no trouble."

The foreign trainees, of course, must have worried about their friends and family back home, some living under Nazi bombs, some under actual occupation. But for a few years their presence livened up the prairies. They organized sports, including boxing, cricket, soccer and track and field. They grew gardens and put on plays. After 1941, married men were allowed to bring their families if accommodation could be found. From the start, unmarried men were welcome additions to local dances. Many married Canadian girls and returned after the war. And occasionally some young hothead stuck instructing even younger pilots would commit a misdemeanor in an effort to get reassigned to the front—something like flying a Tiger Moth under a bridge.

Over the course of the war, the Commonwealth Air Training Plan eventually graduated 72,835 Canadians, 42,110 British, 9,606 Australians and 7,002 New Zealanders, as well as about 5,000 French, Czech, Norwegian, Polish, Belgian and Dutch crewmen. They flew everywhere battles were fought. You might even say the dogfights of Europe were won in the skies over the prairies.

Indian Legend Tells of Brave and Terrifying Sacrifice

Highway 2, 20 miles (32 km) south of Moose Jaw at Highway 36 intersection, then drive 5 miles (7.7 km) southwest on Highway 2 to Old Wives Lake

---

Buffalo were plentiful back in the days before Europeans came to the plains. But that doesn't mean the hunting was always good. And when something interrupted the normal patterns of game and caused people to move outside their usual territories, the results could be violent. The story of how Old Wives Lake got its name is an example.

One season long ago, a prairie fire blackened the grassland across the Regina plains and the Qu'Appelle Valley. The buffalo drifted west in search of pasture and a party of Cree from the Qu'Appelle area followed them. Their hunt was successful and the band, camped by a large lake, soon had all the meat they could carry back to their regular territory. But before they could leave, they were spotted by a party of Blackfoot. The Blackfoot attacked, and the Cree, burdened by their entire camp as well as the meat they had butchered, were unable to flee so defended themselves from where they were. Soon, the Blackfoot disappeared into the hills, but the Cree knew their enemies would return with reinforcements. They held council in their camp and pondered their situation. Outnumbered and trapped, the Cree warriors were preparing to make a stand to the death when one of the band's old women spoke out.

She suggested that the band's men, young women and children sneak out during the night. The old women would remain in the camp, keeping the fires burning to fool the Blackfoot scouts into believing that the camp was still occupied. The plan was accepted. All that night the old women heaped the fires with buffalo chips while the rest of the band stole off into the dark-ness. When the Blackfoot attacked in the morning, only the old women remained. Angry at having been tricked, the Blackfoot killed them all.

Because of the old women, the rest of the band made it safe-ly home and the scene of their sacrifice became known as Old Wives Lake. It was renamed Johnstone Lake after a titled Englishman who spent some time hunting in the district, but the original name was restored in 1953.

On windy nights, from an island in the middle of the lake, legend holds you can still hear the laughter of the old women mocking the Blackfoot.

Prairie Archaeology Leaves Much to the Imagination
Highway 2, 3 miles (5 km) south of Moose Jaw, south of military airfield area east of highway, Parkhill Archaeological Site

If the word *archaeologist* conjures up images of Indiana Jones swinging through ancient temples, give a thought to the archaeologist working on the prairies.

Ancient Indians were nomadic people and left no great build-ings or stone idols. Their settlements were temporary and left little imprint on the earth. Most of what they needed they made from wood, leather, rock or bone—materials that either don't last or blend in so well that what were once tools now just look like more debris. Scientists must piece together the rich history and culture of hundreds of years through the bits and pieces that remain, like trying to rebuild a car with only an old tire and a rusty carburetor.

At the Parkhill site to the east, there's nothing for the unedu-cated eye to see (and it's private land, anyway). But research has shown that the top of the low rise in the east was a popular pre-historic campsite.

It's not hard to imagine why. The spot would have given paleo-Indians an excellent of view of any nearby game. The ele-vation would have made the most of any breeze to help keep the bugs down. The small sloughs nearby used to be a stream, which would have provided water. The stream channel also could have been used to drive buffalo, which regularly migrated through here. It would have been a great spot to set up camp for few days, butcher a kill, maybe fix a few tools broken in the hunt.

And it seems that's exactly what early Indians did. Past excavations have turned up about 300 blades, points and knives made from rock that came from North Dakota and southern Manitoba. That's all that was found.

But it's enough to conjure up an image of an ancient hunter sitting by his tepee, flaking a new spearpoint out of a broken one, getting the most out of the valuable stone. He pauses and squints, maybe from the campfire smoke blowing into his eyes or maybe from the setting sun as he gazes across the prairie, thinking about where to look for game tomorrow and giving thanks for today's hunt.

Finnish Homesteader Builds Little Ship on the Prairie
Highway 2, 7.5 miles (12 km) south of Moose Jaw, Tom Sukanen's Ship

---

Most of the throngs of immigrants attracted by Saskatchewan's Last, Best West eventually fit happily into their new lives. But many must have felt the tidal tug of the Old Country long after they broke their sod. They must have felt, despite new friendships and new opportunities, like ships adrift from their moorings. Like Tom Sukanen.

In 1898, Tom Sukanen emigrated from Finland to the United States to settle in Minnesota. There was little call in his new home for a skilled shipbuilder, so Tom took up farming. He worked at it for 13 years, marrying and fathering four children, but it was tough going, and in 1911, at age 33, he left his family with a promise to return and came to Canada. He walked the entire 620 miles (1,000 km) from Minnesota to Saskatchewan and homesteaded near Macrorie, about 93 miles (150 km) northwest of Moose Jaw.

Here, Tom became a successful farmer, with a farmer's ingenuity. He made himself a sewing machine to fix his clothes and knit himself a suit of work clothes out of binder twine. When small threshing machines became popular, Tom had a look at his neighbor's and built his own. Tom , at 6'2" (188 cm), 270 pounds (122 kg), was hugely strong and was often seen walking the 6 miles (10 km) between town and his farm carrying hundreds of pounds of supplies. By 1916 he had saved $9,000—a lot of money back then. Two years later Tom decided to fulfill his promise to his family and walked back to Minnesota. He hoped to return to Saskatchewan with his wife and four children, but found his home deserted and his wife dead of influenza. Tom tracked down his son, but when the two tried to return to Canada the authorities would not let the boy leave his foster parents. Tom returned alone.

Tom worked his farm and on railway crews, where he could lift a 600-pound (272-kg) rail by himself. In 1929, he remarked that he was thinking of returning to visit Finland. No one thought much of it, but when he disappeared for a month it was later discovered that he had built a rowboat, paddled up the North Saskatchewan to Hudson Bay, got a job on a freighter and visited his old home, bringing with him a homemade violin on which he played tunes he had learned in Canada.

He returned to Saskatchewan that same year. Soon after, a shipment of steel cable and copper arrived for Tom at the Macrorie rail station. Neglecting his farm (not that it mattered in the first year of the drought of the Dirty Thirties), Tom began building a steamship. By hand, he forged gears, pulleys, anchor chain and propeller. He bent thick planks onto the oak hull and caulked them watertight. Tom's forge blazed and his hammer rang constantly through the dusty Great Depression years. The project bankrupted him. He became a recluse, lost weight and stopped caring about his appearance—his face was constantly blackened from working over the forge. Tom's neighbors called him "Crazy Finn" and maybe he was, but the ship took shape—more than 33' (10 m) long and 13' (4 m) wide, complete with cabins, a wheelhouse and storage space. By 1941, the ship's boiler and engine were complete. His plan, which he had carefully charted out with government maps, was to float the ship in sections down the North Saskatchewan River to Hudson Bay. From there he would sail it home in triumph to Finland. He never made it.

For some time Tom's neighbors had become increasingly concerned about what they thought was his strange behavior. But it wasn't until vandals stripped the ship in his absence that Tom's spirit finally broke. His neighbors convinced the authorities to take him to an institutional hospital in North Battleford, where Tom died in 1943. What was left of his ship was towed onto a friend's farm. There it remained until 1972, when it was towed to its present site and restored. It is now on display, the vessel of Tom Sukanen's unquiet spirit.

White Mud from Claybank Brick Plant Bricks up Hotels, Locomotives, Warships
Highway 339, 32 miles (53 km) southeast of Moose Jaw

When Tom McWilliams stuck his spade in the dirt back in the 1880s, he didn't anticipate that the contents of his shovel would wind up everywhere from the front of a historic hotel to the warships of the Canadian Navy. But that's what happened.

McWilliams, a local homesteader, was among the first to realize that the pale gray muck of the Dirt Hills near his farm was actually a vein of high-quality clay. Part of the Whitemud Formation, the rare and rich deposit was high in quartz and other minerals that make it particularly heat resistant and suitable for fire bricks. McWilliams applied for a permit to mine the clay in 1886, shipping it to a fire brick factory in Moose Jaw.

The coming of the railway in 1910 encouraged local businessmen to build a fire brick plant right on the site. In 1912, that's what they did. Under various owners the Claybank brick plant produced bricks steadily for the next 75 years. Claybank brick came to cover the central tower of the famous Chateau Frontenac hotel in Quebec City. Many of Saskatchewan's public buildings, including the Gravelbourg Cathedral, are faced entirely in Claybank brick. The fireboxes of both Canadian National and Canadian Pacific rail locomotives used them. So did the submarine-hunting Corvette-class ships of the Canadian Navy during World War II.

The plant closed in 1989, a victim of changing markets and technology. But the Claybank site is now open to visitors, providing insight into 19th-century industrialism and the scenic land that provided the raw material.

Chapter 3

Horizon Region

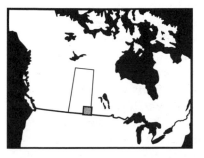

Visions and Dreams Mark Horizon Country

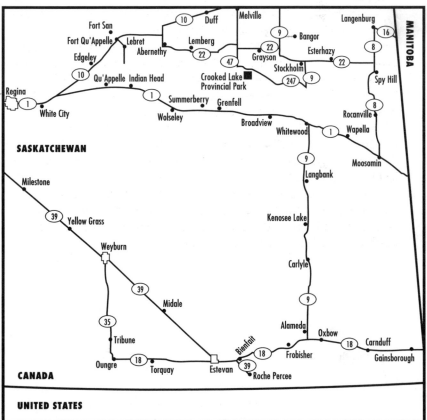

HORIZON COUNTRY they aptly call this southeast corner of the province. This area is full of stories about people who came here with their eyes on future horizons, full of hope and faith that they could create here the community they saw in their dreams.

There was the little piece of England that was Cannington Manor and its Gallic counterpart, the gracious French Counts of neighboring St. Hubert. There were Welsh nationalists in Bangor and to the south, the Jewish refugees of Hirsch. Other kinds of community began here, too, based on ideals rather than ethnic roots. Saskatchewan's cooperative movement traces its start to the Harmony Industrial Association south of Langenburg. And it was here that farmers banded together for the first time to fight for their economic interests with the Territorial Grain Growers Association.

Saskatchewan's future arrived first in Horizon Country. Some of the earliest fur trade posts were built here. The fledgling policemen of the North-West Mounted Police entered the province here in 1874 on their epic March west and began to learn what the prairie was really all about. The railroad came through here, too.

It's fair to say that in this country of visions and beginnings prairie agriculture began to take shape. Angus Mckay at Indian Head headed a research station that developed the use of summer fallow and shelterbelts, two of the agricultural techniques that still determine much of the look of the prairies. And one of Saskatchewan's most durable icons—the prairie grain elevator—appeared here first.

Some of the people most associated with the province also got their start here. The writer W.O. Mitchell, author of the beloved novel *Who Has Seen the Wind,* grew up in Weyburn. That's also where Tommy Douglas, the politician remembered today as the Father of Medicare, came as a freshly ordained Baptist minister for his first congregation. And although the Bronfman family may not be associated with Saskatchewan these days, it's here, in the province's prohibition past, where the roots of the family fortune lie.

Behind it all lie generations of native prehistory, and perhaps the best way to contemplate all that began here is from that perspective. There's an ancient burial mound, one of a few in western Canada, on a bluff overlooking Crooked Lake and the Qu'Appelle Valley. With all that's changed here, that view may be the only one those buried here would still recognize.

ALONG HIGHWAY 1

Bad Luck, Bad Weather Break Would-be Emperor of Bell Farm
Highway 1, Indian Head

The year 1882 was a great one for empire builders on the plains. The railway was coming through, easing the movement of goods and people. The federal government was eager to see settlers move into its empty western lands. And the fading of the buffalo hunts and the fur trade left the land wide open for men with big ideas. Such a man was Major William R. Bell.

Born in Brockville, Ontario, Bell was a veteran of the Fenian raids of the 1860s. Afterward he farmed in the United States and lived in Winnipeg. He knew about both agriculture and the West when he approached the government with his plan. Promising to move in hundreds of tenant farmers, Bell got 23,000 acres (9,308 ha) from the government and another 29,111 acres (11,781 ha) from the Canadian Pacific Railway that included the land on which Indian Head now sits. Bell began industrial farming on a grand scale.

His men began breaking land on June 25, 1882, and by the next year he already had 4,320 acres (1,748 ha) seeded to wheat, oats and potatoes. By 1884, he had 14,000 acres (5,666 ha) under cultivation and had spent about $400,000 (a fortune in those days) putting up about 90 buildings, including granaries, a veterinary clinic, a smithy, a stable, an icehouse, a chicken house, a cow barn, bridges and roads. The operation could marshal as many as 45 binders to harvest a single field. About 106 settlers lived on the Bell Farm, now incorporated as the Qu'Appelle Valley Farming Company.

Bell commanded the whole enterprise from his great 16-room stone farmhouse, where he sat and barked orders to his tenants over his newly installed telephone, an invention then less than a decade old.

The first sign of trouble came in 1885, when the North-West Rebellion virtually shut the farm down. As well, wheat varieties adapted for the short growing season of the plains hadn't yet been developed and heavy frosts hurt harvests. Bell was having trouble with both his financiers and the Canadian Pacific Railway, and the original farm went under in 1889. Bell hung on,

managing to retain control of 12,700 acres (5,140 ha). But more bad luck came his way. A fire in 1893 destroyed his mill, office and elevator. Two disastrous crop years followed from 1894 to 1896. Finally, Bell was sued into receivership by Scottish creditors and everything was auctioned off. In 1887, part of his land became the nearby Dominion Experimental Farm, which was to help develop the farming practices and crop varieties that might have made it possible for Bell to prosper.

The Bell Farm's round stone stable, the only vestige of a farming empire in a land that's been tough on would-be emperors, still stands about 1.9 miles (3 km) north on Highway 56.

Hiring Out Horses Leads to Revolution in Farming at Indian Head Experimental Farm
Highway 1, Indian Head

The practice of summer-fallowing (leaving a field unsown for a summer so it can replenish its nutrients and moisture) is so

Work on the Bell Farm around 1885 with 5 sulky plows and 23 reapers.

common on prairie farms that even city folk know what it is. Summer-fallowing practically defines prairie agriculture, and that definition was written here.

Angus Mackay, who had begun farming this district three years before, was getting ready to start his field work in the spring of 1885 when the North-West Rebellion broke out. The militia and the North-West Mounted Police needed horses to move equipment and supplies to Battleford, and the offer of $10 a day for a man and his team was too good to pass up. Mackay got most of his newly broken land seeded before he headed out to help the forces, but he didn't have time to seed 400 acres (162 ha) that had produced a frozen crop the year before. Mackay eventually got around to plowing it and occasionally worked it over through the summer to keep down weeds.

The summer of 1886 brought a cruel drought. Crops through-out the district died—except for the field that Mackay had left unseeded the previous year, which yielded 35 bushels per acre (.4 ha).

At about this time the government in Ottawa decided to establish a series of agricultural research stations across the country. When the Minister of Agriculture heard about Mackay's miracle crop in the face of a drought, he offered the farmer the job of heading up the Indian Head Experimental Farm in 1887. Mackay went right to work refining the phenomenon that had given him such a bountiful harvest. And although the practice has changed significantly over the years, the basic idea of sum-mer-fallowing remains.

Mackay and his scientists didn't stop there. One of their greatest achievements was Marquis wheat, bred to mature early and escape the killing frost that comes early on the plains. They planted trees, 23,000 in the first year alone, to shield fields and farmyards from the dry prairie wind as well as add a bit of wel-come green to the landscape. Shelterbelts descended from Indian Head trees still line Saskatchewan. Better-quality live-stock was developed and distributed from here, as were hardier fruit varieties.

For 26 years Angus Mackay served as superintendent of this farm, penetrating in his shrewd, no-nonsense way to the heart of every problem. Mackay had the simple, direct manner of a man who had firsthand knowledge, and he used it often while speak-ing at farmer's gatherings, answering innumerable letters or conducting visitors through the farm. He headed the farm until his retirement at age 73 and lived another 18 years at Indian Head.

No amount of research will ever do away with frost, drought and wind. But the work of Angus Mackay and the scientists at this facility helped make it possible to farm well in spite of them.

Sergeant Bill Both a Hero and a Goat
1010 North Front Street, Broadview Museum, Broadview

Sergeant Bill endured all the horrors of World War I. He was gassed at Ypres. He had shrapnel removed from his neck at Vimy Ridge. He was shell-shocked at Hill 70 but held his ground with the stubbornness of his kind at Passchendaele. He even suffered trench foot. Or should that be trench hoof? By any standard, Sergeant Bill was a uncommon soldier.

Never mind that he was a goat.

He was just plain Bill when he enlisted with the 5th Battalion, Western Cavalry, known as the Red Saskatchewans, on August 24, 1914, the gift of schoolgirl Daisy Curwain. By the following spring he was in the trenches of Armentiers. He was very nearly discharged forthwith, for one of his first actions was to eat the Battalion Nominal Roll and one of his next was to attack a superior officer. Suspicion grew that Bill was a spy, but he was soon to make good.

At the second battle of Ypres, Bill was gassed. Then he received a shrapnel wound to the neck in action around Festhubert. He was seconded to the transport section, where he remained his collected, unflappable self despite any amount of shellfire. But as 1915 marched grimly on, Sergeant Bill suffered trench foot at Hill 63 and finally, his nerve cracking, shell shock at Hill 70.

He stayed with his men, however. One soldier credits Sergeant Bill with saving his life at Neuve Chapelle by butting him into a trench just before a German shell exploded. After this battle Bill was promoted to sergeant. During troop movements, the newly minted officer always rode high on the back of a transport, attracting much notice and heartening the troops with his grave manner. He was a popular comrade, and there was worry in the ranks when Sergeant Bill went missing in the summer of 1918. The Bengal Lancers, noted for their taste for goat meat, were suspected.

But Bill returned unharmed, and although he was characteristically taciturn, the word went around that he had been captured by the enemy and escaped.

With the Allied victory Sergeant Bill was demobilized and sighted Canada on April 18, 1919. The grizzled vet, decorated with the 1914 Star, the General Service Medal and the Victory Medal, returned home.

Sadly, the war had taken a lot out of old Bill, and he died that same year. His body was stuffed and displayed in the provincial museum for many years, but eventually he was shuffled back into storage. In 1980, the Broadview Museum took him home, spruced him up and that's where he remains today, his cool, appraising eye as steady as ever.

Navvies' Hammers Ring in New Era Along Original Canadian Pacific Railway Grade

Junction of highways 1 and 201, Broadview picnic site just east of Broadview

It's a peaceful picnic site these days, but back in 1882 this site rang with the clang of hammer on steel, the shouts of railway navvies and the puffing and churning of steam locomotives. That was the summer the railway came to the prairies and brought the rest of the world with it.

In January 1882, two railway engineers from Minneapolis, Minnesota, named Langdon and Shepard won the contract to build the prairie stretch of the Canadian Pacific Railway—684 miles (1,100 km) of steel from Oak Lake to Fort Calgary. Right away, the contractors advertised for 3,000 men and 4,000 horses, and that summer, from their base in Winnipeg, they got to work.

The hub of the operations was End of Track, a chaotically bustling community with its own administrators, carpenters, blacksmiths, kitchens and dormitories, full of tough-talking navvies who could toss around steel rails like crowbars. The only difference between it and a dozen other pioneer settlements was that End of Track moved about 3.7 miles (6 km) west a day as the railway became its own supply line.

First came the surveyors and grading teams. Bridges had to be built, with every timber shipped through Winnipeg. The tracklayers followed: ties dropped first, then positioned. A team followed throwing down rails, which were placed by another team. More men positioned the spikes and plates. Finally, the spikes were hammered home and a hand-truck rolled over the new rails as the crews worked on the next set. Telegraph teams came next, and End of Track was never out of touch with Winnipeg for more than an hour. The hundreds of men doing dozens of different jobs (the task required 300 subcontractors) had to move precisely as one unit to keep things moving ahead. There was little room for error. The horses alone needed 4,000 bushels of oats every day. But the system worked. One day, the crews laid more than 5 miles (8 km) of track. So fast was track laid that antelope and other game that had migrated north returned in the fall to find they were cut off by the railway. "Terrified by the sight, they gathered in hundreds

Laying Canadian Pacific Railway track on the prairies, around 1900.

on the north side, afraid to cross it," wrote one railway employee. By the end of the first season, the crews made it to Swift Current. By mid-August 1883, Langdon and Shepard's contract was complete.

Soon, towns sprang up where the railway passed and died where it didn't, while fortunes were made and lost speculating on their land. The rails were the thin steel edge of a new age of settlement, and the navvies' hammers rang out the final days of the old, nomadic life of the Indians and Métis. The prairies were never to be the same again.

Fort Ellice–Fort Qu'Appelle Trail Runs Beside Railway That Replaced It
Junction of highways 1 and 201, Broadview picnic site, just east of Broadview

The ruts of the cart trains that once creaked and squeaked their way through what was once known as the Plain Hunters Trail can still be seen near this marker. Linking the major pemmican post at Fort Qu'Appelle with the Hudson's Bay Company hub of Fort Ellice, this route was an important part of the extensive trail system that laced through the prairies of the old North-West from the 1830s on. From here trails connected as far west as Fort Edmonton and back east to Fort Garry (now Winnipeg). Explorers such as John Palliser came through here, as did adventurers like James Carnegie, Earl of Southesk. The North-West Mounted Police rode it on the March west in 1874, and a generation later it came to serve the genteel pioneers of Cannington Manor.

After the railway came through, the old trail fell into disuse. The Canadian Pacific Railway's original grade is just a few yards away, and with the two routes so close, it's not hard to imagine the passing of one era into another. The explorers, traders and hunters, on horseback or hauling loads by squealing Red River cart, gradually faded away to be replaced by the thundering and puffing locomotives hauling settlers, supplies—and civilization.

Helpful Former Fur Trader's Name Remembered in Racette's Crossing
Highway 1, on gravel road heading north from Wolseley, Qu'Appelle River

Anyone who lived near a river crossing in the days of the old North-West could be sure of plenty of visitors, mostly travelers hoping for a little help getting across the water. That was no easy task back then. Carts had to be taken apart and wheels lashed under the box to form a raft. Loads had to be doubly secured. Sometimes, trails leading into the river valley were steep or muddy, making it difficult to even get a team down to the water.

Little wonder, then, that this crossing on the busy Carlton Trail became known as Racette's Crossing, after the former Hudson's Bay Company man who took up living here in the 1870s, when his fur trade days were over. Racette was often called on to lend what must have been a willing hand. A little later, in 1882, another homesteader named Joseph Ellis moved in. He took advantage of the traffic to open a post office and a store, and named the place Ellisboro. Old Racette forgotten, the crossing became known as the Ellisboro Crossing.

For two decades, this was the most common way to get to the farmland north of the Qu'Appelle River.

Invisible Line of Second Meridian Backbone of Land Survey
Highway 1, 1.3 miles (2.1 km) east of Wapella

It's invisible, imperceptible and completely arbitrary, but the line stretching from pole to pole that runs through here is one of the most important features of the province. The Second Meridian is one of two baselines in Saskatchewan used to determine the entire system of townships, sections and road allowances. In the vast checkerboard that is Saskatchewan by air, this is one of the main borders.

Saskatchewan's survey grid was laid out between 1880 and 1905. During that time the teams covered more than 8 million acres (3,237,600 ha) with an unbending rectangular grid. Those rigid squares ignored previous systems of land ownership, such as the river lot system of the Métis. That conflict came to be one of the causes of the 1885 North-West Rebellion. But the uniform, highly precise system made for easy settlement and registration of land title. The free homestead policy that brought many of the province's pioneers would have been impossible without it, and one of the two meridians still forms part of the legal description on every deed in the Land Titles Office.

First Prairie Sentinel Built
Along railway tracks, Moosomin

If Saskatchewan has an icon, a symbol that says *prairie* to people everywhere, it has to be the grain elevator.

The romantic call them prairie sentinels, and that's often how they seem, the tallest thing for miles and miles and miles. The first inkling a prairie driver gets that a town is near is usually the blockish, steeply gabled silhouette of an elevator. A small community may be referred to, disparagingly, as a "one-elevator town." Although the original structure is long gone, the first elevator in the province was built here in Moosomin.

An elevator gets its name from what it does to the grain. It's essential feature is an endless chain of scoops that takes grain delivered at the bottom of the structure and elevates it to the upper cleaning and storage bins. From there the grain can simply be poured into trains or trucks for transport to millers or shippers.

Building an elevator in Estevan, 1907.

It's an old idea. The elevator dates back to 1841, when the first example was built in Buffalo, New York. Elevators came to Canada in 1881 in Gretna, Manitoba, and to Moosomin and Indian Head by 1884. By the end of that year there were 27 elevators along the Canadian Pacific Railway, most owned by private grain buyers or milling companies.

Farmers were never comfortable with that arrangement. Even with a couple of competing grain buyers in town, many farmers believed that elevator agents routinely cheated them on both the grade and volume of their crop. The situation got worse as large corporations began buying out the individual, locally based operations. By 1912, American interests controlled nearly half of Saskatchewan's elevators. Elevators, and the control of prices and access to markets they represented, became a symbol of farmers' fight to control their own economic destiny. In 1911 Saskatchewan farmers, with help from the provincial government, formed the Saskatchewan Co-operative Elevator Company. By 1925, the cooperative had grown into the Saskatchewan Wheat Pool, it owned 450 elevators across the province. By the end of that decade about one-third of the elevators in the prairie provinces were farmer owned.

Elevator numbers peaked in 1933. There were 5,746 across the prairies, most in Saskatchewan. Larger farms, better roads, smaller towns and centralized grain handling have nibbled away at that total ever since. But in 1992, Saskatchewan still had more elevators than any other province. And about 80 percent of them were still owned by the people who grow the grain that fills them.

Red River Cart was Pioneer Pickup
Highway 1, campground just north of Moosomin

Sturdy as the tree trunks it was made from, adaptable as the Métis who drove them, ubiquitous as the buffalo and shriekingly loud as a thousand gulls in a field, the Red River cart was the pickup truck of the old North-West.

In those days everything came hauled in Red River carts: pelts, pemmican, settlers' supplies, buffalo robes, guns and whiskey. The printing press that newspaperman and politician Frank Oliver used to start the *Edmonton Bulletin* was brought in on a Red River cart. The great days of the Métis buffalo hunt saw brigades of more than 1,200 of them. Some say Winnipeg's Portage Avenue is so wide because of the Red River cart trains that rolled through it.

The first carts began to appear about 1801, descended from the two-wheeled carts that French and Scottish fur traders were

Red River cart and camp.

familiar with in Europe. They adapted the design to local conditions and materials: dense oak for axles, shafts and railings; willow for the shakes; durable elm for the hub. Buffalo rawhide lashed it together and covered the wheels. A savvy freighter could find what he needed to fix a cart anywhere on the plains.

It took about about a month to make a cart that could carry about a half-tonne of freight. Pulled by an ox, it could make about 2.2 miles (3.5 km) per hour, which made the travel time from Fort Garry (now Winnipeg) to Fort Edmonton about 75 days. On the big trails, trains would travel 20 carts wide. A good freighter could handle up to 7 teams at once. At river crossings the wheels would be strapped under the box to provide flotation, and the cart became a raft.

A common nickname for the Red River cart was "Manitoba piano." Why? Red River carts were never greased. Prairie grit blowing into the axle would turn any lubricant into an abrasive. So, louder than the shouts of the freighters, the bellowing oxen and the cracking bullwhips was the unending shriek of dry wood on wood.

Pemmican to Fuel Fur Trade Army Freighted Over Trail
Highway 1, next to service station at the east end of Moosomin

Something had to fuel the army of freighters, traders, factors and paddlers that the Hudson's Bay Company deployed over its vast territories, and most of the time pemmican was it.

So vital was this staple food of the fur brigades that supply routes to pemmican were sometimes as important as paths to the furs. The company required tons of the stuff. Wood Mountain harbored some of the last large buffalo herds on the plains, and the trail from Wood Mountain made Fort Ellice an important provisions post for the company.

Here's a recipe for pemmican:

Take one buffalo, slice meat thinly, dry over fire, then pound with stones until pulped. Meanwhile, sew the animal's hide into rawhide sack, then take the pulped meat and half-fill the sack. Melt the animal's fat, pour on top of meat, stir in 15–18 pounds (7–8 kg) of berries and sew sack shut.

Said to resemble dehydrated dog food, pemmican was nutritious (the berries added vitamin C) and so high-calorie that 2 pounds (1 kg) a day was enough to keep a fur trader paddling from dawn to dusk. It could be served raw, sliced, floured and fried, or chopped into a thick soup called rababoo. It also lasted forever. One Manitoba farmer discovered a bag of pemmican that had been cached on his farm 80 years earlier. After taking a bite, the farmer said, "It tasted like meat and retained some of its flavor." Of course, there's also the description of pemmican given in an account of the time:

Take the scrapings from the driest outside corner of a very stale piece of cold roast beef, add to it lumps of rancid fat, then garnish all with long human hairs and short hairs of dogs and oxen and you have a fair imitation of common Pemmican.

Along with the supply wagon trains, John Palliser also used the Fort Ellice–Wood Mountain Trail on his way to Roche Percee in 1857. The pioneers of Cannington Manor also traveled it to get to Moosomin.

ALONG HIGHWAY 22

Qu'Appelle Valley Named for Indian Legend
Highway 10, take Highway 210 turnoff, drive 9 miles (15 km) to Echo Valley Provincial Park

The touching story of how this beautiful valley got its name is one of the best known of all prairie legends. The story goes that a young Indian man was paddling across one of the valley's lakes to visit his bride-to-be when he heard his name ring out in the still air. He cried, "Who calls? Who calls?"—or, in French, *"Qu'appelle? Qu'appelle?"*—but received no answer. When he got to the other side, he found that his beloved had died, calling his name with her last breath.

One version of the story dates back to at least 1804 and to the visit of a North-West Company fur trader named Daniel Harmon. He wrote in his journal that "The river is so named by the superstitious natives who imagine that a spirit is constantly going up and down it; they say they often hear a voice distinctly which resembles the cry of a human being." Harmon makes no mention of a lover's death, and the popularity of the current version may have much to do with Pauline Johnson's poem, which ends with the bereft Indian saying, "I listen heartsick, while hunters tell / Why white men named the valley Qu'Appelle."

Of course, the young hunter would have called out in Cree *"Awina Katepwet?"* That phrase is preserved in the name of Katepwa Lake, the easternmost in the valley.

Cynics maintain that the name comes from the echoes the valley walls throw back to anyone who raises his voice. But even the least romantic don't doubt the valley's beauty. Harmon's trip was marked by food shortages, bad weather and, as he described, "the constant fear I was in of being torn to pieces by wild beasts." All that faded when he stopped and rested at Qu'Appelle, which he called "beautifully situated and over-spread with buffaloes and other kinds of animals, as well as many other delightful objects."

Modern visitors agree.

Qu'Appelle Crossing Crossroads of the Old North-West
Highway 56, .25 miles (.4 km) west of Highway 35 intersection, Fort Qu'Appelle

Back before the days of highways and bridges, rivers weren't so easy to cross. Depending on the time of year, banks could be a swampy morass, or the water could be high and wild. Even getting to the riverbank could be a problem because so many prairie rivers flow between steep valley walls. Getting down to the river was difficult for the drivers of heavily loaded Red River carts.

Travelers of the day had ways of coping. Carts could be turned into rafts by removing the wheels and lashing them under the cargo box. Getting down the valleys could be made safer by blocking up the cartwheels or dragging logs behind; sometimes the oxen were even hitched onto the back of the cart. Even so, it could mean a day's work just to get across a river, and the easiest places to ford were much frequented. The Qu'Appelle Crossing was one of the busiest.

At Qu'Appelle Crossing, trails converged from Wood Mountain, Fort Qu'Appelle, Fort Pelly, Fort Ellice, the Elbow on the the South Saskatchewan, the Red Deer Forks, Battleford and Prince Albert. The presence of the crossing probably influenced the Hudson's Bay Company to build Fort Qu'Appelle near here in 1864, and the place became an even more important link to the north when the railway passed about 20 miles (33 km) to the south.

Man of Steele Commanded Fort Qu'Appelle North-West Mounted Police Post
Highway 56, on golf course, Fort Qu'Appelle

In 1875, a detachment of North-West Mounted Police was sent here from Fort Walsh in the Cypress Hills to establish a new post. The community, established about 10 years earlier, was thriving as one of the pemmican posts producing and shipping the foodstuff that fed the North-West. It was surrounded by camps of Métis and Indians, and was the site where Treaty No 4 was signed; there was plenty for the police to oversee. The men built a crude log post from lumber shipped from Swan River to the east.

Fort Qu'Appelle, from a drawing made in 1877.

After 1879, the fort was commanded by Inspector Sam Steele, one of the force's legendary figures who always managed to be where the action was. The aptly named Steele, known for his great strength and endurance, was already a veteran of the Fenian raids, the Red River Rebellion and the North-West Mounted Police's grueling March west when he received the promotion. Placed in charge of the detachments supervising the building of the Canadian Pacific Railway, he was military through and through, and orders were orders. When Sitting Bull came here in 1881 to plead one more time for his people, Steele was told to send him packing with just enough provisions to get the Sioux chief back to Wood Mountain. That's just what he did. When Steele fought the Métis during the North-West Rebellion, some say his enthusiasm for battle prevented a peace parley that might have gotten Big Bear to surrender a couple days earlier.

Years later, in 1898, Steele was sent to the Klondike to establish Canadian authority during the gold rush days. After that he commanded Lord Strathcona's Horse during the Boer War in South Africa. Still not done, it was Sam Steele who commanded the second contingent of Canadian soldiers who went overseas in 1915. He died in London on January 30, 1919, shortly after his 70th birthday.

Inspector Sam Steele.

Steele's first command here at Fort Qu'Appelle, however, was not nearly so long-lived. The post ceased being an independent command in 1882 when it was reduced to two or three officers attached to the Regina headquarters. These cellars off the golf course fairway are all that remain.

Southern Third of Province Signed Over in One Treaty
Corner of Company Avenue and 5th Street, Fort Qu'Appelle

On this spot, with a few strokes of a pen, life changed forever for the Indians of Saskatchewan's southern plains. Here, on September 15, 1874, after two years of tough negotiations, Treaty No 4 was signed. The Cree, Saulteaux and Stoney could no longer call themselves masters of the prairie they had roamed for generations. Land from Moose Mountain in east to the Cypress Hills in the West, from Lake Winnipegosis in the north to the American border in the south—the bottom third of the province, an area larger than some European nations—had just been ceded to Her Gracious Majesty, Queen Victoria.

The chiefs well knew what was at stake and had bargained hard. One government negotiator later wrote

> *Any one who, in negotiating with these Indians, should suppose he had mere children to deal with, would find himself mistaken. In their manner of expressing themselves they make use of a great deal of allegory, and their illustration may at times appear to be childish enough, but in their actual dealings they are shrewd and sufficiently awake to their own interests.*

He also said that one Indian at each meeting memorized the proceedings, and on one occasion one such record keeper repeated arguments, word for word, made two years before.

Treaty No 4 offered its signatories the usual grants of land, to be selected by the government, as well as gifts of clothes and cash for the chiefs, who were also eligible for "a suitable flag." But the Indians won some concessions that the government hadn't intended. Every family cultivating land was to get some farming tools and enough seed to plant whatever land they had broken. Ploughs, oxen and carpenter's tools were to be distributed to and shared among each band. Schools and teachers were to be provided. Treaty No 4 also recognized trapping as a feature of native life, the first treaty to do so, and guaranteed Indians the right to hunt and trap on their former lands.

Still, the 13 chiefs who made their mark that day couldn't have done it without some reluctance. The Cree leader Piapot didn't think they were getting enough in return for their lavish land grant, even with the extra concessions, and he refused to sign until a year later. It took still longer for all the bands to settle on reserves. The chiefs and their people knew what they were giving up.

Busy Fort Qu'Appelle–Touchwood Hills Trail Still Presented Challenging Travel
Highway 35, 3 miles (4.8 km) north of Fort San turnoff

Part of the Carlton Trail system, these old ruts mark the path of hundreds of carts that once rolled out to the Touchwood Hills, one of the most important early settlements on the plains. The Hudson's Bay Company fur post in the Touchwood Hills was originally built in the 1850s as a satellite of the larger post at Fort Pelly. But it soon captured lucrative business of its own, and it shipped out a lot of pemmican. Before long, Touchwood Hills was a well-known stop on the Carlton Trail.

By 1870, settlers began to ply this path. Attracted by the rolling, wooded countryside, adventurous farmers had established one of the first agricultural settlements in the old North-West around here. Mail service ran along here as did the West's first telegraph line, its operator stationed in the Hills in a small, lonely shack.

Despite its importance, the Carlton Trail was still a prairie trail. Major-General Frederick Middleton found out what that meant in 1885, when he was moving 900 men north from Fort Qu'Appelle on their way to confront Louis Riel's rebel Métis. It was a particularly nasty April. The deeply carved ruts became icy hard and slippery one day and full of deep gluey mud the next. Adding to the hardships was the harsh alkali from local streams and marshes that burned horses' hooves. It took 400 horses to heave the army through this stretch.

High Hopes, Tragic Results in Story of Residential Schools
White Calf Collegiate, 1 St. Mary's Avenue, Lebret

High hopes. Good intentions. Tragic results. Too often that was the story of Canada's Indian Residential School system, a system that began here over a century ago.

As the old way of life faded for the plains Indians, the chiefs began to look ahead to see what was next for their people. They knew their children would need education to live in this new world and saw to it that schools and teachers were promised in the treaties. Schooling was important to them; when Governor-General Lorne visited Fort Carlton in 1881, the Cree leader Mistiwasis told him bluntly, "We want teachers for our schools."

Mistiwasis and other chiefs probably had day schools in mind. The government, however, felt residential schools would ensure better attendance and tighter control over the children's development. In addition, religious schools would have the advantage of building on a system that was already partly in place and cheaper to administer. So, in 1883, Prime Minister John A. Macdonald stood up in the House of Commons and told the assembly that "secular education is a good thing among white men but among Indians the first object is to make them better men." The schools, he said, should ensure that the native child "be dissociated from the prejudicial influence by which he is surrounded on the reserve of his band." His government then voted $44,000 to build three such schools in the Northwest Territories. One of them was at Lebret.

The Qu'Appelle Indian Industrial School was built in 1884 and run by the Oblate order of priests. For 30 years Father Joseph Hugonnard was its principal. Hugonnard was not unsympathetic to Indians. He admired the dignity of chiefs like Sitting Bull, and former students praised his vision for their future, describing him as genial, engaging and diplomatic. Still, he knew what was expected of his school.

The young students, fresh off the reserve, were dressed in school uniforms—dresses for the girls, jackets and pants for the boys, whose hair was cut short. One student remembered that he was renamed after Hugonnard ruled that no "civilized" tongue could pronounce the name his parents had given him. Some schools forbade the use of Indian languages or any expression of Indian culture; at Lebret, children were allowed to dress in traditional clothes for pageants and plays, which often celebrated the achievements of whites. Cricket, at least in the early days, was the school sport.

Many of the teachers were poorly qualified, which contributed to academic problems at the school. In one year during the 1920s, the school had 235 students in its first level and a total of only 87 in the higher two. In addition, boys were taught farming and trades such as carpentry and blacksmithing, and girls learned how to be housewives. The students also maintained a market garden, the produce of which was sold in town and used to finance the school.

In 1901, Hugonnard became involved in the nearby File Hills Colony, intended as a model Indian agricultural village. Lebret graduates were preferred colonists, and couples were preferred even more. After 1909, government policy encouraged graduates to intermarry, and in some cases partners were selected for each other. Hugonnard himself once married six couples at once. Although some colonists were successful farmers, most failed.

Meanwhile, the Indians back on the reserve knew what was going on. One Indian agent wrote the following:

One old man told me in confidence, 'If my children go to school and learn the ways of you white people, when they die they will go to the heaven you talk of while I, an Indian, will go to the happy hunting ground. I love my children and want to see them again when I die.'

The purpose of the schools was clear to others, too. In 1945, a visiting American official wrote in his report on the Canadian system that "the extinction of the Indians as Indians is the ultimate end."

Some former students praise the residential schools for giving them the tools they needed to enter mainstream society. Some say that here, they learned to set high goals. One wrote,

When the buffalo had vanished and our spirits were broken, we thought the Manitou of our forefathers had forsaken us. But Father Hugonnard inspired us with a new vision—a vision of a greater future for our race in a better and happier world.

Others look back on the residential schools as a time of cruel separation from their family and their roots, and as a deliberated attempt to wipe out a culture. Some schools have become notorious for the abuse that children suffered. In 1998, the Canadian government offered native people an apology for the treatment they suffered at these schools and created a $350 million fund to help with their healing.

Here, the federal government turned the operation of the school over to the local Starblanket band in 1968. Now called White Calf Collegiate, it accepts students from across Canada and is famous for its hockey program. Most of its students go on to post-secondary institutions.

Motherwell Fought for Rights of Farmers

Off Highway 22 on Municipal Road 606, drive 1.9 miles (3 km)
south of Abernethy to Motherwell Homestead

> *I took a vow to myself that if I ever got in a position where*
> *I could do it, I would try to reverse the idea that farming*
> *is a subservient position.*
> –W.R. Motherwell

It would be hard to imagine William Richard Motherwell subservient to anybody. He fought all his life to improve the lot of prairie farmers, helping break the back of the monopoly held by grain buyers and calling the mighty Canadian Pacific Railway itself to account. And when he wasn't at political meetings or fighting legal battles, he was running as brisk, efficient and scientific a farmyard as any in the territory.

W.R. Motherwell, the fourth son of an Ontario farmer and a fresh graduate of the Ontario College of Agriculture, came west in 1882. Drawn like so many others by the promise of free land, he came at a time when rural discontent was building on the prairies. Farmers felt that private elevator companies, which held a monopoly on grain buying, were cheating them. And even after they sold their grain, they couldn't necessarily get it to the customer because the Canadian Pacific Railway favored certain elevator companies. Then there was the National Policy of John A. Macdonald's government in Ottawa that forced western farmers to sell their grain at depressed world prices but buy high-priced supplies from Ontario manufacturers who were protected by high import tariffs.

Farmers tried several times during the 1880s and 1890s to organize and fight the system they felt exploited them. Finally, on December 18, 1901, they formed the Territorial Grain Growers Association, with Motherwell as its first president. Almost immediately, the association was able to win farmers the right to obtain platforms and railway cars to load their grain. Motherwell and the Grain Growers then took on the Canadian Pacific Railway, and the Supreme Court of Canada found the railway guilty of violating the Manitoba Grain Act.

Motherwell wasn't done. He entered politics and served as Saskatchewan's first Minister of Agriculture, holding his seat from 1905 to 1918. Bluntly honest and incapable of compromise,

W.R. Motherwell, as minister of agriculture.

he resigned from provincial politics on principle: he opposed his party's support of conscription and its attempt to curtail French language rights. He then entered federal politics and became Wilfred Laurier's minister of agriculture for the better part of the 1920s.

Throughout, he ran his homestead on the latest scientific

principles of agricultural stewardship. Lanark Place was divided into four quadrants: domestic, garden, water supply and barnyard. To preserve moisture he devised an elaborate system of shelterbelts. Visitors could count on finding the most efficient new machines at Lanark Place. Motherwell bought a thresher as early as 1911. Nor did he forget the graces of more settled areas. Lanark Place had a lawn tennis court, ornamental gardens and a lovers' lane.

Motherwell was the picture of an Edwardian man of substance: big, burly, bearish, bowler-hatted and waistcoated even out in the farmyard. He believed that hard work and enterprise coupled to scientific principles made for progress, and he embodied those no-nonsense virtues.

Motherwell resigned from politics in 1939, the Grand Old Man of Canadian agriculture. He returned to Lanark Place and died in Regina in 1943.

Religious Dissidents Rejoin Mainstream
Off Highway 10 on Municipal Road 617, drive 2 miles (3.2 km) northeast of Duff to picnic site

Some settlers in Saskatchewan grouped themselves by nationality. Others, like the Primitive Methodists, were more concerned with spirituality. Dating back to the early 19th century, the Primitive Methodists were a reaction to what they considered the stifling regimentation and respectability of mainstream Methodists. Emphasizing fervor and simplicity, the Primitives held camp meetings and prayed long, rambling, impassioned prayers. They also used women as regular preachers.

The movement had already begun to die by 1883 when 120 Primitive Methodists came here to set up their own colony. The following year the sect rejoined the general Methodist Conference of Canada. But for a while their colony here thrived with a church, school, hall, smithy, post office and store. The Pheasant Forks Agricultural Society had up to 172 members and held an annual exhibition every year until 1901. The agricultural pioneer and later federal Minister of Agriculture W.R. Motherwell was one of the original directors.

Burial Mound Undisturbed For Nearly a Millennium
Highway 47, 19 miles (30.5 km) south of Melville, then east on
Highway 247 for 11 miles (17.7 km) to Cedar Cove turnoff

One of the few prehistoric burial sites in Canada that has been scientifically excavated, the Moose Bay Mound rested undisturbed for nearly 1,000 years until it was discovered in 1951.

Sometime around 1040 A.D., the ancestors of today's Indians built this mound to house nine burials. Two of the dead were men (one was about 80 years old) and the rest were children. The mourners painted the bodies with red ochre and laid them directly in the earth. Along with them were birchbark containers cut from a single piece of bark and stitched together with spruce root, all beautifully preserved. The dead also took turtle shells, pipes, pottery, projectile points and a bone knife with them to the spirit world. Then the mourners built a low, tepeelike structure of logs over the bodies and covered them with earth.

A little later a tenth grave was dug into the center of the mound to house the body of a little girl about 10 years old. She was buried with goods including pottery vessels engraved with turtles, birchbark baskets, pipes, scrapers and stone awls.

Perhaps because of its distance from other burial mounds, this one was never robbed. Archaeologists say the mound shows the influence of tribes to the east, who were vigorous traders, and tribes to the south, who practiced agriculture. Others might say the mound, on the crest of a hill overlooking Crooked Lake and the Qu'Appelle valley, shows the influence of beauty.

Welsh Settlers Take Scenic Route to Saskatchewan
Off Highway 9, Bangor turnoff, drive east 6 miles (10 km) to
Bangor

Of all the groups that settled Saskatchewan, few took as roundabout a path to get here as did the Welsh farmers that homesteaded in the Bangor area. The story begins in 1865 in Wales, when 153 settlers left Britain for Patagonia, the southernmost province of Argentina on the tip of South America. They were fleeing coal mines, a failed independence movement, cultural assimilation and a British ban on the teaching of Welsh in schools. They wanted to get as far from Englishmen as possible, and they couldn't have gotten much farther. For more than a generation they lived and thrived along the Chubut River. But although the Argentine government had originally welcomed the settlers, arguments with officials over land titles, military service and education in Welsh became more and more frequent.

In the late 1890s, a Welshman named Evan Jenkins came to examine the good things he heard about Saskatchewan. He must have liked what he saw, for after 1899 and 1901 brought devastating floods in Patagonia, 230 ranchers and farmers headed north. The fervent nationalism of the original settlers had faded and the Welsh- and Spanish-speaking settlers sought no language rights. They wanted only one concession to their nationality. When the Grand Trunk Railway came through the area six years later, it wanted to name the community Basco. Instead, the Welsh wanted Bangor, the name of a city in Wales. Since both names began with *B*, leaving intact the Grand Trunk Railway's alphabetical scheme, the railway agreed.

For a while Bangor was known for its skilled choir and unbeatable soccer team. Although there remains a Welsh presence in certain areas of Patagonia, little trace of the Saskatchewan colony's origins remains.

Mysterious "Count" Leads Countrymen to Canada
Highway 22, Summer Street, 3 miles (5 km) south of Esterhazy, Kaposvar Historic Site

In the mid-1880s, large groups of Hungarian peasants left the Old World for the New, only to find themselves trapped as laborers in the grueling coal mines of Pennsylvania. A benevolent countryman, living in New York under the name Count Paul Esterhazy, took up their cause. He looked for a new land for them, and in 1886, he led a group to this site on the Qu'Appelle River valley. More immigrants came directly from Hungary in 1888, and the town that grew up in the area was named for its founder. But who was he?

Historians now suggest that the man who called himself Count Paul Esterhazy was born in Hungary as Johan Baptista Pakh in 1831. It was, however, rumored in the court of the ruling Hapsburg monarchy that he was the illegitimate son of Count

Nicholas Esterhazy, a wealthy and powerful aristocrat. Johan was to spend much of his colorful, world-wandering life fighting to have that connection acknowledged.

Johan joined the army and quickly rose to the rank of lieutenant. But after he joined a failed revolution against the Hapsburgs, he was forced to flee to Turkey, then England. He then joined the British army and wound up in a garrison near Cape Town, South Africa. That wasn't enough action for young Johan, so in 1857 he volunteered for service in the Indian Mutiny. After that conflict he became a paymaster of a West Indian regiment in Kingston, Jamaica.

Johan's superiors called him diligent, zealous and punctual, and his comrades described him as a gentleman—a great sportsman, scholarly, cultured and thoroughly honorable. That, however, did not prevent him from abandoning the West Indies the day after Christmas, 1866, with the 22-year-old daughter of a fellow officer in tow. Granted amnesty by his homeland, he returned to Hungary and somehow got a passport under the name Count Oscar Esterhazy.

Despite his career (or perhaps because of it) the Esterhazys still refused to recognize Johan/Oscar. He left Hungary a final time, aided, it was rumored, by Esterhazy money as a way to be rid of him. He moved to New York and began helping Hungarian immigrants adjust to the New World. After founding settlements in both Saskatchewan and Manitoba, he died in 1912.

ALONG HIGHWAYS 39 AND 18

Charismatic Young Preacher Enters Politics
T.C. Douglas Calvary Centre, 400 – 10 Avenue S.E., Weyburn

Before Tommy Douglas became the head of the first socialist government in North America, before he introduced Medicare to Canada and before he headed the federal New Democratic Party, he was a popular, fiery young Baptist preacher in Weyburn. The building on 10th Avenue, now renovated into an arts center, was his church.

It was August 1930 when the freshly ordained Douglas, aged 26, arrived on the train from Winnipeg with his wife, Irma, and

Tommy Douglas as a young politician in 1944.

$5.26 in his pocket. His congregation greeted him at the station, and a brass band serenaded the couple to their apartment. It wasn't long before Douglas was making a little noise of his own.

As the Dirty Thirties began to squeeze Saskatchewan tighter and tighter, Douglas started to publicly question the economic system that he thought was part of the problem. His sermons had titles such as "Jesus, the Revolutionist" and "Would Jesus Revolt Against Our Present System of Graft and Exploitation?" A gifted speaker who had helped pay his college tuition by writing and delivering comic after-dinner speeches at community events, he knew how to hold a crowd. Attendance at Calvary Baptist grew markedly.

Nor did Douglas restrict himself to the pulpit. When coal miners went on strike in Estevan in 1931, Douglas collected food for the striking families despite the complaints of mine owners to Douglas's church board. His church, with the help of other clergy, became a center for distributing food and clothing to the legions of unemployed who were blowing across the prairies like dried-out topsoil.

Despite his serious work, Douglas wasn't afraid to laugh at himself. One morning he got a call from a judge about to send 11 boys off to reform school. Could Tommy do something with them? Tommy took them home. "My wife, to whom I'd been married for less than a year, just about went home to mother," he recalled. The couple cleaned up the young scrappers and break-in artists and found them jobs, but they backslid and broke into a store. Douglas made them sit through Sunday evening service, then lectured them good and long in his study. Douglas later recalled what the toughest kid of the lot said after the stirring sermon:

'Mr. Douglas, I'm terribly sorry for what we've done. I'm so sorry. I want to give you back your things.' And he handed me back my watch, my pen knife, my fountain pen and a half-dozen other things he'd stolen off my desk while I was giving my 10-cent lecture.

Douglas had some fun, too. He had been a lightweight boxing champion in Manitoba, and in Saskatchewan he appeared on some amateur fight cards. "I was too short in the arm to be a good boxer," he said. "But I was fast on my feet and could hit fairly hard." Although he didn't smoke or drink, he liked to hang out at the local print shop and chew over the issues of the day with whoever dropped by. He started a boys sports club and appeared in local theatricals. And once a month his church put on a religious drama instead of the evening service.

But increasingly he was drawn to politics. He founded a branch of the Independent Labour Association in 1931 and ran unsuccessfully for the Farmer Labour Party in the 1934 provincial election. The next year he ran for the federal Co-operative Commonwealth Federation (the forerunner of today's New Democratic Party), and this time he won. Douglas remained in politics, both federal and provincial, until 1979. From 1944 to 1961, he was the New Democratic Premier of Saskatchewan. He is remembered today as the father of public health care in Canada.

After 1935, Douglas never returned to preaching. But his political life was guided by something he wrote during his days in Weyburn: "We have come to see that the Kingdom of God is in our midst if we have the vision to build it."

"Billiard Table" Shaped Writer's Work
W.O. Mitchell's Home, 6th Street, Weyburn

"My vision of Canada has all my life been determined by my first 12 years of the Saskatchewan billiard table," said W.O. Mitchell, one of the Saskatchewan's best-loved writers. His house, now owned privately, is the place where he first experienced that billiard-table prairie and gathered the material for his 1947 novel *Who Has Seen the Wind*, now classroom reading across Canada. Here is that book's description of four-year-old Brian O'Connal's first encounter with the prairie:

> *Without hesitation he crossed the road and walked out through the hip-deep grass stirring in the steady wind; the grass clung at his legs; haloed fox-tails bowed before; grasshoppers sprang from hidden places in the grass, clicketing ahead of him to disappear, then lift again.*
>
> *A gopher squeaked questioningly as Brian sat down upon a rock warm to the backs of his thighs. He picked a pale blue flax-flower at his feet, stared long at the stripings in its shallow throat, then looked up to see a dragon-fly hanging on shimmering wings directly in front of him. The gopher squeaked again, and he saw it a few yards away, sitting up, watching him from its pulpit hole. A suave-winged hawk chose that moment to slip its shadow across the prairie.*
>
> *And all about him was the wind now, a pervasive sighing through great emptiness, unhampered by the buildings of the town, warm and living against his face and in his hair.*

Mitchell went on to live, write and teach throughout the West. He wrote many novels in addition to *Who Has Seen the Wind*, although that remains his best-known work. His stories in *Jake and the Kid* about a crusty farmhand and his young sidekick have been popular as radio plays, short stories and a TV series. His play *The Black Bonspeil of Wullie MacCrimmon*, in which a farmer curls for his soul against the devil, is regularly performed. He was a teacher and inspiration to a generation of prairie writers. And to the public, who crowded his public readings and appearances, he was folksy, salty and wise.

Mitchell died in 1998, honored and mourned by an entire nation. But in that passage from his first and probably greatest novel, it's not hard to picture Mitchell himself as a boy back in the 1920s, wandering past the town limits of Weyburn, lifting his face to the sun and leaning into the prairie wind.

Glorious North-West Mounted Police Trek West a Sorry Sight
Highway 35, 2 miles (3.2 km) north of Oungre

The North-West Mounted Police were a sorry sight when they passed by this spot on August 1, 1874. The force's freshly mustered 3-mile (5-km) -long column of 275 officers, 20 drivers, 310 horses, 140 oxen, 100 cattle, 73 wagons, 114 carts, 2 field guns and 2 mortars must have been an impressive sight when it set out from Dufferin, Manitoba, a few weeks earlier to bring British law to the West. But while those Ontario farm boys and city clerks may have started out strong and eager, by this point the prairie was winning.

Plagues of mosquitoes and flies, prairie fires, and 12- and 16-hour days of hard and hungry slogging over the hot, dry plains had taken their toll. The procession was beginning to lose the Boundary Commission Trail, which meant it had to build its own bridges and roads. The relentless sun parched the prairie grass and ruined it for grazing. One night a tremendous thunderstorm blew up that completely knocked over all the tents. So even though some of the heaviest equipment had been sent north to Fort Edmonton via Roche Percee, both man and beast were wearing out. Horses were even dying of exhaustion. To make matters worse the troop's guides had become unsure of where they were. Somewhere between here and the Cypress Hills, one of the men came up with this little song, sung to the tune of "God Save the Queen" and aimed at those who had planned and led the march: "Confound their politics / Frustrate their knavish tricks / And get us out of this damn fix / God save all here."

Still, 11 days after the force passed this point, the men were able to summon up enough spit to polish up their camp and present an impressive front to the first Indians they were to meet, a party of 30 Sioux. The Sioux marched into the police camp chanting in low tones, where they accepted gifts, smoked a peace pipe and listened to speeches. They then spent a day or two nosing around, which the policemen attributed to a desire to trade but which was just as likely a military reconnaissance. The Sioux's opinion of the inexperienced, thirsty, tired and increasingly ragged supposed guardians of the plains was not recorded.

Engineers, Surveyors Lay Out Medicine Line Along Boundary Commission Trail
Highway 39, 14.5 miles (23.3 km) southeast of Estevan

Canada, especially western Canada, was as much idea as reality when the surveyors and engineers of the Boundary Commission began their work in 1872. The 49th parallel had been the agreed upon international border between Canada and the United States since 1818, but where did it run? When, in 1869, the Hudson's Bay Company signed over its holdings to the fledgling country and the Americans claimed that the Hudson's Bay Company's Pembina fort was actually on their soil, it became clear someone would have to draw a line in the prairie.

So in 1872, a joint American, British and Canadian survey party began their work where the last survey had left off, at Lake of the Woods on the edge of Ontario. The British sent 50 Royal Engineers with a Canadian contingent of a geologist, doctor, veterinarian and a party of surveyors. The Americans were accompanied by an infantry company. They soon found Pembina was Canadian, and by the following summer, they were in the plains, following a trail left by buffalo hunters and fur traders. The ruts left by the commission's carts can still be seen along the edge of this coulee east of here.

Here, they suffered the familiar torments of early prairie travelers: lack of wood and shade, alkaline water that gave dysentery to men and animals alike, and mosquitoes and black-flies that came in clouds thick enough to kill a horse already weak from work or illness. On September 23, the British ran into an early snowstorm so powerful it forced them to stay huddled under blankets in their wagons for seven days and nights. By October they made it as far as Wood Mountain, where they left a supply depot that was later to prove invaluable to the North-West Mounted Police as they followed the commission's route on their own march west.

The commission picked up again next summer, with the American military contingent doubling as they entered Blackfoot country. It was buffalo country, too, and while the great herds provided fresh game, the beasts fouled and muddied what little water there was. Once a charging herd endangered the entire wagon train until their Métis scouts fired into the head of the pack and split it so that it thundered by on either side.

The commission finished its job in August 1874, leaving behind a trail of 388 cairns over 1,056 miles (1,700 km) of border. That line marked the end of the American West and the start of Canada's, a distinction many native bands were soon to learn had such importance that they came to call the border the Medicine Line.

Cemetery Marks Philanthropist's Failed Dream of Jewish Colony
Highway 18, 2 miles (3 km) west of Hirsch, 20.5 miles (33 km) east of Estevan

---

This area marks the site of one of Saskatchewan's earliest homesteading colonies. In the 1890s, a Bavarian Jewish philanthropist of considerable wealth became concerned about the oppression of his people in Europe. To bring about their "moral and spiritual regeneration," he formed the Jewish Colonization Association, which encouraged emigration to Argentina, Australia and western Canada. He funded the association with $12 million, a vast sum that made the association one of the largest foundations in the world at the time.

In 1892, the association made its first foray onto the prairies when a group of refugee Russian Jews were settled between Hirsch and Oxbow. Defeated by the harsh winters of the 1890s, all but seven were gone by 1894. The association tried again in 1907, with 60 families near Hirsch. That number grew to 166 Jewish families on 28,160 acres (11,396 ha) by 1909. Still, the colony never became self-sufficient and continually depended on the foundation for support. Harsh weather, debts and rivalries between colonists finally tore Hirsch's dream apart. In the abandoned town of Hoffer, farther west on Highway 18 near Oungre, derelict barns adorned with the Star of David stood as late as the early 1970s.

This site marks the Hirsch settlers' cemetery. Fleeing oppression and violence in their old lands, these pioneers may have finally found peace on the Saskatchewan prairie.

Miners "Murdered by RCMP" During Estevan Coal Strike
Highway 39, 2 miles (3.2 km) south of Bienfait

Coal has been mined in this district for generations. Railroad survey crews noticed these deposits of lignite back in 1853, and they were duly noted by the Palliser expedition five years later. Members of the North-West Mounted Police warmed themselves over Souris Valley coal when they were camped at nearby Roche Percee on their March west, and the first coal mine in the area was opened in the early 1880s. It's been mined ever since, one of the reasons nearby Estevan is referred to as the Energy City. But the industry hasn't escaped conflict. In 1931, it was at the center of what became one of the bloodiest strikes in Canadian history.

Nobody was making any money in Saskatchewan coal that year. The Dirty Thirties and competition from other mines had depressed prices to the point where a ton of Souris lignite sold for about a nickel more than it cost to dig it up. The mine owners wanted to cut costs. Wages were an obvious target, and the average earnings of a Saskatchewan miner fell about 20 percent between 1921 and 1931, even faster than the Depression was lowering prices. As well, the spreading Dust Bowl choked off the farm laboring work that many miners used to pad their paychecks.

They had other concerns, too. Some miners told of working

Violence during the Estevan Riot.

for months in knee-deep water. Others worked through clouds of blasting smoke that poor ventilation failed to clear. Still others complained of Black Damp, a miner's term for high levels of carbon dioxide. A later investigation found nearly every mine broke some provision of the Mines Act. And when the miners came to the surface, they returned to company-owned housing that was just as bad: drafty, run-down, cold and bug-infested. Complaints? "If you don't like it, pack your tools and get out" was the common response from the mines, according to testimony at the same investigation.

When organizers from the Workers Unity League and the Mine Workers Union of Canada appeared on the scene that August, they had nearly everyone signed up—more than 600 men—within days. But the mines refused to negotiate with the union and the union refused to apply for conciliation, so on September 7, the workers walked.

Tension mounted all that month. The Royal Canadian Mounted Police first sent four extra men to Estevan, then another dozen. Patrols were mounted 24 hours a day.

Then on the afternoon of September 29, the strikers organized a parade into downtown Estevan. The caravan of cars and trucks strung out for a mile along the highway, banners reading "We will not work for starvation wages" and "We want houses, not piano boxes" blowing in the breeze. At the corner of Fourth

Street and Souris Avenue, between 300 and 400 strikers met 22 policemen. Words escalated to blows, and a riot began. Then a miner climbed on top of a fire truck that had been called to douse the mob. He was shot dead. A battle ensued, with miners and their wives attacking police with clubs and stones. Another 30 Mounties had to be called in to disperse them. But for miners Nick Nargan, 25, Julian Gryshko, 26, and Pete Markunas, 27, killed during that bloody 90 minutes, it was too late. Eight other miners, 4 bystanders and 10 policemen were wounded either by bullets or clubs and stones.

That evening another 45 Mounties were rushed to Estevan. The 60-man local militia was mobilized and the army alerted. The next morning 60 heavily armed policemen backed up with a turret-mounted machine gun descended on nearby Bienfait and arrested 13 miners. Most later received fines or short prison terms.

On October 4, the dead miners were buried in a cemetery just north of Bienfait, their flower-covered caskets followed by a procession of 600. Some carried banners reading "They fought for bread, but got bullets instead." The inscription on their tombstone reads "Murdered in Estevan September 29 by RCMP."

The strike ended two days later. The owners agreed to most of the workers' demands. A Royal Commission was later struck to examine the cause of the strike and most of Judge E.R. Wylie's recommendations became legislation.

Matoff Murder Marks End of Rum-Running Days
Along railway track, Bienfait

October 4, 1922, was a quiet night at White's Hotel in Bienfait. Fat Earl was hustling strangers, throwing a four-bit piece into a crack in the floor. A few other regulars were nearby, playing some listless hands of poker more out of habit than anything else. A dapper pool shark and sometime bootlegger named Jimmie LaCoste wandered in, greeting the boys with the news that a couple cars were being loaded in the dark down by the grain elevator.

Nobody thought much of it. Everybody knew what was being loaded. Booze.

Liquor had been part of the history of the prairies since the days of the fur trade and the whiskey forts, but by the second decade of the new century people were getting tired of it and the problems it caused in a rootless, pioneer, fast-buck economy. The seriousness of the World War I made Prohibition seem like the right thing to do, too. So on July 1, 1915, Saskatchewan closed down 406 bars, 38 liquor wholesalers and 12 clubs and replaced them with 23 government liquor dispensaries. Drinking is estimated to have dropped by 90 percent. And nobody missed the bars—most were crowded, cheerless, chairless places where patrons had to lean against the brass railing to drink as they dodged other patrons' increasingly inaccurate attempts to hit the spittoon. So the next year, Saskatchewan joined the dry tide sweeping the prairies and declared full Prohibition. Liquor became illegal to sell unless you had a medical prescription. Not that prescriptions were hard to get. In 1917, one doctor prescribed a quart of scotch as a chill preventative to a group of buddies who were going fishing.

But the law had an even bigger loophole than that, one big enough to drive through with a rum-runner's Studebaker. It was not illegal to export booze out of the province, nor was it illegal to buy it mail order. A sharp young businessman named Harry Bronfman noticed that loophole, and in 1919, he formed the Canada Pure Drug Co. and got a bonded warehouse, which happened to be beside a hotel he owned in Yorkton. Bronfman's first shipment of pure drugs (five train carloads of scotch) came December 25. Within weeks he had shipped 30,000 cases of whiskey to warehouses all over western Canada. The Canada Temperance Act made it illegal to ship booze into a province that forbade its sale, but each province had to hold a referendum on the issue, and the earliest that could be done was October 1920. Until then, the exporters could make hay while the boozy sun shone. And they did. By 1920, Saskatchewan alone had 50 export houses.

Shortly after, the interprovincial export business was shut down and the real action moved south. Although it was illegal for Americans to buy liquor, it was fine for Canadians to ship it there. Most of the exports flowed quite openly, but there was substantial smuggling. When a so-called Whiskey Six Studebaker could carry up to 40 cases of liquor at $50 a case, American underworld figures began to pop up in Saskatchewan border towns. Dutch Schultz once spent a week in the Bienfait Hotel.

As it happened, Harry Bronfman owned a liquor warehouse in Bienfait. It was managed by his brother-in-law Harry Matoff, and Harry was on duty that night when Jimmie LaCoste noticed the cars near the warehouse down by the tracks. Matoff was in the office counting the cash he had just been paid by a North Dakota liquor dealer when someone poked a 12-gauge shotgun in the window and blasted him from about 10' (3 m). Jimmie and the boys burst from White's just in time to see a solitary figure carrying a shotgun on the train platform. Not wishing to inquire after the stranger's business, the gang called the Royal Canadian Mounted Police instead.

They never found Matoff's killer. Bronfman said it was simple robbery for the $6,000 the dead man had been counting and the wedding ring on his finger. Others said it was payback after Matoff had a couple American rum-runners returned to Canada and jailed for stealing a Bronfman car and Bronfman booze. Others say it was mistaken identity and the real target was Harry Bronfman. Whatever it was, it worried the Saskatchewan government, which shut the liquor exporters down on December 15, 1922.

It hardly mattered. By 1924, Saskatchewan had gone wet and instituted the system of government control and sale now in use. And by then Harry Bronfman was living in Regina, a millionaire several times over and the founder of one of Canada's great family fortunes.

Fledgling North-West Mounted Police Rests at Roche Percee during March West
Old Highway 39, 4 miles (6.5 km) south of Bienfait to Roche Percee turnoff, drive a few hundred yards (meters) east of Roche Percee to cairn and features

The dramatic, wind-eroded sandstone outcrops and welcoming valley of Roche Percee has made this spot a landmark and way station for travelers for generations. The soft rock has been carved and marked by Plains Indians, members of General George Custer's Seventh Cavalry and surveyors who have paused and rested here. But it was during the North-West Mounted Police's epic March west that Roche Percee won its place in prairie lore.

The future of the fledgling force was dubious when it arrived here on July 24, 1874. It had left Fort Dufferin, Manitoba, a few weeks earlier on its mission to bring law and order to the North-West frontier with high hopes and a 3-mile (5-km) -line of 275 policemen, 20 drivers, 7 guides, 310 horses, 140 oxen, 114 carts, 73 wagons, 100 cattle, 2 field guns, 2 mortars, field kitchens, portable forges and mowers to cut grass. But while the force's recruits included farmers, schoolteachers, clerks and adventurers from several countries, precious few had any experience on the plains.

Water was a constant worry as the men marched through the 86°F (30°C) heat. The men hadn't been issued canteens, and the force had few barrels along, so even when they found good water they had no way to store it. And the muddy, alkaline slough water they were often forced to drink made diarrhea epidemic.

Food was a problem, too. The cattle, intended to be a larder on the hoof, often fell so far behind the main body of the procession that they arrived in camp too late to for the men to have any supper except biscuits and water. Grasshoppers and prairie fires destroyed the prairie grass, and many of the horses weakened and died pulling the heavy carts. Often the men went to sleep at night listening to wolves howl over the carcasses of horses left on the trail. One of the recruits, who kept a diary, described the force's arrival at Roche Percee:

On our arrival at Roche Percee the column resembled a routed army corps. For a distance of several miles the road was strewed with broken carts and horses and oxen overcome with hunger and fatigue.

Here, five days of rest allowed both man and beast to recover their strength. Spirits recovered enough that an impromptu band was formed, featuring a fife and a tin dish drummed on with tent pegs. From here, one party headed toward Fort Edmonton while another kept pushing west. But neither group's trial by prairie was even close to ending. The men wouldn't reach their destinations until October.

The March west tested the mettle of the North-West Mounted Police like nothing else could have. After that, chasing out a few whiskey traders must have seemed like a holiday.

ALONG HIGHWAYS 8 AND 9

Cannington Manor—A Little Bit of England on the Frontier
Off Highway 9 on Municipal Road 603 to Manor, follow signs for 10 miles (16 km) northeast of town

---

The dream of inscribing an ideal vision of society onto the blank slate of an unsettled, unspoiled new land haunted many pioneers of the Canadian prairies. Such were the settlers of Cannington Manor, who sought to recreate an old-fashioned English manorial village in the West.

In 1882, Captain Edward Mitchell Pierce finagled a grant of land from the government in Ottawa for the purpose of starting an agricultural colony peopled by sound British stock. Early the next year, Pierce, along with his family, arrived at what he named Cannington Manor after a place in Somerset and began to break land and sow wheat, oats and barley. Suitable colonists, responding to Pierce's advertisements, soon followed, bringing with them such pioneering essentials as grand pianos, tennis racquets, shotguns and the family silver and household staff to polish it. Cannington Manor began to thrive. Between 1884 and 1889, the Captain's Moose Mountain Trading Co. built a carpenter's shop, a mill, a smithy, several civic buildings and a store that provided everything from postal services to farming supplies to marriage licenses. The stout, red-faced Pierce may have been somewhat bossy and overbearing, but the Skipper, as he was called, was a man to get things done. Before he died in 1888, he even founded what he called an agricultural college (and others called a pup ranch), which offered to teach young English gentlemen the rudiments of farming in the North-West for a mere £100 a year. One attendee of that institution later wrote, "We may have laughed and made fun of these men trying to teach us farming, when, it was so evident that that they knew so little about it themselves." For their part Pierce's instructors were often glad when the high-spirited younger sons of English gentry took off for the day so they could get some real work done.

Cannington Manor certainly offered plenty to distract one from the hard work of extending the Empire. There was dancing, cricket, soccer, tennis, fox hunting, cockfighting and horse rac-

A Cannington Manor fox hunt in 1893.

ing with thoroughbreds imported from England. When Prohibition was repealed in 1892, there was the bar in the Mitre Hotel. The social scene was enlivened by visitors such as Lloyd George, the future British Prime Minister. Bertram Tennyson, nephew of the great poet, lived nearby and published his own verse in the *Moosomin Spectator.* And after 1889, there were the Beckton brothers: Ernest, Billy and Bertie.

The wealthy Beckton boys had been sent west to farm but had no intention of doing any such thing. They built a great stone house for themselves and barn to match for their horses. They imported foxhounds and bull terriers. They held an annual Hunt Club Ball, at which evening dress was required. They became the leaders of the bachelor set, spending money and having fun on a grand scale.

Not all the imported folkways of Cannington Manor were so benign. England's class structure came over with the engravings of the Royal Family. "Many a caustic remark we heard about Canadians," recalled one woman. "The funny thing about the Cannington English was that they called all people of the working class Canadians, though they might be straight from Somerset or the Hebrides. Canadians were supposed to lack culture and education."

In the end Cannington Manor was doomed by the railway's decision to build 10 miles (16 km) south of the settlement.

A group of Cannington Manor lads relaxing. Two of the Beckton brothers are seated at the table.

Bachelors spent all their money and went off in search of new adventures, many in the Boer War. Businesses faded with the lack of rail connections. Gentleman farmers and serious home-steaders alike gradually succumbed to the drought, killing frosts and low crop prices of the 1890s. The prairie turned out to have its own ideas about recreated English villages, and Cannington Manor faded away. Captain Pierce, the old Skipper, remains buried in the churchyard. If there is any corner of the West that remains forever England, this is it.

Moose Mountain Wintering Post Offers Shelter in Winter and Storm

Highway 9, 13 miles (22 km) north of Carlyle, turn west at Kenosee Lake turnoff, Moose Mountain Provincial Park, Government Beach on Kenosee Lake

An outpost of an outpost, this wintering post provided shelter to Hudson's Bay Company men from Fort Ellice who used it to overwinter trade furs with the local tribes. In use for over a decade during the mid-1800s, it was also handy for travelers between Moose Mountain and Fort Ellice, an important Hudson's Bay Company hub of the day. Supplies were also stored here.

French Aristocrats of St. Hubert Provide Gallic Counterpart to Cannington English
Highway 9, just south of St. Hubert turnoff

The English at nearby Cannington Manor were not the only old-world aristocrats drawn to the dream of a new land in the North-West. Here at St. Hubert and nearby Whitewood came a group of wealthy French nobles with their own ideas of how to live.

The counts Roffignac, Jumilhac, Beaudrap and Soras arrived in the mid-1880s. They, along with their compatriots, built a series of gracious homes that became the center of a French colony of flair and élan. One of those houses, the 1895, 20-room, brick and oak dwelling of Benjamin Lomoges, still stands in Whitewood as a museum and antique store. To ease the transition to their new life, the counts imported vintage wines for their tables and Paris gowns for their wives. When they raced horses, usually against the English of Cannington Manor, they arrived at the meet in coach and four. Several were musical and played in the Whitewood town band. And once a year at the Whitewood Hotel, they held an open house for the whole community.

Meanwhile, they raised large herds of purebred sheep and cattle as well as horses for the French army. They brought out families of farm workers from the Ardennes and Ardeche regions of France. They tried a variety of enterprises from cheese factories to sugar beets to chicory farms for use in making French coffee. All these ventures, after a brief prosperity, failed. Eventually, perhaps with a Gallic shrug, the counts returned to France. They were all gone by the World War I, leaving behind them the church of St. Hubert, the nucleus of a permanent community and a romantic memory of things past.

Palliser Follows Moose Mountain–Fort Ellice Trail to Coal Deposit
Highway 9, 1 mile (1.6 km) north of Langbank

When Captain John Palliser was dispatched by London's Royal Geographical Society to the far-off North-West in 1857, part of his task was to identify and assess any valuable natural resources. So when Palliser heard about coal in what is now the southeast corner of Saskatchewan, down he came. This is the trail he followed. Sure enough, at Roche Percee his expedition found a deposit that still keeps miners busy.

Palliser wasn't the first over this trail. It was already well known to fur traders who used it to get into the Moose Mountain country from the Hudson's Bay Company post at Fort Ellice. Later, the North-West Mounted Police followed it, as did incoming settlers.

Ernie Symons' Oiler a Paragon of Rural Ingenuity
Highway 8, Rocanville

They say that nobody is as inventive as a farmer—always out in the shop, fixing this, scavenging parts from that, trying to come up with something that will work a bit better. You couldn't find a better example than Ernie Symons.

Ernie was a farmer about 12 miles (20 km) out of Rocanville when he decided he was better at working metal than working the land. In 1922, he came into town and opened a blacksmith shop. He had no capital, no formal training and only a couple of books to refer to, but he did all right. One thing kept bothering him, though. A blacksmith and machinist is always squirting oil on something, and none of the three oilers he had worked worth beans. Ernie put his mind to it, and before long he came up with his own version. It worked great.

His shop customers agreed and wanted to buy them. Ernie couldn't interest established manufacturers in his design, so in 1924, with no production or machine-shop experience and shoe-string capital borrowed from his parents, he started building them himself.

The first year he sold 24 (one was still in use 40 years later). The next year he sold 400 and the year after that 3,500. Displays at exhibitions took the Symons Oiler all over the West. Symons Metalworks, based in Rocanville, came to sell up to 25,000 a year of the indestructible, reliable, useful little gadgets all over the world. They've been spotted in the United States, the Netherlands, Pakistan, the Arctic, France, Germany, Italy, Burma and on a boat from Israel on its way to Vancouver. During World War II, the plant employed up to 32 people, mostly women and girls, making Symons Oilers.

Ernie Symons ran the shop until he was in his 90s. He sold the plant in the early 1980s and died shortly thereafter. The plant was never the same after that, and it has also closed.

Original Symons Oilers—just like the giant model on the highway, only smaller—are still available at the Rocanville museum.

Fort Esperance Became Scene in Violent Business Battle
Highway 8, 3 miles (4.8 km) north of Rocanville

This site, more than 200 years old, marks the first fur trade post in the Qu'Appelle region. It was, however, far from the last. This valley became a hotly contested region between rival fur traders in the days when business battles were fought more by armed men than lawyers.

The first Fort Esperance, just east of the marker, was built by the North West Company back in 1787. The region's furs were no great shakes, but the Qu'Appelle lay beside the great plains, home to the vast buffalo herds and source of the food on which the fur traders depended. Pemmican—dried buffalo meat mixed with melted fat and berries—was durable, nutritious and some say even tasty, and huge quantities of it were shipped out of here every year, packed in 100-pound (45-kg) buffalo-hide sacks.

The hunting was so good that a rival fur trader, the XY company, built a fort a just to the east of Fort Esperance, but it only lasted from 1801 to 1805. In 1810, the Nor'Westers moved the fort upstream a bit to the Qu'Appelle lakes, then back downstream a few years later, near where Big Cut Arm Creek flows into the river. They called this structure Fort John.

By this time the commercial rivalry between the North West and Hudson's Bay companies was getting violent. In 1816, the men of Fort John burned the nearby Hudson's Bay fort to the ground and marched to the Selkirk Colony to take part in what became known as the Seven Oaks Massacre. When they returned they built a new Fort Esperance, this time higher up the valley (directly behind the marker) to make it easier to defend. The cellar and fireplace remain. A depression marks where the stockade used to stand.

Finally, hostile Indians forced the North West Company to

abandon Fort Esperance in 1819. The Nor'Westers merged with the Baymen in 1821, ending the rivalry, but no new forts were built on the Qu'Appelle until 1831, when Fort Ellice was built to the east.

First Saskatchewan Co-op Formed
Off Highway 8 on Municipal Grid Road on north side of
Qu'Appelle River valley, drive 3 miles (5 km) east of highway

The cooperative ideal—neighbors with common needs pooling their resources to get themselves a better deal—is deeply ingrained in Saskatchewan life. Cooperatives are some of the province's largest businesses. Co-op stores virtually define the small-town downtown and are often the place neighbors meet for coffee and a bit of chitchat. The province's first co-op started and failed here.

The Harmony Industrial Association was founded in 1895 by the brothers J.E. and W.S. Paynter and S.W. Sanderson. The small group of member families became known as Hamona. Hamona's constitution was ambitious, almost utopian. The group was to acquire land to build homes for its members, share agricultural produce to protect members from want, to build and run factories, mills and stores, and to offer schooling and recreational opportunities. Finally, Hamona was to "maintain harmonious relations on the basis of cooperation for the benefit of members and all mankind in general."

Perhaps creaking under the weight of its giant mandate, Hamona lasted only five years. It was unable to renew its charter in 1900 and disbanded.

But perhaps it didn't die. The United Grain Growers Grain Company, the first agrarian co-op, was formed only six years later not far down Highway 1 in Sintaluta. By 1912, the Saskatchewan Co-op Elevator Company owned 46 grain elevators and 10 times that number by 1925. And although humanity in general is not noticeably more harmonious these days than it was back then, most of those other goals are being met in some fashion by credit unions, wheat pools or one of Saskatchewan's other cooperative enterprises.

Business Battle Leads to Open Warfare
Off Highway 8 on Municipal Grid Road on north side of Qu'Appelle River valley, drive 1.5 miles (2.4 km) east of highway

Back in the days of the fur trade, business battles were fought not only in the boardrooms of Montreal and London, but sometimes in the field. Fort John dates from a time when the rivalry between the Hudson's Bay and the North West companies was so fierce that men were killed over it.

Tensions between the two companies had already been growing for years when the Nor'Westers built Fort John in 1814 as their Assiniboine regional headquarters. Where once competing traders had entertained and delivered mail for each other, there were now incidents of violence and even death as the fur trade heated up and the aggressive North West Company continued to press the staid old Hudson's Bay Company.

For two years traders in the nearby Bay fort were harassed from Fort John. The threats became reality in 1816, when the Nor'Westers blocked the Baymen from paddling their furs down the river. The violence would likely have escalated if the Fort John men hadn't been distracted by more serious events in the Red River country to the east.

There, the North West Company and the settlers of the Red River Colony were close to war. The fur traders saw the settlers as a pro-Hudson's Bay Company encampment right in the middle of their supply line, and they were forcing out the Métis, the North West Company's providers of pemmican. The settlers saw tons of pemmican being shipped out of the country while they went hungry. In 1816, a group of settlers led by a Bayman captured and burned the North West Company stronghold of Fort Douglas. That sent 62 Métis and Saulteaux on the warpath to Red River, joined en route by the men of Fort John. At Seven Oaks the Métis encountered 24 men from the settlement. Shots rang out, and 20 of the Red River men were slaughtered, their bodies stripped and dismembered.

The bloodshed touched off violence in the territories so severe that the British Colonial Secretary called it open warfare and in 1817 ordered both sides to stop fighting and restore captured goods and forts. But the violence continued. Finally, both sides acknowledged that neither could win, and the two companies merged under the Hudson's Bay name in 1821.

After the Seven Oaks Massacre, the Hudson's Bay Company moved closer to Fort Ellice and the Nor'Westers retreated to the site of their earlier Fort Esperance. Fort John never reopened.

Fort Ellice–Fort Carlton Trail Sees Who's Who of the Old North-West
Highway 8, just outside north edge of Spy Hill

The old cart trail that once passed this spot was the Trans-Canada Highway of its day. With Fort Garry at one end and Fort Edmonton at the other, this was the main artery of the fur trade era. Parts of its 932-mile (1,500-km) length were in use by 1799, but the first recorded use of the whole path was in 1815 by John Rowand, the chief factor of Fort Edmonton. Instead of waiting for the ice breakup on the North Saskatchewan River so he could follow the usual canoe route, the impatient Rowand set off on horseback on April 6 and arrived in Fort Carlton three weeks later.

There was still no cart trail when the driven, dynamic governor of the Hudson's Bay Company George Simpson passed this way in 1825. But after 1831, when Fort Ellice was built, traffic picked up and the trail was well established by 1841.

A virtual who's who of the old North-West followed: missionaries Robert Rundle, Albert Lacombe and John McDougall, the artist and writer Paul Kane, the Klondike-bound Overlanders, the Governor-General the Marquis of Lorne, pioneer newspaperman and politician Frank Oliver, and founder of Prince Albert, Reverend James Nesbitt. This was the road they traveled.

Perhaps one of the most colorful people to walk this trail was no explorer, trader or statesman, but a wealthy, aristocratic Englishman with a taste for hunting and adventure. James Carnegie, Earl of Southesk, rambled widely over the plains from 1859 to 1860. He came through here in 1859 with an entourage that included 8 Métis, 15 horses and 4 carts and wagons of guns, ammunition, food and tobacco. He roved from Fort Garry to Fort Ellice, then on to Fort Qu'Appelle. He shot buffalo in the Eagle Hills and potted grizzly in Stranraer. He sledded to Fort Carlton, the Touchwood Hills, Fort Pelly and as far west as the Rockies at Jasper House. He sampled pemmican, dined on bear and skunk, and bathed regularly in cold water. And while his guides prepared meals and pitched camp, Southesk retired to his tepee to read and ponder Shakespeare by firelight. His copy of the Bard's plays, stained with smoke-induced tears, is annotated with comments such as, "Why is it that one is inclined to have more sympathy for Imogene than Desdemona?" Despite the discomfort, the expedition was a great lark for Southesk. He wrote,

This open air life suits me very well, though, when one considers it bit by bit, it does not seem very charming. Long wearisome riding, indifferent, monotonous eating, no sport to speak of, hard bed upon the ground, wet, no companion of my own class; nevertheless, I am happier than I have been for years.

Happy or not, Southesk returned to England in 1860 and wrote the best-selling *Saskatchewan and the Rocky Mountains*. No doubt having collected enough stories for a lifetime of London dinner parties, Southesk never returned.

Chapter 4

The Schooner Region

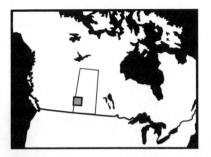

West Central Saskatchewan on the Move

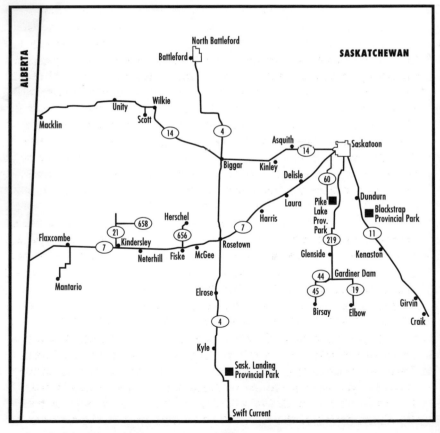

People on the move walk all over the history of this part of Saskatchewan.

Think of ancient hunting camps where the land's first occupants stopped for a while, then roamed on, following the great herds of buffalo. Think of Mistassini, the Big Rock, where Indians paused in their travels to make offerings to the Great Spirit.

Think, a little later on, of the network of trails that laced this land. Think of the brief, busy heyday of the old Swift Current–Battleford Trail, where cart teams took freight off the Canadian Pacific Railway and shipped it north by the millions of pounds. Don't forget the rough-and-ready chain of "hotels" that sprang up to shelter all those travelers, stopping houses that varied from a dugout in a hillside to a rather imposing, two-story field-stone hostelry.

Perhaps most enduring of all are the images of settlement.

Think of the Old Bone Trail, over which so many eager homesteaders poured that one newspaper reporter wrote it was "not an uncommon sight to see an almost unbroken line of wagons and vehicles of all kinds and degrees of richness strung out in a long, snakelike caravan many miles in length. . . ." Then there were the colonization companies that brought in families by the tens of thousands and sold acres by the millions.

Think, too, of a different kind of movement. Sod shacks, built of bricks cut from the same tough prairie soon to be farmed, were the first homes of many of these pioneers. Look around at the prosperous farms and well-established towns, and think of the distance this region has traveled.

ALONG HIGHWAY 7

Battleford–Red Deer Forks Trail Traveled by Many
Highway 44, 2 miles (3.2 km) west of Mantario

For generations the forks of the Red Deer and Saskatchewan rivers to the southwest had been a gathering place for Indians. Early fur traders knew that, and their attempts to trade with those bands date back to the construction of Chesterfield House by Hudson's Bay man Peter Fidler in that area in 1800. Peter Pond, on behalf of the North West Company, built a post near there shortly after. Neither post lasted, due largely to Blackfoot hostility.

Métis freighters and traders had better luck, and by the middle 1800s they had established trails from the forks heading in all directions. This trail, the ruts of which can still be seen, was the route to Battleford. Along this path in 1882 traveled hundreds of Cree and Assiniboine being escorted by the North-West Mounted Police from their camps near Fort Walsh in the Cypress Hills to their new reserves in the Eagle Hills and the Battleford area.

After 1883, the Battleford–Red Deer Forks Trail became the quickest way to the railway at Medicine Hat and Swift Current, and many settlers passed this way, loaded with tools, seed, food and a few household effects, to make their new start in a new land.

Addison Sod House Built to Last

Highway 21, 10 miles (15 km) north of Kindersley, then 6 miles (10 km) east toward Kiyui Lake on Municipal Road 658

The first thought many homesteaders must have had when they stepped onto their new quarter section (65 square ha) probably concerned a home. What to build it out of? In many places, the only material in abundance was the prairie sod itself. So that's what they used.

The sod today has all been plowed and cultivated. But then, it was knotted together by the roots of hundreds of years of grasses and weeds. It was tough.

"That stuff was like carpeting," one old-timer recalled to another writer. "I have actually seen a strong man, a brawny Highlander, take a piece of sod about a foot by a foot and try to tear it in half, and the muscles in his arms bulged and he got red in the face but I'm damned if he could."

So here was how the pioneers used it to build their homes: First, you'd plow out your floor plan, 16 x 26' (5 x 8 m) or so. Then, you'd cut some poplar trees from some hills or a nearby coulee and put up a frame. You'd plow out some more because the sod you were lifting up was going to be bricks and you were going to need lots of them—4,000 or so. Besides, you'd want a plowed-out area around your house as a firebreak against the inevitable

Sod houses on homestead, 1907.

prairie fire. Then you'd start stacking up the sod bricks against the poplar frame. Each brick would be 1.6 or 2" (4 or 5 cm) thick, about 16" (40 cm) wide and twice as long, piled up with a slight inward tilt to help bear the weight. You could put doors and windows anywhere. The roof was made by stretching poles side by side between the walls, then putting down a layer of hay, a layer of sod, another layer of hay, then some more sod. Some homesteaders referred to that top layer as "government shingles." Boards on the ground would make the floor, and cloth was pegged into the dirt walls. Blankets were hung to make rooms. This was the little home on the prairie, warm in winter, cool in summer, although not particularly dry.

The Addison sod house, however, is special. When James Addison arrived from England in 1909 with his wife, Jane, and three children, he saw that many sod dwellings had a tendency to collapse within a year or two. He resolved to build one that lasted.

Addison chose sod with plenty of dry roots from a dry slough bottom. He interlocked the bricks double-thick, hollowing the center of each wall and narrowing them as he built upward. This way, the house slumped down instead of in. He built a second story using sod walls and a gabled wooden roof. Jane Addison planted vines along the exterior, weatherproofing the walls. In the 1940s, the vines were replaced by wood siding, then asphalt siding in the 1960s.

The work was done by 1911 and the Addisons, now with five children, moved in. Jane died in 1929 and James lived until 1963. Their daughter, Edith, lived in the house into the 1990s, making it the oldest continuously occupied sod building in the province and a tribute to the ingenuity of the prairie pioneer.

Herschel Petroglyphs—A Ceremonial Focus For 1,300 Years
Off Highway 7 on Highway 656, 12 miles (20 km) to Herschel, drive gravel grid road 2.5 miles (4 km) to petroglyphs, signed

---

For over a dozen centuries, Indians visited this site, conducting important ceremonies near a limestone boulder intricately inscribed with hundreds of dots, lines and circles, mysterious to us today but full of meaning to them.

Archaeologists who have excavated around this boulder, a ceremonial site centuries old, say the dig reads like a history of the West written in layers of earth.

Nearest the surface, stone items made by the natives mingle with European glass beads, bits of brass and china shards, especially on the west side of the boulder, where literally thousands of china fragments were found. A little deeper, the imported material disappears, and the stone implements are of a style made between 1100 and 1400 A.D. Deeper yet, a fragment of bison bone has been dated to the seventh century. Few artifacts have been found anywhere else but around the boulder, and almost no domestic refuse has been found anywhere at the site, indicating that this was not a campsite but a place of visitation where offerings were left.

The people who made the earliest carvings were of a culture widespread across the plains. These so-called Avonlea people lived in hide-covered tepees and were the first in this region to use the bow and arrow. They followed the buffalo, their goods carried by dogs instead of horses, using buffalo jumps and corrals to hunt many animals at once.

Archaeologists and local Indians suggest the bisected circles carved into the boulder represent buffalo hoofprints. The Herschel boulder drawings resemble other petroglyphs in Alberta referred to as ribstones because the abstract lines and dots are said to represent a buffalo's rib cage and spine. Most of these ribstones, from the right angle, even look like a buffalo.

To some natives the Herschel petroglyphs still hold their ancient significance.

Otter Marches Along Swift Current–Battleford Trail to Relieve Battleford
Highway 7, 1 mile (1.6 km) east of Fiske

In the spring of 1885, the residents of Battleford gazed anxiously south along this trail as Colonel William Otter and about 500 militiamen made their way north, passing by here in a column 4.3 miles (7 km) long. The North-West Rebellion had broken out, and after the Battle of Duck Lake, the residents of the small community feared a massive uprising. When a group of Cree and Assiniboine approached Battleford in late March to present grievances and find out what had happened at Duck Lake, the citizens abandoned their homes and businesses, and barricaded themselves in the police stockade. The local Indian agent would neither meet with the natives nor issue rations. Angry and frustrated, some band members looted and burned buildings in the abandoned town; two settlers were killed in separate incidents. Although most of the Indians returned to their reserves or joined Poundmaker's camp at nearby Cut Knife Hill the next day, the 200 men and 300 women and children of Battleford remained in the stockade, poised for and fearing an attack, and praying for help.

That was Otter's job. His troops, one of three columns to engage the rebels, arrived by rail at Swift Current and marched overland on April 13. The column must have been an impressive sight as it filed past. Along with the troops, clad in their various regimental colors, the line contained 500 horses, 200 teamsters and wagons, artillery pieces, a Gatling gun and tons of munitions, supplies and fodder. It was a cold spring. A week earlier it had been –22°F (–30°C) at Fort Qu'Appelle, and it snowed three days later, but the column moved fast. It was ferried across the river by the steamer *Northcote* and reached Battleford on April 24 to the wild cheering of the nervous citizens.

Despite his triumphant arrival, Otter and his men were soon routed after an abortive attack on Poundmaker at Cut Knife Hill. They spent the rest of the North-West Rebellion in Battleford.

The Old Bone Trail for Settlers Going Out, Bones Coming In
Highway 7, 1.5 miles (2.4 km) northwest of Delisle

By the end of the 1800s, buffalo herds no longer shook the plains. But it's not quite accurate to say they disappeared. No, their slaughter left thousands upon thousands upon thousands of buffalo bones littering the land. And those bones were worth money.

Along this trail the Métis hunters who once sought the living animals went out to scavenge for their skeletons. The hunters would haul them back by the cartload to the rail head at Saskatoon, where they'd be shipped to the United States to be made into fertilizer or used for bleaching sugar. Buffalo bones were worth about $15 a ton. Just as the size of the old herds is hard for us imagine, so is the number of bones they left. Bone scavengers would pile them up beside the tracks, using hundreds of skulls to form a compound and tossing the rest of the bones into it. In three weeks one homesteader gathered up three rail cars of bones off his new land—its first cash crop. It's estimated that 3,000 carloads of bones went south from Saskatoon alone.

After 1900, traffic on the Old Bone Trail reversed. Bone pickers returning to the growing city were replaced by homesteaders heading out to their new land. From 1904 to 1906, more than 10,000 settlers passed through here, looking for their virgin quarter section (65 square ha). In 1909, the *Saskatoon Phoenix* looked back on the spring of three years earlier:

That particular spring the traffic was so steady and continuous it was not an uncommon sight to see an almost unbroken line of wagons and vehicles of all kinds and degrees of richness, strung out in a long snakelike caravan many miles in length. At night around every slough, campfires blazed. . . .

Indeed, about .6 miles (1 km) from here was the old Schell Stopping House, one of many places that catered to travelers heading west. Joseph Schell, who filed his own homestead in 1902, served the public until 1908 when the railway came through, closely following the original path of the trail.

That didn't kill traffic immediately, though. The Old Bone Trail was used right up until 1919, sometimes by the then new Model T Fords.

Buffalo bones gathered by homesteaders being shipped out by rail.

The Bentley Brothers Burn Up the Ice
Highway 7, 21 miles (35 km) southwest of Saskatoon at Delisle, Water Tower

Look up. Those crossed hockey sticks on Delisle's water tower commemorate of one of the National Hockey League's all-time great brother duos, Max and Doug, Delisle's flying Bentley boys.

Doug was the elder, born in 1916, four years before Max. The boys came from a family of 13 children, and hockey was a religion with them. Doug was playing Junior hockey for Delisle when he was only 16, and at one time there were five Bentleys playing for a team in Drumheller, Alberta.

It was Max and Doug who were destined for the big time, however. Both were small, tipping the scales at a featherweight 145 pounds (66 kg), and there were many who thought the NHL's tough guys would wipe the ice with them. The Bruins passed on Max, and Montreal's team doctor told him he had a bad heart and shouldn't be playing at all. Finally, Chicago took a chance on him, and Max teamed up with Doug and Bill Mosienko to become one of the league's great forward units, the Pony Line. Max, the line's quick puck-handling center, became known as the Dipsy Doodle Dandy of Delisle. Over on left wing, Doug added his own speed, stamina and showmanship, and the Ponies were unbeatable.

For a while the Blackhawks had a third Bentley when Reg joined Max and Doug on right wing. Reg's career, however, was short. He played just 11 games, managing one goal and two assists.

The Pony Line broke up in 1947. Max had won the league scoring title two years in a row, and the Toronto Maple Leafs wanted him enough to trade an unheard of five players for him. Max played six seasons with the Leafs, helping them to win three Stanley Cups. He spent one season with the New York Rangers. Along the way he also earned the Hart Trophy, the Lady Byng Trophy and the Art Ross Trophy twice in a row from 1944 to 1946.

Doug was to spend almost his entire career with the Blackhawks, 1939 to 1951. He scored 219 goals and won the 1942–43 scoring title. Although he never won a Stanley Cup, in 1950 a Chicago newspaper gave him the Half-Century Award as the team's best player up to that year. In 1953, at the age of 37, he made a brief comeback with the New York Rangers.

Max played until 1954, when he retired to run the family wheat farm. In 646 NHL games Max scored 245 goals and had 299 assists. Doug died in 1972. Max lived until 1981.

Both Bentley brothers are members of the Hockey Hall of Fame.

ALONG HIGHWAY 14

Giant White Mushroom Really a Russian Legacy
Junction of highways 14 and 17

What is that great white thing looming beside the prairie like some sort of giant mutant mushroom? That, as anyone from nearby Macklin can tell you, is a 33' (10-m), 98-times-enlarged fiberglass, steel-and-chicken-wire model of a horse's anklebone. At night it's illuminated bright orange and can be seen for miles. The locals call it a bunnock. And bunnocks are both a game and a story.

Back in the early 1800s, say the old-timers, Russian soldiers posted to the frozen Siberian frontier found time weighing heavily on their hands. The ground was too frozen most of the year to even play horseshoes; nobody could bang a post into the permafrost. So one day, perhaps out of sheer desperation, some-body realized that a horse's anklebone could be set upright. There were lots of such bones around, so anyone could afford to gather some. One thing led to another and the game of bun-nocks was born.

Each game has 52 bones. The eight heaviest are the Schmeisers (throwers) and another four are marked as guards. The rest are soldiers. The guards and soldiers are divided equally and set into two straight lines 33' (10 m) apart. Opposing players try to knock down the lines with the Schmeisers, knocking the guards down first.

Bunnocks came to Canada with Russian Germans who set-tled the area. Today, Macklin hosts the World Bunnock Cham-pionship every long weekend, complete with a festival.

Incidentally, Macklin is one of the few towns in the world named for a reporter. Harry Macklin was covering the construc-tion of the Grand Trunk Pacific Railway for the *Winnipeg Free Press* and wound up with a town named after him. This is also why the town's streets were all given newspaper names: *Leader, Post, Empire, Herald, Telegraph, Tribune* and *Times.*

Ethel Catherwood's Great Leap Carries Her too High
Highway 374, 5 miles (8 km) east of Wilkie, 2.5 miles (4 km) south of Highway 14 turnoff at Scott

---

It was quite a leap from a backyard in the tiny community of Scott to the 1928 Olympic games in Amsterdam. But Ethel Catherwood, the high jumper who "sailed like a bird," special-ized in big leaps.

Ethel, born in 1908, was a gifted athlete from the start. Her father, Joseph, who in his day had been a professional barn-storming athlete himself, noticed her gift and began coaching her in the family backyard when she was nine years old. She was the best around, excelling in sprint, broad and high jump, hock-ey, basketball and baseball. But it was in the high jump that she reached her peak. One day in 1924, in the jumping pit behind the family home, Ethel jumped just over 5' (152 cm). The world record for women was then 5'1.5" (156 cm). Ethel's life took off from that jump.

The coach of the Canadian Olympic team heard about her

jump and decided he wanted Ethel for the 1928 Olympics. She, along with her mother and two sisters, moved to Saskatoon to continue school and training. That training paid off. On August 31, 1926, in a stadium at the University of Saskatchewan, Ethel sailed over a bar 5'2.4" (158 cm) high. It was the best in the world, but Ethel wasn't overawed in an interview with the *Saskatoon Daily Star:* "Naturally I feel quite elated over breaking the record, but I am quite sure I can go even higher."

She was right. The next year, at the first-ever Canadian Women's Track and Field Championships in Toronto, she won the high jump, placed third in the discus and set a new record in javelin with a throw of 114'7" (34.9 m) breaking the old mark by 8' (2.4 m). The year after that, at the Canadian Olympic Trials in Halifax, she broke both her old records with a javelin toss of 118'8" (36.17 m) and a jump, using the old-fashioned scissors style, of 5'3" (1.6 m).

Ethel was a star. The *Toronto Globe* called her the "Queen of the Women's National Meet." Sportswriters wrote that she "sailed like a bird" and she "landed as easily and lightly after her jump as though she had merely leaped a hurdle." The fact that she was tall, slim and graceful, with a manner of understated confidence, didn't hurt her popularity with newsmen, either.

Her fame went international in Amsterdam, the first Olympics to include women's track and field. After dueling for three hours with American and Dutch jumpers, wrapping herself in a Hudson's Bay blanket between jumps to keep warm, Ethel finally won gold with a leap of 5'2.5" (1.59 m). She was carried to the podium on the shoulders of her teammates. Again, the press loved her. "The prettiest of the girl athletes," beamed the *New York Times.* The *Globe* said she was the most photographed athlete at the games. Back in Saskatoon, September 28 was declared Ethel Catherwood Day.

That jump, however, was to be the high point of her career. By 1931, the best she could manage was third place at the Canadian championships with 4'9.5" (1.46 m). The bloom was coming off her public image, too. In 1929, she had secretly married James McLaren, a bank clerk, only to file for divorce in 1931 and to be re-engaged to Byron Mitchell, the manager of the U.S. rowing team she had met in Amsterdam. It was considered a scandal. She and Mitchell were wed in 1932, and Ethel moved to San Francisco. There, she cut herself off from her athletic past, disparaging all sports, refusing interviews and wishing Canadians who remembered her past glory would leave her alone. Eventually, she and Mitchell split. From 1960, Ethel lived alone in San Francisco, working as a stenographer. She never gave another interview and died in 1987.

Maybe Ethel's sister Beatrice had it right when she told an interviewer that it had cost Ethel dearly to maintain that cool, confident facade and that the effort became too much. Maybe she was tired of jumping and wanted to come back to earth.

Nevertheless, Ethel's records stood up well. She held her javelin record until 1936. And until 1954, no woman jumped higher.

Rail Opens New Territory for Freighters
Highway 51, 6 miles (9.6 km) west of Biggar

When Swift Current became the Canadian Pacific Railway's end of steel in 1883, a whole new set of markets opened up for ambitious freighters to ship goods to. By April 30 of that year, a Métis named Marchand left Battleford with a party of men, 35 horses, a string of carts and a wagon carrying a scow to help with the river crossing. Looking for a practical, profitable route to reach Swift Current, they returned less than a month later on May 22, laden with provisions, enthusiastic about the new trail to the south and the Canadian Pacific Railway. Within months the Saskatchewan Coal Company expanded the ferry at the South Saskatchewan River crossing and built a store. The following spring the government further upgraded the trail by building a bridge over Eagle Creek.

The Swift Current–Battleford trail, which passed here, grew into one of the busiest north–south arteries in the old North-West. It saw almost 4,410,000 pounds (2 million kg) of freight between the spring and fall of 1886. A stagecoach route ran along it. A string of way stations also sprang up to shelter travelers for the night. In 1885, Colonel Otter and his troops used this trail to travel into the Battleford country during the North-West Rebellion. Many homesteaders, including some who pioneered this area, drove their wagons along these dusty ruts.

Although parts of it were used until 1925, the trail's heyday ended in 1890, when the railway came to Saskatoon, making that city the best jumping-off point for people and goods headed north.

Cree couple with Red River cart along the Swift Current–Battleford Trail at the bridge over the Battle River, 1904.

Prince Albert–Red Deer Forks Trail Links River Systems
Highway 14, just outside east edge of Asquith

Fur traders probably established this trail in the early 1800s as a way to get between posts on the North Saskatchewan River and the fork of the Red Deer and South Saskatchewan rivers. But because of Blackfoot hostility, those posts didn't last long, and traffic over this path remained light until midcentury. Then, it was frequently followed by Métis hunting parties. The North-West Mounted Police used it for patrols, and many early homesteaders followed it to their new quarter sections (65 square ha). It was gradually replaced by railway branch lines and surveyed road allowances.

ALONG HIGHWAY 4

Popular Stopping Place and River Crossing Becomes Homestead
Highway 4, 31 miles (50 km) north of Swift Current

Travel between prairie towns is a matter of hours these days. But back when the trip between, say, Swift Current and Battleford was undertaken on horseback or Red River cart, any such journey meant days on the trail. Stations such as Goodwin House brought wayfarers in from the cold or wet, or just offered a night of relative comfort and companionship after a day on the lonely prairie.

As the usual place to cross the South Saskatchewan River, this spot has been a gathering point for travelers for generations. Those on horseback simply waded across (the river was narrower before the Gardiner Dam was built), while Métis freighters and buffalo hunters tied the wheels of their Red River carts up under the box and rafted across. By 1883, a government ferry was in operation, just in time to move troops across en route to relieving Battleford during the North-West Rebellion. In 1887, W.E. Russell opened an inn here that he called the Russell House. Built of logs and timber, and offering meals at all hours, one old-time freighter gave it the backhanded compliment of "not half bad for the times."

So heavy was the traffic that ruts worn into the prairie sod by the carts coming over the south bank hills can still be seen. But traffic declined seriously after 1890, when new railway construction shifted freight traffic to Saskatoon.

Still, when the Frank Goodwin family came to the area in 1898, they decided to offer their home as a stopping place as well. Their residence, built of fieldstone collected from the surrounding hills, became a popular stopping place from about 1904 on. An inn was certainly needed. In the spring or autumn, travelers could be delayed for days until the ice either strengthened enough to walk across or melted enough to run the ferry. In autumn, after a good cold night, one man would step gingerly out on the ice to see if it held. If he made it, sand would be spread on the ice and horses would be led over one at a time. Finally, wagons would be drawn over on ropes.

This spot was handy for the police, too, and the Royal North-West Mounted Police (the *R* for *Royal* was added in 1904 in recognition of the service many of the force's men saw in the Boer War) kept a detachment here from 1904 to 1914. The ferry remained in operation until 1951, when it was replaced with the bridge.

Doctor Fords River on Folding Boat
Highway 4, north bank of South Saskatchewan River

In the generations that this spot has been the preferred crossing point for the South Saskatchewan, these hills have seen all manner of traveler, from prairie-wise Métis freighters to optimistic homesteaders, from lone horsemen to the mass transport of Colonel Otter and his men on their way to relieve Battleford during the North-West Rebellion of 1885. But among the oddest to pass this way was Campbell Mellis Douglas.

Douglas was born in 1840 in Quebec City. A doctor by training, he joined the British Army and earned the Victoria Cross in 1867 for the rescue of 17 men from the pounding surf off Little Andaman Island in the Indian Ocean. Upon retiring in the early 1880s, Douglas returned to Canada to farm in the quiet, picturesque village of Lakefield, Ontario.

Perhaps it was a bit too quiet. When the North-West Rebellion broke out, Douglas, then 45, immediately volunteered for service. Among his effects when he hopped off the train at Swift Current was a collapsible boat of his own design. Mellis took it to the south bank of the Saskatchewan River, unfolded it and rowed blithely across, much to the astonishment of the ferrymen. He then paddled more than 186 miles (300 km) to Saskatoon, where he served briefly, treating the wounded from the battles of Fish Creek and Batoche.

Douglas returned east, but he wasn't finished yet. A few years later he paddled across the English Channel in that same collapsible boat, which he had named the *Saskatoon*. Eventually, Douglas moved to England and died in Somerset in 1909.

End Of Swift Current–Battleford Trail a Sweet Sight
Old Highway 4, 1 mile (1.6 km) northwest of Red Pheasant

The ruts visible here are from the old Swift Current–Battleford Trail. Here, northbound travelers were almost at the end of their 200-mile (320-km) journey from Swift Current, and near this spot was the last stopping point before the home stretch into Battleford.

No doubt many were glad to see it. By this point a cart train loaded with goods from the rail yards at Swift Current would have been on the trail for about two weeks. The traveling was hard, and some of the stopping places were even harder. There were other hazards as well. On September 29, 1883, a Battleford newspaper reported on one of them:

> *When about 40 miles from this place on their way in from Swift Current last week, Mr. Prince and the party were caught in a fierce prairie fire, and in fighting it to protect his outfit he was seriously burned about head and face. A yoke of oxen and a horse were so badly burned that fresh animals had to be sent for to bring in their loads.*

For a few months in 1885, during the North-West Rebellion, there were human hazards as well. About 6.2 miles (10 km) north of here, a cart train freighting in supplies for Colonel William Otter's militia troops in Battleford was captured by Poundmaker's Cree.

ALONG HIGHWAYS 11 AND 219

Early Indians Leave Evidence of Stay Along River
East off Highway 45 at Birsay, then follow Municipal Road 646 12 miles (20 km) southeast to Camp Rayner along shores of Lake Diefenbaker

It would have been hard to imagine life for the ancestors of today's Indians without the North and South Saskatchewan rivers. The rivers themselves were a transportation route and a dependable source of water in a climate where it was a precious commodity. Wood for fires and tools could be cut in the cool, damp coulees along their shores. Erosion exposed stone that could be shaped into all kinds of useful tools. And as game came down to drink, hunting was always good along the riverbank. Small wonder, then, that the South Saskatchewan basin has one of the richest concentrations of archaeological sites on the Canadian prairies. This site, Camp Rayner, is one of the best of them.

The Rayner site was found because of the Gardiner Dam. While its reservoir probably drowned hundreds of other sites, erosion along the shores of Lake Diefenbaker has exposed several new ones.

Artifacts have been found at this site that date back 10,000 years, far older than classical Greece, more than twice as old as the pyramids. The size of the site is impressive, extending around a few thousand feet (hundreds of meters) in all four directions. Even more remarkably, the archaeological record is almost continuous for at least 6,000 years.

What has been found? Charred bones from buffalo, bear and other animals, cracked open so the last nutritious bit of marrow could be sucked out. Broken bits of pottery. Tools and weapons, along with the flaked-off bits of stone and fire-cracked rock used in their manufacture. Not fabulous buried treasure or golden statuettes, perhaps, but clues to how families lived on these plains thousands of years ago.

The Saskatchewan Archeological Society has operated a field school here since 1987, which usually runs for two four-day sessions every summer. The school offers amateurs a chance to join in a professional dig, but participants must register in advance. Casual visitors are welcome, but collecting artifacts from the beaches is prohibited.

Camp Rayner is owned by the Saskatchewan 4-H and the Girl Guides of Saskatchewan. They were attracted here, as were the Indians of old, by the waters and cool refuge of the South Saskatchewan River valley. After thousands of years it's still a good campsite.

Jack Hitchcock Lived Frontiersman's Life
Rayner Center, east off Highway 45 at Birsay, then follow Municipal Road 646 12 miles (20 km) southeast to Camp Rayner along shores of Lake Diefenbaker

The old North-West was made for people like Jack Hitchcock. Tall, lean, laconic and resolutely self-sufficient, Hitchcock was

the kind of man people mean when they say "rugged individual-
ist."

Born Orville Arthur Hitchcock in Quebec in 1870, Jack first
came west in 1894. He liked it, but knocked around California,
Mexico and back east. He got married in Vermont and fathered a
daughter, but couldn't stay. "I felt cooped up. I could not forget
the freedom of the West," Jack told a local historian. "I had to go.
She wouldn't go with me. She thought more of her father than
she did of me."

He returned for good in 1903, crossing the Saskatchewan near
Elbow at around Christmas. He started building his log cabin, but
was only four logs high when winter halted his efforts. He spent
the rest of the season in a tent and finished the cabin in the spring.
That cabin remains on the site today, pretty much as Jack left it.
Built with ax and saw, it's complete with furnishings, the floor
made of wooden discs, the wooden door with wooden hinges and
wooden handle as well as the special opening for Jack's cats. It has
a rough wooden table, a pair of bunk beds, apple boxes for shelves
and a low armchair made of willow and deerhide thongs. It was
barely tall enough for the 6' (182-cm) Jack to stand in.

Jack called himself a rancher, and he did run cattle although
he never owned much for land and always seemed to manage to
avoid paying grazing fees on the community pasture. He had
horses and raised colts for sale and had a purebred Percheron
stud. That kept Jack in enough money to buy what he couldn't
provide for himself, which wasn't much. He shot game, caught
fish, picked berries, collected shrubs and even tapped his own
maple syrup. He built his own smokehouse and dressed in buckskins that he prepared and sewed himself. He found a use for
everything from tin cans (handy for patching walls) to calendars
(just as handy for brightening those same walls, even if the pages
are 20 years old). He was a fine hunter (they say he could hit a
quarter tossed in the air from 26' / 8 m) and expert horseman,
but he's remembered just as much for the old bicycle he used to
get around on and the motorcycles he replaced it with.

Jack lived alone for the rest of his life, but he was a great
reader of everything from the *Western Producer* newspaper to
science fiction magazines. He had plenty of visitors, too. They
remember his calm, appraising eyes, his even voice, his confident manner and his love of spinning yarns. He was happy to
play up to the role of the untamed frontiersman, keeping his hair

long and sporting a six-gun. When he returned from his last trip east, he loved to tell how he sat at dinner, buckskin clad amidst his white-shirted and gowned companions, inventing tall tale after tall tale, them believing every word.

Jack lived the rest of his life in this little cabin except for the last few years spent in a senior citizens home in Saskatoon. He died in 1964.

Dam Writes Modern Ending to Cree Legend
Highway 19, in parking area of Elbow marina along waterfront, Elbow

---

Long ago, goes the Cree legend, there was a chief with several wives. The chief was very jealous, and when one of the wives accused a young man in the band of bothering her, the old chief attacked him. But the young man was too strong, and he killed the chief.

The young man was banished from the band. For years he wandered on his own far into the lonely prairie. Eventually, the people of the band began dreaming of the young man, dreaming that he still lived, that he was being cared for by a great white buffalo known as Old Man Buffalo.

One day a band elder dreamed the young man had died. He dreamed that the young man had been turned into a great rock as a symbol of the white buffalo's mercy and kindness. The band traveled west and sure enough, there was great rock. They called it *Mistassini,* or "big stone."

That's the way some people tell the story, illustrating the evils of jealousy, the price of crime and the importance of acknowledging kindness received. Another version holds that *Mistassini* was dropped from the sky by a great eagle. Either way, this rock became a place of pilgrimage for generations of Indians. In 1858, the explorer Henry Hind observed beads, bits of tobacco and fragments of cloth placed near it in offering. John Palliser noted groups of Indians near it in a trancelike state. But in 1966, *Mistassini* became a glacial erratic about 75 square feet (7 square meters) and 13' (4 m) high, just 224 tonnes of rock about to be submerged by the Gardiner Dam. A small campaign was mounted to move the giant rock, but the money couldn't be raised. So *Mistassini* was dynamited, and in 1967, a few bits of it became part of this cairn. Other fragments became part of the memorial to Chief Poundmaker on the Poundmaker Reserve. The rest of the big rock—or, if you prefer, the monument raised by Old Man Buffalo—lies under the waters of Lake Diefenbaker about 9.3 miles (15 km) to the east.

Saskatchewan Valley Land Company Markets a Dream
Highway 11, 3.5 miles (5.6 km) south of Kenaston at picnic site

It had to be one of the greatest challenges in marketing history: sell not just a car, a line of clothes or a sports team, but an entire country and the dream of a new life. That's pretty much what Canada's colonization companies had to do to fill the West with settlers.

Colonization companies have a long tradition in this country. The first one, dating back to 1628, was founded to settle New France. Generally, this is how they worked: the government would sell a company a tract of land at reduced rates. The company would publish brochures, advertise, set up offices from which they hoped to attract settlers, arrange for transportation, assist settlers in picking land, buying supplies and helping them build their first home. Once the land was partly settled, the remaining land would become more valuable to the company.

The first great bloom of colonization companies came in the late 1800s under John A. Macdonald. Most of those companies collapsed when the great prairie real estate bubble burst in 1881.

The Saskatchewan Valley Land Company had better timing. By this time Canada's great immigration boom had begun, and the demand for land was raging. So in 1902, the Canadian government quietly approached Colonel A.E. Davidson, a onetime Canadian who had moved to Minnesota, with a very attractive business proposition. He was offered 1,750,000 acres (708,225 ha) of Crown and railway land if he promised to settle 16 families per township on it within five years. A township being 23,040 acres (9,324 ha), Davidson thought that wasn't too onerous and formed a syndicate with nine others to take on the task.

The company organized a special rail tour for 200 American businessmen, merchants and reporters to look over the land. It built hotels and stables for its settlers. It spent $40,000 in advertising that first year and had 2,200 sales agencies in 12 states.

That high-powered marketing paid off. The company eventually sold over 5.5 million acres (2,225,850 ha) of land for between $6 and $10 an acre (.4 ha) after paying between $1 and $1.53. And much of that was paid with Métis land scrip, which the company bought at a steep discount and redeemed at face value. The original investment has been estimated as low as $50,000.

The settlers flowed in. On land that other companies had passed up as marginal, the Saskatchewan Valley Land Company eventually settled more than 50,000 families. Near Kenaston (named for one of the company's principals, F.E. Kenaston) one of the first homesteaders plowed a 43-mile (70-km) furrow all the way to Outlook for the steady stream of new arrivals to follow like an arrow to their future.

The great majority were Americans, experienced farmers with the money and know-how to set themselves up right. So many came north that although Davidson took the colonel's name, the town's streets were named for American presidents. Some officials back in the States even proposed measures to halt the Canadian exodus.

A few Canadians worried that so many Yankees might eventually tilt the West toward being annexed by their southern neighbor. They needn't have. The former Americans knew a good deal when they saw one and were quick to transfer their allegiance to the country that had given them such a good new start. Here's what one told a Canadian journalist:

> Four years ago, I lived in Iowa with a $2,000 mortgage hanging over me. Taxes and interest were eating me up. I came up here, got 160 acres of land as a gift from the Canadian government, and for two years I lived in that shack. Now I own that house. . . . Eighty acres of my land are under cultivation. My wife and children are well fed and well clothed for the first time in years. Do we want to be annexed? I guess not!

Elbow–Prince Albert Trail Links North with Transport Hub
Highway 60, 20 miles (32 km) southwest of Saskatoon, entrance to Pike Lake Provincial Park

---

One of many provision routes that spiderwebbed the prairies, this path was a link from Prince Albert to the Elbow of the South Saskatchewan. The Métis, fur traders, Indians, settlers and Mounted Police who used this trail could then join up with other trails that would lead them almost anywhere in the North-West.

Dundurn Military Base Built by Army of Unemployed
Highway 219, 19 miles (30 km) south of Saskatoon, Canadian Forces Base Dundurn

By 1932, the Great Depression had bitten hard and deep into households not just in Saskatchewan, but across the country. Work was so scarce that many simply pulled up stakes and hit the road, figuring that wherever they ended up, it had to be better than where they were. They were wrong. It was that bad all over. Great armies of the homeless, transient unemployed— 70,000 of them that year—began to pile up like leaves blown against a fence. Governments began to worry. Left-wing labor groups like the Communist-led Workers Unity League were already active among the unemployed, and that year's May Day parade in Regina drew 10,000. What if those bitter young men were organized to do something more than just march?

So that year Major-General A.G.L. McNaughton pitched the idea of a national system of work camps to Prime Minister R.B. Bennett, and Bennett went for it. All those single, homeless, transient, unemployed men could be kept out of the cities or at least segregated within them. They would be clothed, housed, fed and paid 20 cents a day. In return, they would clear bush, plant trees, build roads and perform other public works.

Entering a camp was voluntary, if that had any meaning to someone denied relief payments if he didn't. Camp inmates could leave whenever they wanted, if they had somewhere to go or were willing risk arrest for vagrancy.

As camp populations rose, so did tensions. When officials tried to move some men from the Saskatoon camp to Regina, a riot broke out. Dozens were injured and a policeman was killed. McNaughton decided a new camp was needed—one outside any major city and one big enough to handle the numbers. He built it here, or rather, the inmates built it for him.

Dundurn was already an existing militia base when the unemployed moved in. Plans to accommodate 1,000 had to be doubled, and there were rarely fewer than 1,500 inmates here, most young men in their twenties. It was one of the largest camps in the country. During the four years the camp was operating, the inmates erected 45 buildings, a railway spur, a landing field, rifle range, power and telephone lines, bridges and miles of road. Since the idea was to create work, most of the labor was done the hard way, with picks and shovels.

The men were being housed in what was meant to be permanent facilities, so the Dundurn camp was more comfortable than most. As well, the men had recreation and sports facilities. There was a hospital, too. Food was based on the standard military ration.

There were other signs of the military presence. Complaints were forbidden, whether voiced in collective petitions, individual speeches, letters to newspapers or to any outside authority other than the camp foreman. Anyone deemed breaking the rules, refusing work or being an agitator could be turfed out, blacklisted from other camps, cut off relief and not even transported back to the nearest city. From May through December 1933, 115 men were expelled, one for reading a book judged socialist.

Under such conditions, with the sense of wasted years building, it's not surprising that grievances festered: the pay was low, the hospital never had a doctor and the government effectively robbed the men of their vote by insisting they could only cast ballots in their home constituencies. So when two inmates, aged 18 and 19, were about to expelled December 12, 1935, in the dead of the Saskatchewan winter, about 70 inmates stood up for them and refused to allow them to be taken. When authorities came back the next day to arrest them, they and 800 others went on strike, and the military lost control of the camp for about 10 days. The strike held through most of January, when it ended with few changes in working conditions. Soon after, the camp was transferred to the Department of Labor, and the workers got a 50-cent raise.

By then it hardly mattered. The camp was closed in June 1936. But the legacy of those workers remains—a military base built by an army of the unemployed.

Chapter 5

The Old North-West Region

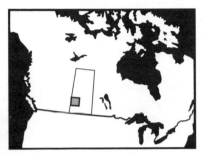

Ghosts of Rebellion Haunt Region

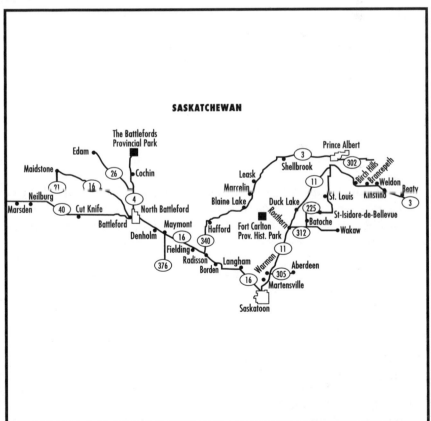

153

A LTHOUGH THE STORIES from this part of Saskatchewan range from the education of a hockey hero to the introduction of medicare, ghosts of the North-West Rebellion are inescapable.

Here, between the North and South branches of the Saskatchewan River, the Métis made claim to their homeland. Here they established the river-lot farms that became flash points of conflict, here Louis Riel returned from Montana to lead the Métis, here they chose to fight, here they fought most of their battles and here they suffered their decisive loss to Canadian troops and policemen at Batoche.

Historians have argued that the North-West Rebellion changed little. After the fighting, the federal government did create seats in the House of Commons for representatives from the territories, but that would probably have happened soon anyway. The violence didn't help the discontented farmers any. High freight rates for shipping grain remained, as did tariffs that protected Ontario while inflating the cost of farm supplies. Nor did the lot of the Cree improve significantly. And the Métis, who fought hardest and suffered most, faced the same pressure on their land and culture as before. The rebellion's strongest echo came not in the West but from Quebec, where outrage over the decision to hang Riel as a traitor increased English–French tension and cost John A. Macdonald's Conservatives the province's support for years to come.

But the failure of those in the rifle pits to win concessions doesn't diminish the fact that the Métis loved their people, their land and their way of life enough to fight and die for it. Perhaps that's why Louis Riel—passionate, fervently religious, patriotic and of wobbly sanity—as well as his able and courageous general Gabriel Dumont, remain Saskatchewan folk heroes.

ALONG HIGHWAYS 16, 40 AND 26

Shiloh Baptist Church Marks Search for Freedom

Highway 21, 13 miles (22 km) north of Maidstone, then 3 miles (5 km) east, then 1.6 miles (2.5 km) north, on left side of road

Mattie Mayes was born around 1853, a black slave on a Georgia plantation. She lived through that, through the Civil War that followed and through homesteading on the American frontier. But she and many like her still didn't feel they had found freedom. In search of it, they came here.

By the turn of the century, the new state of Oklahoma, where Mattie lived, was becoming increasingly segregated. Laws had already been passed forcing black children to attend separate schools, and some politicians were talking seriously about removing their parents' right to vote. Meanwhile, the Canadian government was advertising heavily for immigrants to fill its vast western plains. Some of those ads found their way into widely circulated black newspapers, and to many readers the thought of starting over in a land without the historical baggage of slavery sounded good. But Canada had racism of its own, and the government was suddenly unsure about the desirability of these immigrants, despite the fact that they were experienced dryland farmers. Officials from the great white North came to Oklahoma to discourage blacks from emigrating. Nevertheless, from 1909 to 1911, several parties decided to move.

Mattie Mayes, then 52, was in one of them. She and her husband, Joseph, took carts and wagons to Tulsa, Oklahoma, and from there rode trains to Winnipeg. The group filed for homesteads, then hitched up oxen from North Battleford to take up their new lands near Maidstone. One of the first things they built was this Baptist church, made of logs and stones from the riverbank, chinked with a mix of local lime and mud. Joseph was the first pastor.

Life was difficult for the immigrants. Southern crops like soybeans wouldn't grow up north, and the new farmers had to relearn many things. To get by, many of the men hired out to work on threshing gangs for their neighbors. And yes, there was discrimination here, too. "The settlers are considerably worked up about having to send their children to school with the Negroes," MLA John Lyle wrote in 1914. Despite repeated attempts to work out a compromise, an all-black school district was formed and remained so until 1919.

Still, the colony persevered. Mattie Mayes, who could remember listening to Abraham Lincoln reading the proclamation that freed the slaves, was a community matriarch and midwife, dressed in her long skirts, white apron, high-button boots and copper bracelets to ward off stiff joints. Much of the community's life centered around this church. At other times people enjoyed horse racing and hunting coyotes with greyhounds.

The little colony shrank during the 1940s, when many drifted off to city life and some returned to the south. But Mattie and Joseph stayed, and Mattie lived to be over 100. One of her sons, George Mayes, lived on the family farm until his death in 1975.

Cart Trains Pass Halfway Mark on Fort Pitt–Fort Carlton Trail
Highway 26, just northeast of Edam at picnic site

Old-time cart trains making their way along the Carlton Trail from the east were a little bit more than halfway to Fort Pitt when they passed this spot.

Indians probably traveled along here for generations before the days of the fur trade. But after forts Carlton and Pitt were built in 1810 and 1831, this became part of the main overland route that linked Fort Garry (now Winnipeg) with Fort Edmonton and ultimately the Rocky Mountains. Traffic definitely picked up along the path, which passed near the present towns of Blaine Lake, Alticane and Prince, then stayed fairly close to the north bank of the North Saskatchewan. But many creeks and valleys made travel along this original north bank route difficult. By the 1880s, several alternate paths between the two forts had opened up.

Along with the hundreds of anonymous freighters, traders and trappers, this route, and this site, saw a virtual who's who of the old North-West. Hudson's Bay Company head Sir George Simpson, missionaries Albert Lacombe and George and John McDougall, the artist Paul Kane, journalist and politician Frank Oliver, members of the Palliser expedition, survey teams under Sandford Fleming, Captain William Butler, gold miners heading to the Klondike—they all passed along here. In 1840, the young Gabriel Dumont, later general to Métis rebel leader Louis Riel, came through here as his father, Isidore, took the family back to their old home near Fort Pitt.

Poundmaker Tries, Then Gives Up on Whites
Highway 40, entrance to Cut Knife, at highway turnoff

Nobody tried harder than Poundmaker to build a good relationship between his people and the Europeans. Treaties, he knew, were inevitable, and he fought hard to get the Cree the best one he could, sometimes in the face of opposition from other Cree leaders. Once he signed, he tried to make it work and even doffed his hunting buckskins for a farmer's overalls and swapped his rifle for a hoe. If his fellow chief Big Bear represented Cree attachment to the old ways and distrust of the new, whites saw Poundmaker as the well-spoken, smiling chief, the one they could deal with. But like Big Bear, Poundmaker wound up in jail for his part in a rebellion he did his best to prevent.

Pitikwahanapiwiyin, or Poundmaker (the name, inherited from a relative, refers to the building of buffalo pounds for hunting) emerged as political force among the Cree in his midthirties during the 1876 negotiations for Treaty No 6 at Fort Pitt. Again and again, it was his voice that spoke up, asking for details to be explained, complaining that the treaty was not good enough. Despite the fact that the tough negotiations had won the Cree concessions that no other treaty had, Poundmaker was disappointed with the final treaty, but he signed it. Sarcastically using the government's own flowery rhetoric, he noted, "From what I can see and hear now, I cannot understand that I will be able to clothe my children as long as the sun shines and water runs."

If Poundmaker's tough talk impressed his fellow Cree, his persona impressed the whites even more. He was handsome, dressed and spoke well, had real influence among his people and seemed to get along with Europeans. With his 3' (1-m) -long braid of hair entwined with mink skin and brass wire, and his brass-studded vest, he was, they thought, a true Noble Savage. "He is a noble-looking Indian, and reminds one more of Fenimore Cooper's heroes than do the great majority of North-West Indians," wrote a newspaper reporter.

Poundmaker, with 182 followers, took a reserve about 43.5 miles (70 km) west of Battleford in 1880. He tried to lead his people into agriculture. Here is how another reporter found him in 1882: "Their chief, dressed as becomes a Canadian farmer, with sleeves turned up, was busy, fork in hand, in securing his excellent crop of wheat."

But that was not the whole story. Government help in making the switch to farming was slow and grudging. Indian agents were often contemptuous of the people they served. Food aid was given only in return for work, even for the orphaned, sick or aged. Despite the hard-won famine clause in Treaty No 6, the Cree were hungry and getting hungrier.

All Poundmaker could do was encourage his people to stick together. On New Year's Day, 1882, he pleaded with them: "Oh! Allow me to ask you all to love each other; that is not difficult. We have faced the balls of our enemies more than once, and now we cannot bear a word from each other."

Poundmaker reentered politics. The spring of 1883, after planting his crop, he headed south to talk with Big Bear. The next summer more than 2,000 Cree under Big Bear's guidance gathered on Poundmaker's reserve for a Thirst Dance and council. The event nearly ended in violence against the authorities. Even the peaceable Poundmaker threatened a Mountie with a war club.

When fighting finally broke out in March 1885, many Cree bands gathered under Poundmaker. Now was the time to move, thought the chief. On March 28, Poundmaker had told a young farm instructor he had given up on whites:

Of old, the Indian trusted in his God and his faith was not in vain. He was fed, clothed and free from sickness. Along came the white man and persuaded the Indian that his God was not able to keep up the care. Hunger followed, and disease and death.

Two days later the terrified citizens of Battleford awoke to see a Cree army camped outside town. Poundmaker told a messenger they had only come to town to learn about the fighting at Duck Lake. But while its inhabitants huddled behind the palisades at Fort Battleford, the Cree looted and burned the village, eventually returning to their reserve.

Here they remained, and more and more Cree bands came to join Poundmaker. Despite pleading messages from the Métis for help, Poundmaker felt he had secured his territory and his role in the fighting was over. When his camp was attacked on May 2 in the Battle of Cut Knife Hill, it was War Chief Fine Day who led the Cree, not Poundmaker. After the troops were routed, Poundmaker stepped in to prevent the warriors from chasing the fleeing militia. His ability to influence the War Chief is a measure of his stature.

Poundmaker surrendered on May 26, 11 days after Riel. Like Big Bear he was charged with treason–felony and defended himself by saying he had little control over his warriors once Fine Day had taken charge. Like Big Bear he received three years in prison. "I would rather prefer to be hung than to be in that place," Poundmaker said as sentence was passed. Sure enough, he was released within a year, his health broken. He died July 4, 1886, and is buried on the Poundmaker Reserve.

Army Retreats after Battle of Cut Knife Hill
Highway 40, 20 miles (32 km) west of Battleford; turn north on gravel road, drive for 4 miles (7 km), park at Poundmaker Museum, battlefield about .3 miles (.5 km) away

---

Colonel William Otter was a young officer on the rise in 1885, and when he marched in at the head of about 500 troops to relieve the citizens of Battleford during the North-West Rebellion, he thought he'd finally found his main chance.

About 500 townsfolk and police had been cooped up in the old North-West Mounted Police fort for weeks in fear of the nearby Cree, who had taken the opportunity to loot and burn most of the settlement's homes. The citizens wanted the Cree punished, and Otter, knowing a good career move when he saw one, wanted to lead his men in battle. So on May 1, after informing his commander Major-General Middleton that he was setting out on a reconnaissance mission, he headed out with 300 soldiers toward the camp of Chief Poundmaker.

Early the next morning Otter had his men climb this hill across from Cut Knife Creek for breakfast. Unknown to him, Poundmaker's camp was just on the other side. At about 5:15 A.M. the two sides more or less bumped into each other, much to their mutual surprise. If Otter had advanced, the Cree might have surrendered right there to protect their families in camp, but instead Otter halted his men at the crest of the hill.

Before long it was clear they were in a bad spot. War Chief Fine Day, although not much more than a teenager, deployed his men with great skill, using mirror signals to shift squads of four or five around from place to place, keeping up a steady fire from three sides and never giving the army a solid target for their artillery or Gatling guns. Every time the soldiers moved, they were clearly outlined against the sky and made easy targets for the Cree in the wooded coulees and ravines below. The Cree were poorly armed (many had old fur-trade muzzle-loaders and some only had bows and arrows), but it was clear the Cree were getting the better of it.

The troops, originally itching for a scrap, knew they were

beaten. One later wrote, "I never felt afraid, but quite made up my mind I was to be hit and wished myself back in Toronto." At about 11:00 A.M. Otter began to organize a retreat. He'd suffered 8 dead and 14 wounded, and only Poundmaker's intervention stopped the Cree from chasing the army and making the total higher.

Otter spent the rest of the rebellion in Battleford. The Cree, with six dead and three wounded, headed to Batoche for one more doomed battle.

Big Bear's Failed Dream a Tantalizing "What If?"
On gravel road in Poundmaker Reserve, just north of Cut Knife

One of the most powerful of all Cree chiefs, Big Bear (in Cree, *Mistahimaskwa*) was a tough, shrewd and deeply spiritual man who fought to unite all Indians to preserve their way of life in the face of the encroaching Europeans. The tale of his bloody failure leaves one of the most intriguing "what ifs?" in the West.

Big Bear was born about 1825, the son of an Ojibwa chief and was marked as a future leader even as a bright, precocious boy. His special aura was enhanced by his roots with the Ojibwa, who were considered to have a closer relationship to the spirit world. Sure enough, as a teenager he dreamed a dream of great power: he saw the coming of the whites, saw them purchase the land, saw the bounteous gifts of the Great Mother. Big Bear's vision was retold again and again in the years to come.

By the 1870s, Big Bear was the leader of up to 2,000 Cree around the North Saskatchewan River. Renowned for his ability to shoot accurately astride a horse at full gallop, he had a commanding presence and a rich, sonorous voice. In 1875, the government sent the missionary George McDougall to sound out the Cree on what was to become Treaty No 6. Big Bear told McDougall, "When we set a fox trap we scatter pieces of meat all round, but when the fox gets into the trap we knock him on the head. We want no bait. Let your chiefs come like men and talk to us." When most of the chiefs signed in 1876, Big Bear was not among them.

Big Bear had come to believe that all Indians had to unite. He tried to get bands to select a string of adjoining reserves that would have run from Swift Current to Gleichen, Alberta, creating

an Indian territory. But he failed to overcome old tribal hostili-
ties, and finally the government blocked the move. He then tried
to get chiefs to cluster their reserves around Fort Pitt, near
Battleford.

By 1884, hunger was becoming a problem on the reserves
and the chiefs felt the government wasn't doing enough about it.
Big Bear called a Thirst Dance here on the Poundmaker Reserve
to discuss the problem, and on June 7, more than 2,000 Cree and
their leaders gathered. Big Bear wanted the meeting to select a
single spokesman for all Indians to go to Ottawa; he also wanted
the Cree to select one large reserve on the North Saskatchewan.
Not only was the council unable to reach those goals, but Big
Bear was barely able to prevent violence from breaking out
against the North-West Mounted Police

Things didn't improve when Big Bear finally took a reserve in
1884 near Battleford. His people remained hungry; his young
men, led by War Chief Wandering Spirit, remained angry. Then,
the following March, came the news of the Métis uprising and
victory at Duck Lake. Big Bear had always worked to keep his
people from fighting, but now he saw his worst fear come to
pass. Five years before he had dreamed this, too:

I saw a spring shooting up out of the ground. I covered it
up with my hand, trying to smother it, but it spurted up
over my fingers and ran over the back of my hand. It was
a river of blood.

Moving fast at the news, Wandering Spirit took control of Big
Bear's camp. On April 2, tired of being denied rations by Indian
Agent Tom Quinn, Wandering Spirit led Big Bear's former followers into the town of Frog Lake. They took its white inhabitants
prisoner and began looting various stores and supply depots.
Big Bear initially got Wandering Spirit to agree to not harm the
prisoners. But the war chief, a volatile and violent man, had
finally had enough of Quinn and shot him dead, triggering the
massacre of nine whites. Hearing the shots, Big Bear rushed
onto the street shouting, *"Tesqua, tesqua!"* ("Stop, stop!") But it
was too late. His dream of a peaceful coalition of Métis and
Indians was as dead as the Indian agent his war chief had shot.

Wandering Spirit was to lead the Cree in the burning of Fort
Pitt while Big Bear kept counseling peace. But after his people's
defeat at Loon Lake, Big Bear and his youngest son, Horse Child,
walked in alone to Fort Carlton and surrendered to a surprised

sentry. He was arrested, convicted of treason and served three years in Stoney Mountain Penitentiary. Sick and brokenhearted, he died January 17, 1888, only a few months after his release.

The man who dreamed of preserving the Indian way of life through common land and leadership is buried on the Poundmaker Reserve.

Cochin–Green Lake Trail Connects Southern Fur Trade with North
Highway 4, 3 miles (4.5 km) south of Cochin

Father Louis Cochin with two friends.

This is the southernmost point on a trail that stretched about 93 miles (150 km) north to the remote Hudson's Bay Company post at Green Lake. Along the way it touched native settlements at Chitek Lake and Birch Lake. From here the trail also connected to the Carlton Trail and other northbound trails.

This village is named after Father Louis Cochin, a Catholic missionary who lived many years among the Cree of Chief Poundmaker's band. Father Cochin refused to leave his flock when the North-West Rebellion broke out. After Colonel Otter's abortive attack on Poundmaker's camp at Cut Knife Hill, it was Cochin who tended to the dead that Otter left on the field. It was also Cochin who acted as a go-between as Poundmaker and Major-General Middleton discussed the terms that led to the Cree chief's surrender.

Cochin stayed by Poundmaker even during his trial. He testified in court that Poundmaker had been a moderating influence on his people and had seen to the safety of the prisoners in the Cree camp. He attended the trial of another Cree chief, One Arrow, and wrote to his bishop in disgust that the jury "without a doubt, have no schooling, and understood nothing of the lawyers' speeches, for or against."

Finally, it was Cochin who stood on the scaffold in Battleford on November 27, 1885, beside the eight natives who were hanged, singing their war songs, for their part in the rebellion.

Fur Trader Shelters Quarreling Explorers
Highway 4 at turnoff to Battlefords Provincial Park, 24 miles (40 km) north of North Battleford.

The Palliser expedition, headed by the dashing, handsome Captain John Palliser, was sent to the North-West in 1857. For three years the expedition was to survey the plains, report on their suitability for farming, look around for valuable resources and find out what was there.

All that summer the party roamed the prairie from Fort Garry to Fort Carlton. When the season ended, Palliser made his way back to Montreal to confer with Sir George Simpson of the Hudson's Bay Company and left his men to overwinter.

James Hector, the party's geologist, naturalist and doctor, decided to head to Fort Edmonton. He passed this way on December 17. He spent that night in a leather-walled wintering post just built by William McMurray of the Hudson's Bay Company very near here on the shores of Jackfish Lake. The two were joined by a group of independent traders, and the party spent a merry night talking, playing the violin and perhaps draining a cup or two of Hudson's Bay Company rum.

Hector had a more convivial time of it than the group at Fort Carlton. Thomas Blakiston, Eugene Bourgeau, James Beads and John Sullivan had set up a weather station and were sharing round-the-clock, six-hour watches taking hourly readings of temperature, atmospheric pressure, star movement and magnetic declination. Perhaps it was the isolation or perhaps it was the grind of the same routine for months on end, but before spring the men were at each other's throats, Blakiston and Sullivan in particular.

That may explain why, when Hector returned this way in May, he found McMurray's post expanded by a two-room cabin and Sullivan and Beads staying here. The three returned to Fort Carlton, where Blakiston and Bourgeau had completed the observations on their own. When Palliser rejoined them, the party set out for another season.

Fort Battleford a Shelter for Rebel-Fearing Settlers
Highway 4, 3 miles (4.8 km) southeast of North Battleford

Its log palisades may not look all that reassuring to modern eyes, but in 1885, when it looked as if Poundmaker's Cree were going to join Louis Riel's Métis in open rebellion, this fort provided some much-needed peace of mind.

Battleford was already beginning to wind down by then, the decision in 1883 to move the capital to Regina having blown a chill wind across the town's brief summer. It retained, however, a sizable North-West Mounted Police detachment living in a sizeable fort. After the battle at Duck Lake, not too far southeast, the citizens of Battleford began to quietly consider where they could take refuge if things came to the worst. At first the old police fort, built back in the late 1870s, didn't look too promising. Its stockade gapped like a hockey player's smile, it had no internal water source and in spring it was cut off from the main settlement as the bridge across the Battle River was taken down during breakup.

But on March 29, when a messenger rode into town with news that Poundmaker's Cree were camped 8 miles (13 km) away, the fort began to look pretty good. Most of the town moved in. "Gathering some clothing, etc. together we hastily took a meal and prepared to take refuge in the Police barracks," recalled merchant James Clinkskill. "My wife carried her jewel case and an old family bible, an heirloom, in her hands, the clothing on our backs was all we could take." About 460 policemen and settlers crowded shivering through a cold, wet night while they waited to see what the Cree would do.

Early North-West Mounted Police Band at Battleford.

Poundmaker's plan was to present a show of force, hoping to squeeze concessions from the government while he was dealing with Duck Lake. But before the situation could be defused, some Cree began to loot and burn the deserted houses in Battleford. Their former occupants could only watch in rage and fire off angry telegrams to whoever would listen. "The devilish ingenuity displayed in the destruction of things that were of no use to them would put to the blush a city mob. . . . They had a high time generally," reporter P.G. Laurie told the *Manitoba Free Press.* Although the town was slowly destroyed over the next few weeks, the fort was never attacked. Nor was the telegraph line cut, and Battleford's terrified cries for help were echoed across the West. The *Manitoba Free Press* wrote

> *The suffering of the poor women and children, hemmed within the walls of a dilapidated barracks, and momentarily expecting to be hacked to pieces by a blood-thirsty horde of yelping savages, can better be imagined than described.*

Even after the Cree moved back to their reserve on April 2, the townsfolk stayed within the fort. It wasn't until Colonel William Otter's column arrived on April 24 from Swift Current that they began to breathe easier. Back in town, the scene wasn't pretty. "Scarcely anything has escaped: what could not be taken has been destroyed," wrote one soldier. "About us we see scattered in dismal confusion feathers, photos, books, tins, furniture, and desolation reigns supreme."

But the fort had done its job. None of its inhabitants had been harmed.

Over the next decades the importance of Fort Battleford declined. Peaceful times meant fewer police, and the officers that were needed were slowly parceled out to the growing towns around Battleford. Finally, Fort Battleford was abandoned in 1924. It languished in the prairie winds and snows until 1951, when it was declared a national historic site and extensively refurbished.

Government House Democracy's First Home
Old Highway 4, 1.5 miles (2.4 km) south of Battleford

This building, erected in 1878, was democracy's first real home in Saskatchewan. Two administrations had already governed this land. The first was the Hudson's Bay Company, which, from 1670 to 1870, more or less ruled all the lands that drained into Hudson Bay. Then it was sold to a just-born, wet-behind-the-ears country called Canada. Lieutenant-Governor Adams Archibald came out from far-off Ottawa to run the show, but he had no power to even appoint, much less elect, a local council. And to someone in say, Qu'Appelle, Archibald's headquarters in Manitoba might as well have been back in Ontario. The real outposts of government were the local Mountie detachments.

In 1875, the Northwest Territories Act provided for a five-person local council to advise the government, with limited power to enact legislation (subject to the federal cabinet) and try cases. The council was appointed, but was to become elected and gradually evolve into a real legislature. And so it did.

The new Lieutenant-Governor, David Laird, must have been relieved to move to these relatively sumptuous headquarters for the council's second session in August 1878. The first session of the council had been held at Fort Livingstone, a North-West Mounted Police barracks near the Manitoba boundary. The fort was drafty and cold, and its log walls were so badly warped that daylight could be seen through them. Laird lived there for a year before he was able to move to Battleford.

Newsman First to Cover Land Full of Stories
Highway 4, just south of Battleford at crossing of Battle River

It was a land full of stories with no one to tell them, and a newsman like Patrick Gammie Laurie couldn't resist. So, on this site, he started the *Saskatchewan Herald,* the first newspaper in the Northwest Territories.

Laurie had already done considerable kicking around the West. He had worked in Winnipeg and had even known Louis Riel in 1869 and 1870 back in his Red River days. He knew an opportunity when he saw one, and when the new government of the Territories moved to Battleford in 1878, Laurie wasn't far behind. Someone would have to cover the council's meetings, write the high-minded editorials and furnish the gossip on which every capital, no matter how modest, thrives. And don't forget all those juicy government printing contracts, either. So he hauled in his printing press from Fort Garry—72 days by oxcart—and the first issue came out August 25 with outside news supplied by telegraph. Subscriptions were $2 a year.

Like all editors of the day, Laurie was anything but objective. He was a staunch Conservative of the John A. Macdonald stripe and supported the Old Chief enthusiastically. But he also spoke out for the West, singling out for criticism Ottawa's inconsistent and sometimes cruel policy toward natives. "At one time encouraged to believe that the Government would do everything for them, they were at another bidden to go and hunt for themselves; so that they did not know what to do," he wrote.

Before long he was joined by other pioneer journalists. *The Prince Albert Times* and *Saskatchewan Review* started up in 1882. Next year the redoubtable Nicholas Flood Davin fired up the presses on the *Regina Leader.* By 1886, the territory had seven newspapers.

The biggest story of Laurie's career was the North-West Rebellion, and his energetic, if highly colored, coverage is still often cited by historians. When his own paper was shut down as the Battleford townsfolk cowered in fear of Poundmaker's Cree, he filed by telegraph to the *Toronto Mail.* His references to "murderers of half a hundred men and women and destroyers of hundreds of homesteads" were among the least exaggerated dispatches filed from inside the fort.

Laurie passed the newspapering bug on to his children as well. During the Rebellion his son William filed copy from Fort Carlton,

Office of the Saskatchewan Herald, *first newspaper in the Northwest Territories, 1878. Patrick G. Laurie, editor and owner, stands in front.*

and the family took over the *Herald* after Laurie's death in 1903. They continued to publish until the *Herald* shut down in 1938.

Satchel Paige Pitches Last Saskatchewan Game
North Battleford

It was a hot, dusty August day in 1963. Two local baseball teams were midgame in North Battleford's Abbott Field when a pair of old cars pulled up and about a dozen black athletes piled out. Excitement rippled through the park when someone found out they were a team of barnstorming ballplayers, the Satchel Paige All Stars, led by none other than Leroy "Satchel" Paige, the greatest pitcher never to play in the major leagues.

Paige, whose race kept him out of the then segregated big leagues, wasn't exactly a stranger to Saskatchewan. He'd pitched his first game here back in 1931 and was a regular with touring black teams, including his own All Stars. This day, however, he was down on his luck. He and the team were broke, hungry and couldn't even afford gasoline to get to their next game.

The local ballplayers stepped up to the plate. They put Paige's men up in a hotel and saw that they were fed. One of the two local teams, the Unity Cardinals, arranged an exhibition game for the next night against the All Stars, with all the proceeds going to them. Paige, then 57, pitched one inning that night, maybe the last inning he ever pitched here. The game raised enough money for the All Stars to return home. It also marked the twilight of a long and colorful chapter of Saskatchewan's sporting history.

Baseball goes back here almost as far as settlement. The first recorded game took place in 1879 outside Fort Battleford. The *Saskatchewan Herald* wrote

> *On May 31 a baseball match between two scratch nines captained by Rbt and Richard Wyld respectively and resulted in favor of the latter by a score of 18–15. The play was very good particularly Mr. Scott's on first base.*

The fort had a permanent club that year and often saw games between Mounties and civilians.

And almost as soon as there was baseball here, there were black teams traveling up from the United States to play it. Shut out of the white professional leagues by the color barrier that lasted until 1947, they formed teams and earned their living by touring and taking on the locals. The first record of such a team in Saskatchewan—the Hottest Coon In Dixie company, which traveled with its own band—dates back to 1905. Such games, featuring legendary teams like the Kansas City Monarchs, were a huge draw. One night in 1935, a crowd of 2,500 gathered in Prince Albert to watch Satchel Paige pitch against Al Eckert. That same night the big-league Reds and Cardinals drew only 807 in Cincinnati.

White barnstormers came through, too, including the famous House of David team, often used by the major leagues to rehabilitate injured players. Even the Japanese came. The Tokyo Giants played in Regina and Saskatoon in 1935, featuring pitcher Eiji Sawamura, the first professional inductee to the Japanese Baseball Hall of Fame.

Saskatchewan also saw at least three members of the Chicago Black Sox, disgraced and banned from the big leagues for fixing the 1919 World Series. Hap Felsch, Swede Risberg and Eddie Cicotte all played for a Montana team that toured here. Felsch and Risberg both played for the Regina Balmorals in 1927. There's even a legend that "Shoeless" Joe Jackson played for a while in the Cabri area during the early 1920s under the name Johnson.

For decades, touring ball teams were cheap and popular

entertainment for small towns and cities alike. In 1951, Saskatchewan saw 34 touring teams, most of them black. But by the time those ragged All Stars pulled into Abbott Field, changing times were catching up to the barnstormers, and their glory days were over. Ironically, the colorful Paige's most-quoted line remains, "Don't look back. Something may be gaining on you."

River Junction Draws Many Fur Traders
Dike Road, 2 miles (3.2 km) southeast of Battleford near junction of North Saskatchewan and Battle rivers, near Battleford Regional Care Centre

By the end of the 1700s, the fur trade was expanding west. The Cree were looking for new trapping grounds, and small independent fur traders weren't far behind them. As always, the cautious old Hudson's Bay Company was a few years behind.

William Holmes was drawn by the strategic junction of two rivers and built the first fur post here back in 1785. Another inde-

Baseball has a long history in Saskatchewan. This game, played in the Qu'Appelle Valley, took place in the 1890s. Walter Scott, who later became Saskatchewan's first premier, is thought to be the pitcher.

pendent company followed along shortly, which merged with the North West Company. The Baymen showed up in 1805 and built a rival fort across the river from the Nor'Westers. After the two companies merged in 1821, the Hudson's Bay Company kept various forts here on several locations for many decades.

Bad Liquor Hard on Everyone's Health at Eagle Hills Post
Highway 376, 8 miles (13 km) south of Maymont, Glenburn Regional Park

Bad trade liquor was not only hazardous to the health of the native trappers who drank it. Sometimes it endangered the traders, too.

This post was built on the banks of the North Saskatchewan River in 1778 by a number of independent traders including Peter Pangman and John Cole. While neither the North West nor the Hudson's Bay companies were above trading a little rum or using it to lubricate a deal, booze figured much larger in the stock-in-trade of the free traders.

In a cold, calculating kind of way, it made sense. Liquor was easy to transport and brought a high return. And it did not need to be of high quality. It was routine to dilute one part rum with at least three or four parts water, adding anything from cayenne pepper to tobacco juice to restore the desired bite. The Baymen had their own specialty, "English Brandy," made from raw gin, water and iodine to give the right color. It's estimated as much as 50,000 gallons (227,300 liters) of liquor were imported into the North-West each season. Diluted, that produced at least 250,000 gallons (946,350 liters) of trade booze at a time when the population of the area wasn't much more than 120,000.

Still, the trappers must have known they were being taken advantage of and probably resented the disastrous effects liquor was having on their society. Here at Eagle Hills things came to a head in April 1779 when someone back in Montreal put too much opium in the brandy. There was violence, and Cole was killed. Pangman fled and lived to rejoin the Nor'Westers. He stayed in the West and marked a spruce tree within sight of the Rockies in 1790.

The post was never rebuilt. The liquor trade, however, flowed on.

Steamboats Ply the Saskatchewan River
Off Highway 16, 7 miles (12 km) east of Borden on riverbank at Borden campground

---

The rivers of the prairies had long been the main ways of getting around in the days of the fur trade. In the late 1800s, a variety of companies tried to bring these historic transportation routes into the Age of Steam. Here was a common place for these wood-burning steamers to stop and take on wood.

The first paddle-wheeler chugged its way up the Red River from the United States to Fort Garry in 1859. By the 1870s, there were a good half-dozen stern-wheelers plying the waters from Fort Garry and Cumberland House all the way to Fort Edmonton.

Crowds gathered and the band played when the steamboat Saskatchewan *docked at Prince Albert.*

Although they could only sail in summer (and then only when the water wasn't too low) the big boats were a much more efficient and pleasant way to travel than the cart train or York boat. *The Princess,* launched in Winnipeg in 1881, could carry 600 passengers and boasted two bridal suites and a $5,000 piano. Steamboat passage from Fort Garry to Fort Edmonton cost about $70 for a cabin and $35 on the deck. Freight rates were 6.25 cents a pound (.5 kg). A good speed was about 16 miles (26 km) an hour.

To allow them to float in the shallow prairie rivers, the boats were built wide and long. The ill-fated *Northcote,* damaged beyond repair in the North-West Rebellion, drew only 40" (102 cm) of water fully loaded. Still, sandbars were a problem. A steamer could push over the little ones just by taking a run. For bigger ones the pilot would turn the boat around and thrash the water with the boat's paddle, washing the bar away. The final resort was "grasshoppering"—jamming a pair of sturdy spars into the sand and using the engine's power to lever the boat along a few yards at a time.

It was the railway, another steam-driven contrivance, that eventually spelled the end of the steamboats. When the paddle-wheeler *The City of Medicine Hat* was destroyed in 1908 only a year after it was launched by crashing into the concrete piling of one of Saskatoon's bridges, it marked the end of an era as well as that city's worst, and probably only, maritime disaster.

Make-Work Project an Index of Depression Desperation
Highway 16, 25 miles (43 km) northwest of Saskatoon at crossing of North Saskatchewan River

Government make-work projects are nothing new. That's how this bridge just upstream of the newer one at this site was built back in the Great Depression. In fact, the story of the old bridge's construction is a good index of how desperate times were back then.

The government was so anxious to create jobs in Depression days that it supplied 90 percent of the money for any public works projects that got workers off the dole. And when Chalmers Mackenzie, an engineering professor at the University of Saskatchewan in Saskatoon, drew up the blueprints in 1934, he deliberately chose a more expensive concrete bridge over a steel truss design because it would use more local materials and provide more jobs for unskilled labor.

Most of those laborers were local farmers, hard hit by drought and low wheat prices. To keep the job numbers up, as much of the work as possible was done by hand. The men hauled sand and gravel with horse teams and moved about 60,000 tonnes of concrete in wheelbarrows. They worked three shifts, twenty-four hours a day, summer and winter, sometimes standing shin-deep in icy water at 37°F (3°C).

"Great credit is due to the courage and tenacity of the local farmers, inexperienced in such work, who cheerfully took this opportunity of avoiding the alternative—relief," wrote Chalmers.

ALONG HIGHWAYS 11 AND 3

City Rises from Teetotalers' Dream
East end of Broadway Bridge, near Five Corners, Saskatoon

The year was 1882. A teetotaling businessman with an eye for frontier real estate stood here on the banks of the South Saskatchewan River, heading a party of likeminded souls. The surrounding plains were lush with late-summer green, and the river flats below seemed just the place for steamboats and a ferry.

This was the spot, John Lake decided. This would be where he founded his city, free of the demon rum. But what to name it? Perhaps after those purple berries, so thick along the water's edge. He asked one of his Cree guides what they were called, and thus was this city dubbed.

"Arise, Saskatoon, Queen of the North!" Lake exclaimed.

At least, that's the story.

We know that it was Lake who chose the spot for Saskatoon. We also know that today's city is the result of a combination of greed and idealism perhaps unique to the Canadian frontier. In the early 1880s, the federal government was increasingly anxious to encourage settlement in the North-West, if only to make the Canadian Pacific Railway start to pay. So Prime Minister John A. Macdonald looked around and came up with a scheme. Since the land was all surveyed, he proposed to sell blocks of odd-numbered sections more than 22 miles (35 km) from the nearest railway for $2 an acre (.4 ha) to any company that could convince the government it was legitimate. The government would keep the even-numbered sections to distribute free to homesteaders. All the company had to do was settle two homesteaders on both odd- and even-numbered sections, and it got half its money back. Not only that, but once the free land started to fill up, the value of the company's land could rise to anywhere between $3 and $15 an acre (.4 ha).

Not surprisingly, this offer provoked considerable interest. Dozens of colonization companies formed, some strictly to make a buck, some with the idea of furthering a social or religious aim. The Temperance Colonization Society, of which John Lake was the commissioner, was a little of both.

As its name suggests, the society planned to create a liquor-free settlement in the hard-drinking West. Any applicant for the society's land had to swear off booze. At the same time, the company's members were not averse to profit. "There's millions in it!" exclaimed one principal.

So in 1882, the society advertised heavily in the Toronto papers and printed up 35,000 lavishly illustrated brochures. One reader later described those enthusiastic illustrations:

Tall chimneys were emitting volumes of smoke, there were wharves stocked with merchandise and huge steamers such as adorn the levees at New Orleans were taking on cargo. Subsequently, I found Saskatoon to consist of six houses at intervals and a store.

Nevertheless, the society got 300 applications and a land allocation of 200,000 acres (80,940 ha). By 1883, it had settled 57 homesteaders, but the dream of a dry colony was gone. There was simply no legal way to keep settlers on the government land from drinking.

Overall, Macdonald's colonization company scheme was sunk when the speculative bubble in western land prices burst. By 1885, the program was canceled.

It was enough, though, for Saskatoon. In 1886, the fledgling community had a tinsmith, a brick hotel, a dressmaker, a school, a Methodist church, a post office, a doctor, a lawyer, a realtor and insurance agent and a detachment of Mounties. The City of Bridges was on its way.

Barr's Lambs Get Fleeced
Spadina and 17th Street W, Saskatoon

The colonization agent stood on the railway station platform to address hundreds of colonists who had just tumbled from the train. Spring that year, 1903, had been remarkably hot, and today, April 17, it was nearly 86°F (30°C). The agent's rhetoric was equally overheated.

"I have a vision of teeming millions in the great valley to the West where you are going and you are the forerunners," he orated. "You will not be disappointed. . . . March westward ho!"

It's unlikely his audience was in the mood for such sentiments. Over the past weeks, they had endured a rough, cramped sea crossing from England and a cross-country train trip through land whose vast, empty expanse shook them to the core. They were the Barr Colonists, more than 1,500 middle- and working-class immigrants seduced by the Reverend Isaac Barr into leaving Britain's gritty, industrial cities for what they imagined was a green and pleasant land on the Canadian prairies. But what they had experienced so far was anything but pleasant.

By this time, it was clear to the colonists that Barr was a better salesman than organizer, and this day he was running true to form. All the baggage—mountains of it, containing everything from a portable organ to formal evening wear to essentials like tents—was a day late. Fortunately, the government had foreseen trouble. On this site, the colonists erected a white canvas city of

Barr Colonist tents in Saskatoon along the river flats, 1903.

nearly 500 government-provided tents. The next day, Sunday, they held service. "The wilderness and the solitary place shall be glad for them and the desert shall rejoice and bloom," Archdeacon Mackay, the North-West's ranking Anglican churchman, told the congregation in their Sunday best tweeds and linens.

Then it was to work. The muddy streets of Saskatoon bustled as never before as it became the staging area for the colonists' trip to their homesteads at present-day Lloydminster. Here they were to get organized, purchase supplies and load up their wagons for the trail. And there was, of course, trouble. When their baggage arrived, it was unceremoniously dumped on the train platform. The stagecoaches that were supposed to take the women and children to Battleford were nowhere to be found. The crew that was supposed to ready the colony site got lost, mired their cattle in muskeg and returned to town after wandering the plains for three days. Saskatoon, which they had been led to believe was an impressive, well-established town, was a heap of "large boxes rushed up without regard to architecture or comfort," its population a mere 600.

The colonists were a gold mine for local merchants. More than $250,000 worth of bank drafts were cashed to pay for supplies. Estimates of their purchases include 1,000 horses, 800 plows, 500 wagons, 150 mowers and binders. Barr took a 10 percent commission on top of the already inflated prices, and the colonists, who had begun calling themselves "Barr's Lambs," complained loudly about getting fleeced.

As well, it was immediately clear to immigration officials that few of the supposed homesteaders had enough money to set themselves up and fewer still knew how to farm. An employment bureau was set up. Farming classes were hurriedly convened.

Meanwhile, life in the 100-acre (40-ha) tent city went on. People tripped and stumbled over the cat's cradle of ropes and pegs. Women, some wearing elegant gloves, cooked supper. Men chopped chunks of ice for drinking water from the great blocks thrown up along the river. Tiny lap dogs yipped and yapped. Recently purchased oxen and horses protested as the inexpert colonists tried to figure out how to hitch them up. One night, the orange glow of a prairie fire lit the sky, but the firebreak of the village road kept the colonists safe.

Finally, by April 23, the first colonists were ready to leave. The boggy spring roads and the colonists' inexperience—some chalked hitching diagrams directly on their animals' hides—meant they were barely out of sight of Saskatoon before they stopped for the first night. But the exodus to the promised land had begun. By May 5, the last of the Barr colonists had hit the trail.

As for Saskatoon, it was about to enjoy the same land speculation boom that was to sweep the prairies. But those profits were in the future. For now, there was plenty of time to sit back and count the money taken off the lambs.

Mr. Hockey Starts Off on One Skate
Highway 16, 6 miles (10 km) southeast of Saskatoon, Floral

It's shrunk to not much more than a community hall and a baseball diamond, but the tiny community of Floral has given Canada one of its greatest hockey stars.

Gordie Howe was born here on March 31, 1928, the sixth of nine children. But father Ab Howe's farm wasn't working out, and the family moved nine days after Gordie was born. They didn't move far, however, just up the road to Saskatoon, where Ab found work as a mechanic. This is how the boy who later became known as "Mr. Hockey" got his first pair of skates.

It was the Depression by this time and things were tough. The Howes were eating a lot of oatmeal—it was cheap and filling. One day a neighbor woman came to the door with a grain sack full of household items and offered to sell it to mother Katherine Howe so she could buy milk to feed her baby.

"I didn't have much to offer but I reached into my milk money and gave her a dollar and a half," Mrs. Howe later told an interviewer. "We dumped the contents of the sack on the floor. Out fell a pair of skates. Of course, Gordie pounced on them. 'They're mine,' he yelled."

Not quite. Gordie had to share them with his sister Edna. Not only that, but they were a man's size six and neither could fit into them without the aid of several pairs of socks and yesterday's newspaper. That didn't stop them. For a week, out on the slough behind the Howe home, Gordie and Edna skated on one blade each.

"They kept coming in cold, bruised and crying but they'd go out again," said Mrs. Howe.

Finally, said mom, Gordie bought out Edna for a dime, a deal closed through the help of a maternal loan. Gordie remembers this a bit differently: *"Edna* got cold and went in and took the skate off, and that was the last she ever saw of it."

Either way the hockey bug hit Howe hard. Every weekend would find him at the nearest stretch of frozen water in an unending game of pickup hockey with 30 or 40 playmates.

Gordie went on to play an amazing 32 seasons of professional hockey in the National Hockey League and the now defunct World Hockey Association. Fast, strong and tough, with a wrist shot once clocked at 114 miles (183 km) per hour, he scored 869 NHL goals with 1,141 assists, mostly with the Detroit Red Wings. His physical, elbows-up style also earned him 2,419 NHL penalty minutes. He played long enough to have his sons Mark and Marty as teammates with the WHA's Houston Aeros. He didn't retire until 1980, when he hung up his NHL Hartford Whalers jersey at age 52.

Coulee Hid Many Ancient Stories
Highway 11, 3 miles (5 km) north of Saskatoon, follow signs

They came to hunt buffalo. They came for shelter and good camping. They came for what has become the name of this place: *Wanuskewin,* an old Cree word meaning "seeking peace of mind." Indians have been coming to this wooded coulee along the South Saskatchewan River for almost 6,000 years, leaving behind artifacts that are older than Egypt's pyramids. There are 21 different archaeological sites here, 19 of them predating European contact. They give a remarkably complete picture of how these people lived, and they tell many stories.

There are two buffalo jumps at *Wanuskewin,* the oldest dating back 2,300 years. Before the arrival of the horse and rifle, hunters would skillfully stampede a carefully directed herd of buffalo over a steep bluff. The herd's momentum would make it impossible stop in time, and the bellowing animals would plummet over the bank. Bones and worn stone tools at the bottom remain to show where hunters would butcher the stunned and injured buffalo by the hundreds.

There are many tepee rings left by hunters seeking shelter, wood and water. It can be blowing a gale up on the prairie, but you'd never know it tucked into the coulee. The tiny valley is also rich in berries, birds and small game.

And there's a 1,500-year-old medicine wheel here, one of 100 known on the plains, perhaps the site of ancient and still mysterious religious ceremonies.

Wanuskewin's survival is almost as remarkable as its existence.

The area was used by aboriginals right up until Treaty No 6 located them on nearby reserves in 1876. It became a farm in the early 1900s, owned for several decades by an eccentric dairy farmer named Mike Vitkowski, who believed the tepee rings and medicine wheel were landing pads for spaceships. Local archaeologists had known about the wheel since the 1930s, and in 1975, Ernie Walker, a graduate student from the University of Saskatchewan, came to visit Vitkowski. The two spent a lot of time talking and walking the land, and Vitkowski eventually came to realize how unique his property really was. When it came time to sell it, Vitkowski spurned lucrative offers from developers and sold it to the City of Saskatoon. He had never plowed the land, and its archaeological heritage had remained intact.

That heritage is still being excavated. Since then, *Wanuskewin* has been developed in close consultation with area Indians into a heritage park considered a model of its kind in the world.

Freighter Loses Coin Toss, Swims for Scow at Clark's Crossing

Highway 41, 19 miles (32 km) northeast of Saskatoon, take Grid Road west at junction of highways 41 and 27, drive 4 miles (6.7 km) west, then turn south on grid road for 1 mile (1.6 km)

River crossings were such a problem for freighters and cart trains in the days of the old North-West that they would do almost anything to make the crossing easier. Here's what two young men came up with to ease their trip across the South Saskatchewan River at Clark's Crossing.

Everitt Parsonage and his partner, Sandy McPherson, had already been on the trail from Fort Garry for weeks with 19 cart-loads of oats when they reached Clark's Crossing in the summer of 1877. This was supposed to be an easy crossing, not like when they crossed the Assiniboine back at Fort Ellice. There, the cart behind the last horse in the train sank, allowing its load of oats to float away in the current. Then, suddenly lighter, the cart began to float, too, pulling the horse along behind, its wheels revolving like a paddle boat. There was nothing for it but to strip down and swim out after the rig and the load. Those oats, after all, were worth $135 at trail's end in Fort Pitt. The two couldn't get going again until after they'd spread the oats out to dry in the sun.

So Parsonage and McPherson were greatly relieved to see the Mounted Police ferry scow at Clark's Crossing. One problem—it was on the other shore. For an entire day they sat on the east side, waiting for someone on the west side to come and get them. Nobody came. The freighters weren't about to go through what they had endured at the Assiniboine, so they tossed a coin. The loser would swim across and row the scow over. No matter how cold, fast or wide the water, it had to be better than trying another ford.

Parsonage lost. Off came the clothes, in went the swimmer and, in due course, over came the scow. After that the crossing was quite simple. The Mounted Police, who had been at the post all along, checked the oats for smuggled liquor by poking the sacks with sharp rods and sent the lads on their way.

At Fort Pitt the long-suffering oats were sold for about $5 a bushel, including freight costs. After selling 15 of the carts for a total of $300, they started back home. Parsonage and McPherson made it back to Fort Garry on September 12, about 100 days on the trail, covering 1,553 miles (2,500 km).

After 1881, the old police ferry was taken over by John Clark, for whom the crossing is named. One can only hope he was a more conscientious ferryman than the North-West Mounted Police.

Patience and Persistence Crowns Wheat King
Off Highway 11 on Highway 312, 4.3 miles (7 km) east to Seager Wheeler Road, then a few hundred yards (meters) north on grid road, follow signs

---

Patient, painstaking and persistent, Seager Wheeler was the very model of the pioneer farmer. And those qualities took him from a fishing village in Great Britain to world renown as the Wheat King of the Prairies.

Born in 1868 on the Isle of Wight to a fishing family, Wheeler was a keen observer of nature and was said to have the finest collection of birds' eggs on the island. As a boy he worked a few odd jobs and tried to enlist in the British Navy, which turned him down because he was too small. But the bright young lad was looking for an opportunity, so when a relative who had emigrated wrote about the land to be had near Fish Creek, well, that sounded pretty good. Wheeler and his mother and sister sailed from Liverpool on May 5, 1885.

Still, it was years before Wheeler could fulfill his dream. He worked on his uncle's farm and for the Canadian Pacific Railway until 1889 before he and his brother, Percy, were able to set up their own farm near present-day Warman. In 1898, Wheeler moved here to set up the homestead that became world famous as Maple Grove Farm.

It wasn't so grand at first. Wheeler and his mother lived until 1908 in a log cabin chinked with mud and roofed with sod. But from the start Wheeler applied the same principles of observation to farming that he had learned as a nature-loving boy on the Isle of Wight. He grew wheat, forage crops, vegetables, flowers and fruits, selecting all his seed by hand. Self-taught, he read everything he could on crop science and was full of questions at local seed fairs. He got experimental wheat varieties from the research station at Indian Head and began growing his own test plots.

Finally, after more than a decade of careful farming, Wheeler hit it big. A sample of his Marquis wheat won first prize at the World Seed Fair in New York, earning the Wheelers a much-needed purse of $1,000 in gold. It was the start of an amazing string. Wheeler won international awards every year from then until 1926, except for the hailed-out years of 1913 and 1923. Several of those championships were won with his own varieties, and his original Marquis 10B seed was sold as far away as Kenya and Australia. During the drought of the 1930s, Wheeler's experiments with shelterbelts and minimum tillage kept his fields from blowing away, giving him 40 bushels to the acre (.4 ha) in years his neighbors got 10. With five hired men to help run the farm, Wheeler wrote and lectured widely. In 1943, he became a Member of the Order of the British Empire.

Along the way Wheeler found time to move out of that log shack, marry wife, Agnes, and help raise four children. His accordion playing livened many evenings and dances. Wheeler remained a voracious reader all his life and also developed a passion for photography, developing and printing almost all of his own pictures. He wasn't a churchgoer but read the Bible regularly and supported the Salvation Army. Although his fame attracted up to 700 visitors a weekend, the Wheelers never got rich and lived modestly on Maple Grove until 1947, when Seager retired to Victoria, British Columbia. He died there in 1961, aged 93.

Some nicknamed Wheeler the Wheat Wizard, but there was no magic to his success. His explanation?

"One must be observant, ready at all times to learn. No matter how much one knows, there is still always much to learn."

Fateful Oath at Gabriel's Crossing Points Toward Rebellion
Highway 312, 18 miles (29 km) west of Wakaw, between bridge and Batoche turnoff

---

There had been plenty of earlier signs. But it was here, at Gabriel's Crossing on March 5, 1885, that the leaders of Saskatchewan's Métis committed themselves to the armed struggle that became the North-West Rebellion.

The place's name comes from Gabriel Dumont, a Métis who had operated a ferry here since 1877. Dumont was one of the undisputed leaders of his people; in fact, he was a legend. His

Louis Riel, leader of the Métis in the North-West Rebellion and author of the pledge to arms taken at Gabriel's Crossing. Taken in New York, 1878.

hunting and leadership skills saw him elected chief of the buffalo hunt in 1862, back when that meant commanding and organizing a camp of hundreds of hunters and their families. He never relinquished that post, the highest in Métis society. Here, at this crossing, he had built a substantial house on the east side of the river, complete with a billiards table, at which he was expert.

But racking a few balls was not on the agenda that night. The Métis, as well as the Indians and quite a few white settlers, were becoming increasingly afraid of the avalanche of newcomers they knew was coming. What was to happen to their current farms, unregistered by any survey? Who would compensate them for land given to new settlers? Who cared about their rights?

Less than two weeks before, Louis Riel had stood in a packed church and listened to a crowd demand that he lead them in their struggle. When he asked in quiet voice, "And the consequences?" the reply had come, almost to a man, "We will suffer the consequences!" A couple days after that, Riel had suggested to a priest that the time may have come for the Métis to "bare their teeth."

So here, in a secret meeting, Riel met with 11 Métis leaders and presented them with the following pledge, a typical Riel blend of religious fervor and revolutionary politics:

We, the undersigned, pledge ourselves deliberately and voluntarily to do everything we can to
1 *save our souls by trying day and night to live a holy life everywhere and in all respects*
2 *save our country from a wicked government by taking up arms if necessary.*

Only one man refused to sign. Three days later Riel declared his intention to form a provisional government. On March 26, shots rang out at Duck Lake—one of them killing Gabriel's brother Isidore—and the rebellion was on.

When it was over the Métis would be defeated. Gabriel's fine house and prized billiard table would be looted and burned, and he, for a while, would flee the country. But if the fire of the Métis nation ever burned brightly, it was here.

Métis Dream of Revolution Dies at Batoche
Batoche

The Métis dream of revolution in the North-West died here, barely two months after it was born.

After the inconclusive skirmish at Fish Creek to the south, Métis general Gabriel Dumont and rebel leader Louis Riel decided to dig in and make their stand at Batoche. Some historians say this forced the Métis to fight a positional, slow-moving siege they had no hope of winning. But others point out that Dumont had little choice: the Métis had neither the horses nor the supplies nor the hoped-for Cree reinforcements to fight a fast-moving, offensive war. That time, Dumont felt, was past. So he directed his troops to dig an extensive, well-hidden system of trenches and rifle pits around the village and waited for Major-General Frederick Middleton and the Canadian army.

Middleton's plan was to attack the 175 Métis and Cree from the south with 800 men, four cannons and a Gatling gun while the riverboat steamer *Northcote* attacked from the north.

On May 9, the *Northcote*, reinforced against rifle fire, steamed in from Prince Albert. But the rebels were ready for her. They had stretched a ferry cable across the river, which tore off the boat's smokestacks, mast and spars. The *Northcote*'s pilot house came under heavy fire, and the unsteered steamer chugged into a sandbar, where it harmlessly remained, ending the only the naval battle in Saskatchewan history. "We had a charming time for three days," recalled one man pinned down in the steamer. "I expected the old *Northcote* to go up in a chariot of fire at any moment."

Meanwhile, Middleton's men had advanced just past a church south of town and began to lob shells into it, sending women and children fleeing. Métis fire checked their advance, and a chess-piece battle of position, skirmish and reposition took shape, with the Métis dodging in and out of their well-hidden rifle pits.

"It began to get dreadfully monotonous," recalled one soldier, "firing at nothing, making guess shots and hearing the rebel bullets *zipp zipp* all round you, and the everlasting clack as the bullets struck the trees. . . . This sort of fighting is very bad for a young soldier. There is no excitement to rush to keep him up, his blood gets cold knowing that he is fighting at a disadvantage, that the enemy knows his position and he does not know how they are situated."

For the next two days Middleton did little but try the Métis strength from various angles. Meanwhile, Riel stole from rifle pit to rifle pit with his crucifix, praying with and encouraging his men, by now so low on supplies they were loading their rifles with stones and nails.

On May 12, Dumont had sent the bulk of his forces northeast of Batoche, where he feared Middleton was massing. But Dumont had left the south open, and three militia companies—fed up with waiting for the cautious Middleton—rushed the rifle pits. Despite Dumont's counterattack, Batoche was taken in under an hour. Over the four-day battle, 12 Métis were killed and three wounded. The army lost 10 men with 36 wounded.

The Métis were never again to fight as an army. Dumont fled across the border and Riel surrendered March 15. He was later convicted of treason and hanged. He was buried in St. Boniface, Manitoba, his coffin shrouded in concrete to prevent his followers from digging it up and stealing it.

Gabriel Dumont—A Plainsman's Plainsman
Cemetery, Batoche National Historic Site, Batoche

He needed no last name. In the days of the old North-West, when you said "Gabriel," everyone knew who you meant.

Gabriel Dumont—hunter, leader and rebel general—was born in 1838 in what is now southern Saskatchewan to a French Canadian voyageur and a Sarcee woman. By age 10 he could break ponies and was an accurate bowsman. He matured to a wide-shouldered, barrel-chested 5'8" (173 cm) topped off with long, black, curly hair and a full beard. And if there ever was son of the prairie, Gabriel was it. His first military experience came at age 13 when he helped a party of 200 Métis stand off 2,500 Sioux warriors. Later, he helped negotiate peace with that same band. He was a crack shot and the most hell-for-leather rider on the plains. He was such a good buffalo scout that it was claimed he could call them. He could swim and handle a canoe. His appetite for gambling was prodigious even among a people who could gamble for days. Although he was illiterate, he spoke French (no English) and five Indian languages. He had a head for business that eventually earned him a nice little ferry concession on the North Saskatchewan River, a substantial house complete with billiard table and some of the fastest horses around.

No wonder the Métis looked to him for leadership. In 1862, he was elected the head of the Saskatchewan buffalo hunt, a job

Gabriel Dumont, king of the plainsmen.

that put him at the head of a camp of hundreds of hunters and their families. In 1868, he founded the camp that became the community of St. Laurent. Five years later he was elected the first president of the Métis living along the South Saskatchewan River, a new government run along the same lines as the old buffalo hunt.

It was becoming clear the old free-roaming ways were fading, and Gabriel became increasingly involved in trying to ensure his people's future. He wanted the government to give them a French-speaking judge, schools, help to begin farming and two Métis seats in the territorial assembly. Most of all, he wanted guarantees the government would recognize the way the Métis farmed. In contrast to the square grid being surveyed across the rest of the West, the Métis liked long, narrow lots that stretched back from the river. Dumont's petitions and appeals failed. In 1884, he and several others headed to Montana to convince Louis Riel to return and plead his people's case. The next year Gabriel was one of the men who signed Riel's pledge to "save our country from a wicked government by taking up arms."

Soon after, he had done just that, becoming Riel's general. Dumont was a frontline commander, wounded at Duck Lake by a shot grazing his head, who inspired his men by the example of his own fearlessness. Although he understood positional tactics, he was an aggressive, guerrilla-style strategist, using the hunting skills of his people to move fast, snipe accurately and lay in ambush. He could be brutal, too, and only Riel's intervention stopped him from executing prisoners taken at Duck Lake, a battle in which Gabriel lost four family members, including his brother. Some, including Gabriel, blame Riel for holding the Métis back and not pressing their advantage after they did win victories. Still, once it became clear that the Métis, Indians and white settlers weren't going to unite against Ottawa, the rebellion was doomed. After the final defeat at Batoche, Gabriel fled across the border to Montana.

In 1886, he accepted an offer to appear in Buffalo Bill Cody's Wild West Show as a crack marksman. In 1893, he returned home to Batoche. He hunted a little, farmed some, occasionally made a trade run to Fort Carlton. He died in 1906 of a heart attack, 21 years almost to the day after the Battle of Batoche.

His friends remembered Gabriel as a kind, gentle man. "He adopted me into his family, and . . . invariably addressed me as *mon frere*," recalled one. "Dumont has been painted in lurid colors as a savage, brutal man. He was anything but that, kindly and generous."

Today, he has become something of a folk hero, the subject of songs and legend. Generations after the death of both the man and his dream, both can still be evoked with one word: "Gabriel."

Carlton Trail Approaches Transportation Hub of its Day
Gravel road 783, 2 miles (3.2 km) south of Duck Lake

In the great 932-mile (1,500-km) length of the Carlton Trail, this was one of the busiest stretches of all. Here, the traveler was less than 19 miles (30 km) southeast of Fort Carlton, the transportation nexus of its day. Fort Carlton was about the halfway point between Fort Garry (now Winnipeg) and Fort Edmonton. One was the gateway back to the settled lands of the east, the other the route to the Rockies. And here you could make connections to nearly every other trail in the old North-West. From this Hudson's Bay Company post, you could head north to Green Lake and out into the northern expanses of the Athabasca country. You could wend your way south to the Cypress Hills or Wood Mountain, from there linking up with other trails that would lead to the headwaters of the Missouri River across the border. Every major fur or police post, from Fort Qu'Appelle to Fort Pitt to Fort Pelly to Fort Walsh, had a path to Fort Carlton.

Gradually, the trail was replaced by roads and railways. But parts of it continued to see homesteader traffic well into the 20th century. And one section was still in use quite recently on the nearby Okemasis Indian Reserve.

First Contact with Rebels at Fish Creek Gives Middleton Pause
Highway 312, 9 miles (14.5 km) west of Rosthern, at junction of highways 225 and 312, turn south on gravel road for 9 miles (14.5 km); Middleton's camp is west at sign; battlefield is farther south down road

Major-General Frederick Middleton was the leader of the Canadian troops charged with putting down Louis Riel's rebel Métis, but a month into the rebellion he still hadn't faced the enemy. Here, he got his first taste of what they could do.

At 59, Middleton was a 43-year veteran and an army man through and through. He came from a British military family and was educated at the elite Sandhurst school, which he later commanded. He served the Empire in Australia and India before being named head of the Canadian Militia in 1884, when he quickly became known for his personal courage and his overbearing attitude as well as his stout appearance and walrus mustache. After the rebellion broke out in mid-March, he marshaled his forces and moved them across thousand of miles of barely settled wilderness with admirable dispatch. But it still took until April 23, a miserable near-freezing and rainy day, before he pointed his columns at Clark's Crossing north toward the rebel stronghold at Batoche.

The Métis referred to Fish Creek as Tourond's Coulee and considered it the southern border of their lands. Métis general Gabriel Dumont, hoping to ambush the army, positioned his forces in densely wooded coulees where the trail rose from the riverbank. The surprise was lost when Middleton's scouts discovered Métis campfires, and the battle was joined at about 7:30 A.M. that morning. Middleton's men poured fire on the enemy, but they hit many tree branches and few rebels while the Métis conserved ammunition and shot sparingly and accurately. One party of rebels found themselves stranded on high ground. Alternating between praying and shooting, they beat off repeated attacks until they were reinforced and the army withdrew.

Finally, Middleton retreated. His 430-man force had lost 10 dead and suffered 40 wounded; 4 rebels were killed.

The battle was inconclusive, but Middleton got a good scare. He hadn't expected his opponent to be able to fight a disciplined, positional battle, and the performance of his own troops hadn't exactly filled him with confidence. After Fish Creek, Middleton treated the Métis with caution and respect—respect bordering on fear, some of his subordinates came to feel.

Opening Shots Fired in North-West Rebellion at Duck Lake
Highway 212, just outside north edge of Duck Lake

The winter of 1885 had been a hard one, the latest in a series of hard winters and poor summers, and things were getting desperate over the entire North-West.

Despite the efforts of many Indians to take up farming, crop failures and the collapse of the buffalo had brought many bands to the brink of starvation. White settlers had suffered the same poor harvests and were tired of being squeezed by high freight rates and tariffs on the machinery and supplies they needed. And the Métis were increasingly angry at government stalling on recognizing their farms and lands.

Louis Riel believed the answer was for westerners to speak with one voice. Hoping to unite all three groups, he and his supporters declared a provisional government centered in nearby Batoche on March 8. His general, Gabriel Dumont, immediately set about organizing an army along the lines of the old Métis buffalo hunt, with squads of 10 men under the command of a captain who reported to him. For almost three weeks, that army did not fire a shot. On March 25, that was about to change dramatically.

The settlement of Duck Lake lay strategically between Batoche and Fort Carlton, where Superintendent Leif "Paddy" Crozier commanded the North-West Mounted Police garrison. Both sides wanted the village, not least because of the food, guns and ammunition contained in Hillyard Mitchell's store.

On March 25, the Métis moved and took the town. The next day, at about 5:00 A.M., Crozier marched out with 22 men. The column didn't know the Métis had beaten them to the town until a party of police scouts encountered some of Dumont's sentries. The men scuffled, exchanged threats and Dumont himself fired the first shot by accident when his glove got stuck in the trigger guard of his rifle. No one was hurt, and the police cautiously retreated to Fort Carlton.

But back at the fort, the whites taunted Crozier for backing down. As well, the citizen volunteers who had joined his force were spoiling for a fight. "Are we to be turned back by a parcel of half-breeds? Now is the time, Crozier, to show if you have any sand in you," the proud policeman was told. Stung, Crozier marched out at about 10:00 A.M. with 56 police, 43 volunteers and a field gun. The Métis prepared for them by taking positions in the bush and a cabin just outside the village. Crozier heard about the ambush and had his men set up their lines just short of it. The two armies faced each other across a road, tense as a drawn bow, when an old Cree man named Asiwiyin and Isidore Dumont, Gabriel's brother, stepped forward, unarmed, to parley. Crozier and interpreter Joe McKay met them.

"What do you want?" Crozier demanded. "Nothing," said Asiwiyin, who asked why McKay was so heavily armed if they hadn't come to fight. He then grabbed the man's rifle. The two struggled, then McKay yanked his rifle free and shot both Asiwiyin and Dumont. Crozier ran back to his lines, yelling, "Fire away, boys!" and the battle was on.

Things went badly for Crozier's forces. The well-positioned Métis opened a deadly fusillade on the volunteers, who floundered in deep snow. Riel himself watched the fighting from horseback, exposed to police fire and brandishing a crucifix. For about 20 minutes, the two sides blasted away at each other. Finally, Crozier ordered a retreat. He had suffered 12 dead and 11 wounded, nearly a quarter of his force. Five Métis were killed, four of them close relatives of Dumont, who was himself wounded when a police bullet creased his scalp.

Nevertheless, Dumont had plenty of fight left in him, and only Riel's orders stopped him from pursuing the fleeing police. Riel then insisted the victorious Métis spend the rest of the day praying for the souls of the dead.

Crozier, shaken, shut himself up tight in Fort Carlton, refusing even to authorize a burial party to retrieve the bodies. For four days the dead remained stacked in the cabin from which the Métis had shot many of them.

All Roads Led to Fort Carlton
Highway 212, 18 miles (29 km) east of Duck Lake

In the ancient world, all roads may have led to Rome. But in the days of the old North-West, all roads led to Fort Carlton.

After the Hudson Bay Company's South Branch House was destroyed in 1794 by the Gros Ventre, the company needed to find a new spot for an inland post. Huddling in York Factory or Cumberland House and waiting for the furs to come to them wasn't going to work any more, not with the aggressive North West Company hustling deals right where the trappers lived. It built a post in 1795 near the junction of the North and South Saskatchewan and named it Carlton House after a fashionable mansion that had just been built in London and was being featured in the newspapers. The fort was moved in 1804, then again in 1810, where it was to remain for the next 75 years.

The new Fort Carlton was built to trade furs, but it quickly developed into a central clearinghouse for furs, trade goods and provisions. The location was perfect. Vast herds of buffalo roamed by every autumn, migrating from prairie to parkland and providing plenty of meat for pemmican to fuel the far-flung Hudson's Bay Company empire. The site made it a natur-

Fort Carlton in 1871. Carlton Trail in foreground.

al hub for trails that ran from Hudson Bay to the Rockies, north to the Athabasca country and south to the Cypress Hills.

Before long the place was bustling. Trade goods from the east arrived in the early autumn, originally by York boat from York Factory but later by Red River cart from Fort Garry. The buffalo hunt began as soon as the river froze and there was enough snow to travel by dog or horse sled. There would be trading with the local Indians, and staff from up-country posts would come by for supplies and mail. Spring was pemmican-making time. When the river ice broke up, the season's take of furs were bundled up and shipped east on boats or cart brigades from Fort Edmonton. Summer was downtime, reserved for maintenance, hunting, tending the garden and cutting hay.

Explorers, missionaries, Hudson's Bay Company bigwigs, chiefs, tourists—everyone passed through Fort Carlton. It was a lively place. The missionary John McDougall described the scene in 1862 during Fort Carlton's golden age:

> *The old fort and the plain around was a busy scene—our crews from the boats, hunters from the plain, parties of Indians in to trade, the air full of stories about the southern Indians and the tribal wars to and fro . . . Buffalo-skin lodges and canvas tents dotted the plain in every direction. Horse races and foot races were common occurrences.*

But as the buffalo vanished, the Indians took reserves and settlers began to arrive. The old ways at Fort Carlton began to fade. Both the railway and the new steamships on the North Saskatchewan began to drain traffic from the Carlton Trail, and in 1882, the headquarters of the Hudson's Bay Company's Saskatchewan District was shifted to Prince Albert.

Fort Carlton's story ends ignominiously in 1885 during the North-West Rebellion. Its site may have been great for trade, but the surrounding high hills made it indefensible. The Canadian troops retreated here on May 26 after their defeat at Duck Lake. After a day of tending the wounded (two of whom died) it was decided to abandon the fort. In the early hours of May 28, the troops and North-West Mounted Police began loading the fort's supplies on to sleds in preparation for their retreat to Prince Albert. The men had lit a stove to keep them warm during the work and at about 1:00 A.M., some hay from a mattress caught fire. The fire spread so fast that the fort's head, Lawrence Clark, barely made it out. The column began marching out, leaving Fort Carlton to burn. Eventually, Métis from Duck Lake finished the job, first looting whatever was still usable.

South Branch House Balances Good Business with Unstable Politics

Off Highway 2 on River Road, 12 miles (19.2 km) west of St. Louis along banks of South Saskatchewan River

The fur trade was good around here back in the late 1700s, and this site was the headquarters of the Hudson's Bay Company's growing and increasingly lucrative business along the South Saskatchewan. David Thompson, the famous explorer and map maker, was clerk here from 1786 to 1787. There was, however, a risk. This country was the uneasy scene of shifting alliances and sporadic fighting between several Indian nations. And a trader who dealt with one could be seen as the enemy of the others.

Weakened by disease the Gros Ventre were being pushed southeast by the aggressive Cree and Assiniboine. In 1793, a Cree war party wiped out a band of Gros Ventre very near here. Part of the reason the Cree fighters were so successful was that their stronger trading relationship with the Hudson's Bay men made them better armed. Both the Gros Ventre and Blackfoot resented this and considered the English fur traders allies of their enemies. So shortly after the Cree attack, the Gros Ventre responded by wiping out Manchester House, a Hudson's Bay fort on Pine Island in the South Saskatchewan River. The next year it was the turn of South Branch House.

The attack came June 24, 1794, while most of the men were away on the spring brigade to York Factory. The war party killed three company men as well as a number of old women and children. Several women were taken prisoner. One man, J.C. Van Driel, survived by hiding the cellar for eight hours. Duncan McGillivray, a trader for the rival North West Company, described the attack in his journal, June 27, 1794:

> The Savages, finding no resistance, broke into the Fort and began a Scene full of horror and destruction. After they became masters of the booty which amounted to 60 or 70 Ps [a 90-pound package of fur, called a piece]; they made a diligent search of the unfortunate people; Butchered every soul that came their way in a most inhuman manner; even the Women and children did not escape the merciless cruelty of the miscreants who destroyed every age and sex with the undiscriminating fury that can actuate the mind of a savage.—They afterwards set fire to and demolished the Fort.—Mr. Vandriel was the only person that escaped the general carnage:— he was lucky enough to secure himself amongst a heap of rubbish which was overlooked by the Barbarians, but at length being almost surrounded by the flames, he was compelled to abandon his asylum and rushing out through the Fire the Smoke favored his escape to the River side, where he threw himself into a small Canoe and committed it to the mercy of the Current which soon carried him out of danger.

South Branch House was never rebuilt.

Early Trails Intersect at Elbow–Fort La Corne Trail
Municipal Road 782, St. Louis picnic site

Two early trails intersected near this point. One came from the west and started at Fort La Corne where the two forks of the

Saskatchewan River joined. This trail, probably pioneered by Chevalier de la Corne back in 1753, crossed this coulee, ran on to present-day Batoche, then all the way down the right bank of the river to the rich buffalo hunting grounds of the Elbow. Although Henry Kelsey may have ventured as far west as the forks of the Red Deer River back in 1691–92, la Corne would have been one of the first Europeans to come through here. It was because of activities like his and other independent fur traders that the Hudson's Bay Company finally decided to stop sitting in York Factory and start venturing inland to trade for furs. This trail also came to carry a great deal of the freight traffic from the Métis settlements along the South Saskatchewan.

The other trail was an offshoot of the Carlton Trail that left the main branch at about Humboldt and connected to the Prince Albert area. This trail crossed the river very near here, just below the hill at Mackenzie's Crossing.

Fort Carlton–Fort La Corne Trail a Spoke in Transportation Wheel

River Street Between Central Avenue and 1st Avenue West, Prince Albert

---

Like spokes from a wagon wheel, trails reached out from Fort Carlton to just about everywhere in the old North-West. One of those spokes ran to the fur post of Fort La Corne, and River Street in today's Prince Albert is part of it.

The first leg of the trail ran to a settlement about 2 miles (3.5 km) to the west founded in 1862 by James Isbister, one of the most important leaders of the English-speaking Métis. Isbister was one of the men who went with Gabriel Dumont in 1884 to convince Louis Riel to return from Montana. The second leg went out to the Anglican mission and Fort La Corne.

This trail survived and grew into a modern roadway because of the steam and grist mill built here in 1876, the first in the Northwest Territories. All trails in the area naturally ended or passed by here, and as the settlement founded in 1866 by James Nisbet slowly grew into a town and then a city, this became a nucleus of modern Prince Albert.

North Saskatchewan Has its Own Gold Rush
Highway 3, 5 miles (8 km) west of Highway 2 intersection, west of Prince Albert

Gold dredging operation on the North Saskatchewan River.

The huge Klondike Gold Rush of 1896, which drew thousands of would-be miners north and led to the formation of the Yukon Territory, also produced some distant echoes along the North Saskatchewan River.

The city of Edmonton, located on the river, became the jumping-off point for those heading overland to the Klondike. With all those prospectors crowding the town, it was inevitable that someone would try panning the North Saskatchewan. And sure enough, in the black sand found along the gravel bars, there was gold.

The same held true when the partnership of W.H. Roughsedge and C.M. Ramsay tried it here. The problem was that the source of the gold was somewhere far upstream, meaning that by the time it washed this far down, the particles were very small. It also meant the gold in the gravel bars wasn't replenished very quickly.

Still, Roughsedge and Ramsay incorporated under the grand name of the International Gold Dredging Company, thinking they could make a go of it if they processed enough gravel. Their dredge, powered by two 100-horsepower boilers, could put through almost 35,314 cubic feet (1,000 cubic meters) of gravel a day. For four years they kept at it, until they finally accepted the gold was just too fine and scarce to be worth the cost of mining it.

The strike-it-rich types in Edmonton had come to same conclusion although the city's Gold Bar and Clover Bar (named after prospector Tom Clover) remember those heady days. The only ones still seeking gold in the North Saskatchewan are hobbyists For them, the thrill of a tantalizing sparkle in the bottom of their pan, and not the money, is the real payoff.

Pioneer Prairie Novelist Born on Nearby Homestead
Highway 3, Shellbrook

If Saskatchewan writers have a homegrown holy trinity, they would be Wallace Stegner, W.O. Mitchell and Sinclair Ross, born on a homestead just outside Shellbrook. But if Stegner looked on the prairie and saw an epic of human striving and Mitchell saw the face of God, the solitary and soft-spoken Ross saw loneliness and defeat. Here is a bit from his short story "The Painted Door":

In the clear, bitter light the long white miles of prairie landscape seemed a region alien to life. Even the distant farmsteads she could see served only to intensify a sense of isolation. Scattered across the face of so vast and bleak a wilderness it was difficult to conceive of them as a testimony of human hardihood and endurance. Rather they seemed futile, lost, to cower before the implacability of snow-swept earth and clear pale sun-chilled sky.

Ross came by those feelings honestly. His parents separated in 1911 when he was only three years old. His brother and sister went to live with his father, and he stayed with his mother, Catherine Foster Fraser. Fraser went to work as a housekeeper on area farms; Ross, when he grew old enough, did chores. He later told an interviewer that he never felt more than a guest or a boarder in any of the houses in which he grew up. Life with his mother set Ross apart in other ways, too. Fraser had grown up in a well-educated, upper-middle-class Edinburgh family and never forgot it in the rough pioneer society of northern Saskatchewan. She was a free-thinking Unitarian in staunch Presbyterian country. When the Ku Klux Klan began recruiting near one of the farms where she worked, she bucked the majority to speak against it. She valued education so highly that she scolded her son for reading books such as *Ivanhoe* too quickly and bought him his own horse so he could make it to school even when a horse couldn't be spared from farm work.

Eventually, Ross left school at age 16 and went to work for the Royal Bank to support his mother. He stayed there for 40 years, working in Abbey, Lancer, Arcola, Winnipeg and, after the World War II, Montreal. He never married and retired alone to Greece and Spain. But his years on homesteads and in small towns marked him for life.

"If I have any claim to be considered a 'writer,' it must be based on the stories in *The Lamp at Noon* and *As For Me and My House,* and they are, as you know, one hundred percent Saskatchewan," he wrote.

That latter novel, published in 1941, remains a touchstone of prairie fiction.

"It seemed the only completely genuine *novel* I had ever read about my own people, my own place, my own home," wrote novelist Margaret Laurence. "It pulled no punches about life in the stultifying atmosphere of small and ingrown towns, and yet it was illuminated by compassion."

Sinclair Ross died in 1996. He was 88.

Chevalier of New France Starts Long-Lasting Fur Trade at River Forks

Highway 302, 21 miles (34 km) east of Prince Albert, turn north just before river on gravel road and follow to picnic site

---

New France was still alive when Chevalier de la Corne arrived in 1753 at this vigorous, energetic colony giving the English a run for their money when it came to exploiting the resources of this new northwest land.

That's why la Corne had come, of course: for furs. Here, he built Fort St. Louis, the farthest west the French ever ventured.

It was a natural site for a post. The two forks of the Saskatchewan gave access to both the northern woods, source of the best furs, and the southern plains, where buffalo herds made a plentiful food supply. For four years the French traded with the local bands. Legend has it that wheat was first cultivated here, in what became Saskatchewan. Maybe, maybe not. But when the Hudson's Bay Company built its own fort here long after

Fort St. Louis was abandoned, the builders reported that the patch where the old traders had grown potatoes was quite apparent.

Peter Fidler, a Hudson's Bay Company explorer and trader, wrote in 1792 that when la Corne left to fight the Seven Years War he buried treasure here:

> It is said that a deal of Silver plate and many other Goods was buried under the Ground when they left the place, expecting to return here again—which they never did— some years after a Canadian who lived with La Corne at the time the things were hid made search for it but could not find any part of it—the Grass and young trees having sprung up in the interval, that completely obliterated every mark they had made for its discovery.

La Corne's fort spurred the English to action. Besides, this spot was too good to remain uninhabited for long. A whole series of forts sprang up here with both the North West Company and the Hudson's Bay Company building in the region by 1795. Between the two companies and various independents, there were no fewer than five posts along this stretch of river, a veritable fur trade shopping mall.

It was, of course, the Baymen who lasted longest. By 1846, they had rebuilt a new post called Fort La Corne and kept it staffed until 1932. Back in the old days, the sort of goods and prices a Cree trapper might expect included one rifle, twenty beaver skins; one ax, three beaver skins; one foot of twisted tobacco, one beaver skin; one bottle of rum "not very strong," two beaver skins; half a pint of gunpowder, one beaver skin; a white blanket, eight beaver skins.

Tommy Douglas Announces First Public Health Care in North America
Junction of highways 25 and 20, Birch Hills

Before Tommy Douglas became premier of Saskatchewan and leader of the New Democratic Party in Ottawa, he was a Baptist minister in Weyburn. One day he conducted a burial for a 14-year-old girl who had died of a ruptured appendix. He knew the girl would have lived if she had been admitted to a hospital, and that death helped convince him it was the government's role to ensure all its citizens had access to health care, regardless of their financial situation.

"What do you say to a woman whose family is on relief, whose husband has died because they couldn't get the kind of medical and hospital care he needed?" he asked.

It was here, in April 1959, that he finally came up with an answer. During a by-election speech, he announced cabinet had decided to go ahead with medicare, the first universal publicly funded health care system in North America. As he elaborated in a later speech, it would ensure that patients would never see a doctor's bill, that it would cover everyone and it would be under public control.

It was an evolution, not a revolution. The government had been paying doctor's bills for the poor since 1945. In 1946, Swift Current set up a regional medicare scheme in which doctors worked for a salary from the municipality. But full-scale medicare—"Socialized Medicine"—was anathema to most of the province's doctors. Fearing a loss of control over their practices, they favored private medical insurance, administered by a nonprofit company and subsidized by the taxpayer.

Medicare was the central issue in the 1960 election campaign. Many prominent people opposed it, including Athol Murray, the popular and fiery priest who headed Notre Dame College in Wilcox. The Canadian Medical Association spent nearly $100,000 fighting the plan. But in June, Douglas won a solid majority. He felt the Saskatchewan people had told him to go ahead. On November 1, 1961, the Medical Care Insurance Act was passed, a few days after Douglas had resigned as premier to enter federal politics.

The fight wasn't over. Anti-medicare sentiment cost Douglas his seat in the 1962 federal election, and doctors went briefly on strike to force amendments to the legislation. But medicare stayed and eventually spread across Canada. And the three principles Douglas enumerated remain at the heart of one of the country's most important social programs.

Henry Kelsey, Traveling Salesman, Scores Exploring Firsts
Highway 3, between Kinistino and Beatty

Few western pathfinders racked up the number of firsts that Henry Kelsey achieved. He was the first European to venture into what is now Saskatchewan, the first to spend a winter here, the first to see the Great Plains, the first to hunt buffalo.

And yet Kelsey was not an explorer. His mission, on behalf of the Hudson's Bay Company, was not about map making or new routes to the West. Loaded down with useful trade knickknacks and gewgaws, he was to glad-hand the local natives and convince them to shop at the Bay. He has been called "North America's first traveling salesman."

Still, it was quite some traveling.

He left York Factory on the gloomy shores of Hudson Bay in 1690, setting out with his guides down the Saskatchewan River. It's too bad he wasn't a map maker, for his journal provides few clues about where he went. We know he spent his first winter near The Pas, in what is now Manitoba. We know he reached the Touchwood Hills, south of Quill Lakes, and maybe the Red Deer River. We think he spent his second winter camped out around here before returning home in 1692.

Part of the frustration comes from the way Kelsey kept his journal. Most Baymen were rigorous record keepers, with daily entries including a sextant reading and weather report. Kelsey, on the other hand, preferred to record his observations in a stumbling doggerel that has a sort of oddball charm but lacks hard data:

Because I was alone and no friend could find,
And once in my travels was left behind,
Which struck fear and terror into me,
But still I was resolved this same Country for to see. . . .

Here's Kelsey's idea of scientific observation:

Which hither part is very thick of wood,
Affords small nutts with cherryes very good.
Thus it continues till you leave ye woods behind
And then you have a beast of several kind
The one is black a Buffilo great . . .

Despite his attractive array of trade goods, including tobacco, beads, metal hatchets and kettles, Kelsey's attempts to make treaties and mediate between warring tribes were not notably successful. Perhaps the problem may have been his patronizing sales pitch, which he described in his thankfully nonrhyming September 6, 1691, entry:

This instant I unclosed the pipe which the governour had
sent me telling them that they must Imploy their time in

Catching of beavour for they will be better liked on then killing their enemies when they come to the factory, neither was I sent there for to kill any Indians but to make peace. . . .

The proud Sioux or Gros Ventre must have been amused by this newcomer telling them how to live.

Back in York Factory, Kelsey's employers mustn't have been much more impressed than the natives. There was little follow-up in his lifetime to the trade mission. In all, Kelsey served the company nearly 40 years, all but three of them at York Factory. Eventually, he became chief trader at Albany and governor of all the fur posts. Still, he died poor and alone in East Greenwich, England, in 1724. His unique journal was lost until 1926, when it turned up in Northern Ireland.

Almighty Voice Dies a Warrior's Death
Highway 3, 2 miles (3 km) west of Beatty

Almighty Voice's people were hungry that October in 1895. Their needs were supposed to have been provided for once they signed the government's treaty, their Indian agent wouldn't even allow them to kill some of the reserve's cattle to feed their families. And now winter was approaching.

Almighty Voice (in Cree, *Kah-kee-say-mane-too-wayo*, or "Voice of the Great Spirit"), was a young man, just 19, but he decided to act. He took his rifle into the bush, found a stray steer and shot it. But as he was skinning it, a Mountie rode by and arrested him.

As the Mountie locked him in the jail at Duck Lake, just southwest of here, he told Almighty Voice that cattle thieves were hung. It may have been just a rough joke or an idle scare-him-straight threat, but Almighty Voice took it seriously and was chilled through. He would never submit to that fate.

That night, as the guard slept, Almighty Voice lifted the jail keys through the cell bars and escaped. (That jail still stands in Duck Lake.) The fugitive then visited his father's lodge, took his gun, two horses and his 15-year-old wife and fled north into the bush. The police, of course, gave chase. When Almighty Voice was not found in a search of the reserve, Sergeant C.C. Colebrook was assigned to track him down. A week later he did just that, surprising Almighty Voice very near here as he was about to shoot a prairie chicken. Instead, he shot and killed Sergeant Colebrook. Almighty Voice was now truly on the run.

For two years he and his wife evaded capture, living fast and light off the land, sneaking in and out of the reserve to visit his family, even giving birth to a son. Eventually, Almighty Voice was cornered on May 28, 1897, as he hunted in the Minichinas Hills to the southwest. Now 21, he prepared to make his last stand, accompanied by his 15-year-old cousin, Going-Up-to-the-Sky, and his 16-year-old brother-in-law, Topean. Almighty Voice was not afraid to fight (his father had battled the Redcoats with Wandering Spirit during the North-West Rebellion) so the three dug a camouflaged pit on the top of a bluff. The Mounties charged once, then twice. Two policemen, a civilian volunteer and Topean were killed. The police then tried to smoke out the warriors, but the grass was too damp to burn. Reinforcements arrived until more than 100 policemen and civilian volunteers surrounded the bluff. Eventually, the Mounties brought out field cannon and began to shell the hillside. For several days the three hungry, thirsty Cree withstood bombardment.

As the tragedy played itself out, both white settlers and members of Almighty Voice's band gathered on nearby hills to watch. One of them was Almighty Voice's mother, Spotted Calf. The final morning she stood against the sky and began singing a keening lament. From the besieged hill Almighty Voice could be heard joining her. It was his death song. After a final barrage that day, the police overran the hill. All three of the young men died.

Almighty Voice is buried on the One Arrow Reserve near Batoche.

Chapter 6

Land of the Living Sky

A Little Bit of Everything in Land of the Living Skies

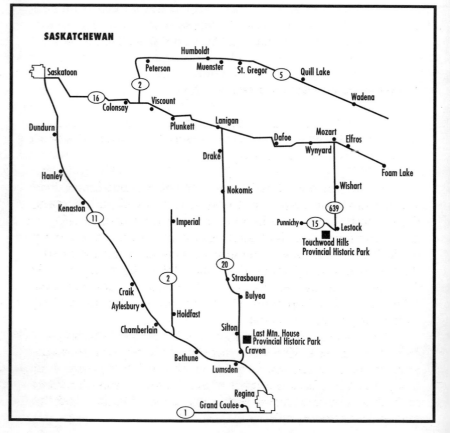

IN THE MIDDLE of Saskatchewan's populated area, the history of this region of parkland and prairie offers a little bit of everything. The pre-railroad network of plains trails laces everywhere through here, telling stories of epic travelers like the gold-seeking Overlanders. Gentleman hunters rode through here, too, suffering the frustration of camp life while enjoying the shooting. And many homesteaders have left behind traces of themselves in the names of their communities. One name recalls the cultural interests of a local settler, another a stubborn farmer, a third a frustrated railway crew.

There's a hint of the Wild West, too. Here's where Saskatchewan's first—and only—stagecoach robbery took place.

But what makes this region unique, and gives it its name, is the bird sanctuary at Last Mountain Lake. Founded in 1887, it was the first bird sanctuary not only in Canada, but in North America, making it one of the touchstones of today's conservationists. Those abundant bird colonies are still around today. And like the living skies over Last Mountain Lake, so are this region's stories.

ALONG HIGHWAYS 16 AND 5

Gentleman Hunters Travel Fort Carlton–Touchwood Hills Trail
Highway 16, 2 miles (4 km) east of Lanigan

With the fur trade headquarters of Fort Carlton at one end and the provisioning post of the Touchwood Hills at the other, the old trail that passed by here once teemed with people en route. But not all were fur traders. Gentleman hunters, following the fashion of the time for lengthy excursions in the old North-West, passed through more than once. James Carnegie, Earl of Southesk, came by here in 1859. William Fitzwilliam, Viscount Milton and his companion, Dr. Walter Butler Cheadle, visited with a party three years later.

They made something of an odd pair. Viscount Milton, then 23, comes across in Cheadle's account of the trip as rather lazy and temperamental, much given to physical complaints and hangovers. Cheadle, although it *is* his account, reveals himself to be both a shrewd observer with a dry sense of humor and the real leader of the expedition.

Although Cheadle praised the beauty of the country around here, this region was not as kind to him and his party. "Messiter and I have caught the itch from our boy," he wrote on September 21. "Pray for sulfur at Carlton."

The next day, Cheadle burned his boots and socks trying to dry them out by the fire and missed everything he shot at. The drinking water in ponds and streams was alkaline. It rained nearly every day and tempers frayed until the party quarreled when their horses balked at a river crossing. Finally, on September 26, they reached Fort Carlton: "Mr. Lillie at Fort very civil and invites us to tea. Fresh buffalo meat for first time; steaks very good. . . . Have famous sleep."

Cheadle, Milton and the rest of the party traveled on to the Rockies, and Mount Milton and Mount Cheadle in the upper Thompson River valley are named for them. The two finally returned to England in 1864. Their book based on Cheadle's diaries became one of the best-selling British travel books of the late 1800s.

Gold Lures Overlanders Across Prairies
Highway 5, 6 miles (9.6 km) west of Humboldt

Free land, adventure on the frontier or a chance at a new life weren't the only things that drew people to the old North-West. Back in the 1860s, the mountains of the Cariboo region in what is now the interior of British Columbia offered a more immediate lure: gold. That familiar old magnet pulled people from all over the continent, and it pulled many hopeful prospectors past this spot. They have become known as the Overlanders.

The Cariboo Gold Rush began in 1860, when prospectors spilling over from the Fraser strike found easy gold in the Horsefly River. Breathless newspaper reports spread the word across North America, and in 1862, news reached the Schubert family living near Fort Garry.

Catherine, her husband, August, and their three children were ready for a change. She an Irish immigrant, he a German, they had met and married in New York, drifted west to St. Paul and now found themselves running what was referred to locally as a grogshop outside the fort. It was not a classy joint—a newspaper the previous December had reported a man's body found at their place after a night of heavy boozing—and it was not an easy life. So when a large party of gold seekers came to Fort Garry to set out for the Cariboo gold fields, Catherine and her husband decided, "Why not?"

The party, led by Thomas McMicking, inspired by the example of the forty-niners and the California Gold Rush, planned to follow the newly developed Carlton Trail across the Canadian West. The Schuberts convinced McMicking to let them join. What Catherine didn't tell him was that she was pregnant.

On June 5, 1862, the McMicking party set out in a half-mile (1-km) -long string that included 97 carts, 110 animals and about 160 men. Catherine was the only woman. They drove every day from 5:00 A.M. to 6:00 P.M., with two-hour breaks at 7:00 A.M. and noon. In the evenings, they headed out for a little hunting, or they gathered around their campfires and sang to music played on cornets, clarinets, violins, flutes and concertinas. Although their guide deserted them, the Overlanders followed a clear trail south and crossed the Quill Plains. One Overlander described walking "under a burning sun and over a vast prairie without a tree in sight as large as your finger." Another wrote, "It was found to be necessary to tie our mosquito nets fast around our necks so as to keep the mosquitoes from flying away with them as they were about the size of humming birds." Sometime toward the end of June, the Overlanders passed this spot.

The Carlton Trail proved to be the easy part of their journey. Past Fort Edmonton and into the mountains, the trail got really rough. Some of the party decided to raft down the raging Fraser River to Fort Kamloops. The Schuberts opted for a land route along the North Thompson, but it was so bad they had to turn back within 62 miles (100 km) of the fort and take their own terrifying raft trip—with three children and Catherine's fourth nearly due. Finally, on October 14, they drifted into Fort Kamloops, and Catherine went into labor within hours. An Indian midwife was found, and the next day Catherine delivered a healthy baby girl. Rosa was the first European baby born in the interior of British Columbia.

Most of the Overlanders went on to the Cariboo gold fields, although few stayed for long and fewer struck it rich. Many, including McMicking went on to become prominent in the burgeoning new province. The Schuberts eventually settled down in Lillooet. Catherine died there in 1918.

Troy–Prince Albert Trail a Supply Line for Bustling Frontier Town—and Tempting Target for Thieves
Highway 5, 6 miles (9.6 km) west of Humboldt

Saskatoon to Battleford stagecoach in 1902, at what is believed to be the Henrietta station near the elbow of the North Saskatchewan River.

Prince Albert, one of Saskatchewan's oldest communities, was one of the few towns of any description during the days of the old North-West, and it was certainly one of the busiest. Fifteen years after its founding in 1866, it boasted hundreds of local settlers tilling the fertile land, serviced by a steam grist mill and a sawmill. Ottawa had opened a Land Titles Office, and the electoral district of Prince Albert was the first in the Northwest Territories to be organized.

But still, it had no railway. Anything people wanted in Prince Albert, they had to have shipped overland from the Canadian Pacific Railway depot at Troy, now known as Qu'Appelle. Here, along a northerly fork of the Carlton Trail, trundled through everything a growing settlement required: load after load of provisions, farm supplies, tools and machinery on groaning wagons and squealing Red River carts. Like other busy commercial routes, the Troy–Prince Albert Trail developed a line of stopping houses, spaced every 40 miles (63 km) or so. By 1883, it had a reg-

First telegraph office in the Northwest Territories, located in Humboldt along busy Troy-Prince Albert trail.

ular mail stagecoach, too—a light wagon pulled by four horses that were changed at every roadhouse.

The stage was a tempting and vulnerable target for bandits wanting to profit from Prince Albert's bustle. On July 18, 1886, someone gave in to that temptation and held up the regular run in Saskatchewan's first and only stagecoach robbery.

The bandit got away with the then huge sum of $1,464.20. Word spread like a prairie fire, and the Mounties, fearing an invasion of desperadoes from across the line, staged a manhunt. The culprit turned out to be George Garnett, a local settler and ferryman who followed this trail north and was arrested near Prince Albert.

While awaiting trial, Garnett told stagecoach hand Peter Smith where the loot was hidden. Smith found it, but perhaps he should have left it alone. He was murdered for the money, and his killer was never convicted. Garnett was sentenced to 14 years in 1886, escaped in 1888, caught shortly after and finally released June 6, 1895.

Buckboards and wagons busily kicked up dust and churned the mud through here until 1891. Then, Prince Albert finally got its own rail line, and trail traffic stilled.

German Settlers Establish St. Peter's Colony
Highway 5, 56 miles (90 km) east of Saskatoon

Anyone looking at a map and reading the names of the surrounding towns—Muenster, Humboldt, Bruno, Annaheim—will not be surprised to learn that this area was settled by Germans. In fact, it was settled by a whole colony of Germans who arrived via the United States.

By the turn of the century, the United States was the source of many immigrants flooding into the West as good homestead land grew scarce south of the border. Many of those were German-speaking Catholics who had originally left Europe for Minnesota. Because nearly all the Catholic priests on the Canadian prairies were French-speaking, some of these settlers began writing back to church officials in Minnesota for priests who could minister to them in their own tongue.

In 1902, Father Bruno Doerfler, OSB, led a group of clergymen around the plains looking for a suitable spot to establish an abbey and an encircling German-Catholic colony. As the party came to the area northwest of where Humboldt now sits, Father Bruno judged the prospects to be good:

> *When we finally arrived at the summit of [a] slope we were greeted by a gently rolling plain studded with beautiful groves and crystal lakes. The soil on the plain was of the very choicest, for it was a deep black humus.*

Returning to Minnesota, the Germans soon worked up an efficiently run, well-organized exodus. The Catholic Settlement Society of St. Paul, Minnesota, arranged for a grant of 50 townships of land around the scouted area, under the condition it establish 500 settlers a year for three years. The German American Land Company bought up another 100,000 acres (40,470 ha) to sell to the immigrants. And Abbott Peter Engel, of an abbey in Collegeville, Minnesota, agreed to look after the spiritual needs of the colony.

The first members of the colony were actually on the land by the fall of 1902. A group of Benedictine monks arrived by the next spring, in time to celebrate the Feat of the Ascension. Near Muenster, not far from the present site of St. Peter's Cathedral, they built their first monastery, a sod-roofed shack with a tent for a chapel.

In that tent, a hollowed stone once used by natives served as a holy water font. Wild flowers decorated the altar. One day, the Benedictines' cow drank the water and ate the flowers and was forever after referred to as the holy cow.

The settlers were coming, too, one a restless young man named Arnold Dauk.

Arnold was 31 when he left Minnesota, an established farmer with a pretty little house and yard on land he tilled with his brother Philip. No one knows why he left all that behind for a tiny settlement in the North-West called Annaheim. But in May 1904, that's what he did.

Like most of the immigrants, he got some land and started homesteading. He built Annaheim's first store, too, and was soon well known in the mostly German-speaking community. Hardworking and enterprising, he was also a railroad land agent and served on municipal councils and later became Justice of the Peace. He bought one of the first gas-powered threshing rigs in the neighborhood and hired it out to neighbors. In 1906, he suffered a bit of embarrassment when he was fined $100 for selling whiskey (three shots for 25 cents) without a license. Arnold insisted he kept the liquor only for medicinal purposes—there was smallpox in the area, after all—and that he made no profit on the sale. The judge, however, was unimpressed.

Together, he and his wife, Frances, fought through the trials of homesteading—like the waterlogged harvest of 1912, when the fields were so wet that farmers had to wait until December so the frozen ground would support the weight of a threshing machine without swallowing it up. Although Frances suffered badly from rheumatism, the couple thrived, living near Annaheim and raising eight children until Frances died of a heart attack in 1927. Arnold continued on, living here until he died in 1964.

Many of their children and descendants still live in the area. The legacy of the St. Peter's Colony remains as well, in the Cathedral and St. Peter's College at the Benedictine monastery and in the strong German flavor of the area.

Sodbusters Honor Composer at Mozart
Off Highway 16, 9 miles (14 km) east of Wynyard

Yes, this tiny community really is named after the great composer. Settlers began to gather here in the late 1800s, after the

Canadian Pacific Railway built its main line through the area. By 1900, enough people lived here that it was time to name the place. The honor fell to one Mrs. Lund, the wife of the hopeful settlement's Canadian Pacific Railway station agent. She and fellow homesteaders may have been sodbusting pioneers, but they were not bumpkins. Mrs. Lund, widely respected in the community, was a talented musician, and when she suggested the village be named after one of the finest composers of all time there were nods of assent all round. Not only that, but the community's original street names played a variation on that theme: Liszt, Chopin and Wagner.

Touchwood Hills a Busy Post
Highway 15, 7 miles (11 km) east of Punnichy

Straddling the boundary of the fur-bearing parklands and the buffalo-rich plains, winter home of the Assiniboine and Plains Cree, the Touchwood Hills were a natural place for a fur post, and the Hudson's Bay Company first built here in 1849. It was to be the first of several posts, the final one constructed in 1879 and remaining open to 1909.

Touchwood—named for the dry, pithy poplar wood of the area, which could easily be sparked into flame—came to be a thriving spot. It was a common stopping house for travelers on the Carlton Trail. It was a mail delivery point, and it was on the telegraph line. And by 1870, trade with Indians was augmented by one of the earliest farming settlements in the old North-West.

It had other advantages, too.

"At sundown, came upon Touchwood Hills," wrote Walter Cheadle, who traveled through here on a two-year hunting excursion in 1862. "Old Fort; pretty situation, rounded hills &c. Autumn hills at sunset very fine."

Of course, the men who worked here had more on their minds than scenery. A few excerpts from Chief Trader William McKay's 1854 diary paints a busy picture. The trader's matter-of-fact recording of the increasing damage done by the liquor trade also is revealing:

Sept 28: the Soldier and the rest of the Indians camped at the fort. Kept all the men busily employed taking in their provisions . . . on the afternoon the Indians commenced

The Old Telegraph Trail in the Touchwood Hills. Still in use in 1923.

Drinking. traded 5 Horses today, 2 of the Horses traded off the Stone Indians, the 3 traded from the Crees.

Sept. 29: Indians still drinking. traded 2 Horses from the Crees while drinking. . . . Pierre Lapierre henry Kennedy and John Stevenson tying up Bulls of Meat to bo sent to fort Pelly. John Pelly and Frank Johnston waying Meat and stowing by. . . .

Sept. 30: Henry Kennedy and John Stevenson and the 2 Indian Boys that came with the Carts started this morning on their way to fort Pelly with 6 Carts loaded with provisions 49,000 lbs Dried Meat in all. . . . Some of the Indians began to trade and some still drinking. George Sinclair and Peter Hourie attending to the Indians still drinking My Self trading in the store. Pierre Lapierre John Pelly waying Meat. . . . finished trading with the Soldier's party and the Little Black Bear's party by Candle lite.

The next day, Sunday, those Cree left and two new bands showed up. On Monday, the cycle of trading, drinking and preparing pemmican started again.

ALONG HIGHWAYS 11 AND 20

Buffalo Rubbing Stone Reminder of Buffalo Days
Highway 11, 2.8 miles (4.5 km) northeast of Aylesbury, north side of road

---

Once, they dominated both the land and the lives of the people who lived here. Now, the only traces of the vast buffalo herds that washed over the plains like floodwaters are mute monuments such as this, a boulder polished smooth where the large animals scratched themselves to relieve the itch of insect bites or to remove their winter coats and wore a depression around the rock over the centuries.

Buffalo were superbly adapted to the prairies. Their thick coats saw them through the winter, and they thrived on forage that left cattle and horses famished. A bull took up to 8 years to reach maturity and could live as long as 20 years.

The buffalo provided the Indians with nearly everything they needed. The lean, tasty meat fed them. The hides clothed, sheltered and warmed them. The skin from a bull's neck could be fire-hardened enough for a warrior's shield. The bladder made a waterproof sack; the sinews made bowstrings. Facial hair was braided into rope. Some bones were shaped into cutting tools while the ribs made sleigh runners and the spine made dice for gambling games. Even the dung was valuable—it was often the only cooking-fire fuel to be had on the prairies.

Buffalo ran in herds that boggle today's imagination. Fur trader Isaac Cowie, writing in 1869, when the buffalo were already in decline, described one of them:

> *They blackened the whole country, the compact, moving masses covering it so that not a glimpse of green grass could be seen, the earth trembled day and night, as they moved in billow-like battalions over the undulations of the plain.*

While the buffalo thrived, the natives who hunted them considered themselves rich. But a population of up to 60 million animals in 1800 had shrunk to 40 million by 1840. And by 1885, methodical hunting had almost wiped the buffalo out. The collapse of the Indians' economic mainstay was a major factor in forcing natives onto reservations in Canada and the United States.

Captive buffalo herds, as well as herds in several national parks, still exist. A few ranchers continue to experiment with buffalo as a commercial animal, and occasionally it is possible to spot a small herd roaming the prairie, a pale example of what once was.

Findlater Origin Still Lost
Highway 11, 25 miles, (42 km) northwest of Regina

One day, so the story goes, a group of workmen set some tools down on the prairie for a moment, intending to return later. Some say the men were surveyors, some say they were a railway crew. At any rate they came back to where they thought they had left the tools and couldn't see them anywhere. This town is said to have been named when the men gave up their search, promising to return and find them later.

Not so, goes another version. In this tale, a homesteader loses some cattle and in searching for them comes across a railway crew. The crew assures the homesteader that he will find his stock later.

Less colorfully, there are those who insist the community was named for George Findlater, a Scottish piper who was awarded the Victoria Cross for bravery during the 1889 attack on Dargai Heights in India.

No version of the origin of the name Findlater can be accepted as fact, making its name even more appropriate.

Stubborn Streak Survives in Name of Holdfast
Just east of Highway 2 at Holdfast turnoff, 12 miles (19 km) north of junction with Highway 11

With tough prairie sod and tougher prairie winters to contend with, prairie homesteaders found a little stubbornness essential equipment. That equipment is commemorated in the name of the community of Holdfast.

The first settlers in the area came in 1904 and settled on the west side of Long Lake. When the Canadian Pacific Railway came through in 1910 and proposed to build on the east side of that village, it found the land owned by John A. Fahlman. Fahlman and the railway dickered and bickered back and forth, but the farmer couldn't get the terms he wanted and refused to sell to the mighty Canadian Pacific Railway, forcing it to build on the west side of the village.

Fahlman's determination to hold fast to his land eventually gave the town its name.

Avian Abundance Inspires Continent's First Federal Bird Preserve
Off Highway 2, 7 miles (12 km) east of Imperial on gravel road

---

An astonishing number and variety of birds have lived at Last Mountain Lake from the earliest days of the frontier. With over a million birds crying and winging through the sky, settlers would have found them hard to miss.

For generations, local Cree hunters were well aware of this abundance. The earliest European to make official note of it was John Macoun, a botanist who came west in 1879 to study the flora and fauna of the plains, including Last Mountain Lake. He came none too soon, too. By 1883, the Canadian Pacific Railway was bringing new settlement to the plains, and tracks reached the south end of the lake by 1886.

Edgar Dewdney, the Lieutenant-Governor of the Northwest Territories, realized the railway could dramatically affect the huge colonies that Macoun had written about. In March 1887, he wrote to Thomas White, the Minister of the Interior:

> I think it would be very desirable to reserve the islands near the north end of the lake . . . these islands are the favourite breeding grounds for almost all the different varieties of wildfowl we have in the North-West, from pelicans to snipe . . . the shores of the islands are literally covered with eggs in the breeding season.

Accordingly, without much ado, Sir John A. MacDonald and his cabinet set aside more than 2,500 acres (1012 ha) as a bird sanctuary, the first federally created sanctuary in North America. Despite considerable pressure from homesteaders in 1911 to open the land for farming, the sanctuary has remained intact ever since and was expanded in 1921 to cover the entire water surface of the lake. It has been expanded several times since then.

Today, over 280 species of birds have been spotted here, including 9 of Canada's 36 endangered bird species. There are flocks of 50,000 cranes and 450,000 geese. Thanks to a good habitat and position on the continent's central flyway, Last Mountain Lake provides respite to birds from 25 different countries, from the Arctic to Argentina.

Buffalo Hunters Follow Fort Ellice–Elbow Trail West
Highway 11, 3 miles (5 km) north of Bethune at picnic site

When the Hudson's Bay Company sent its buffalo hunters out from Fort Ellice, just over what is now the Manitoba boundary, most of them used the Fort Ellice–Elbow Trail. It led straight into the rich hunting territory near the Elbow of the South Saskatchewan River. They had to tread warily, though. The Cree, the Assiniboine and the Blackfoot all used those lands, hunted those herds and fiercely guarded access to them. Still, Hudson's Bay Company parties from the Touchwood Hills, Last Mountain House and Fort Qu'Appelle all regularly traveled this route.

Baymen weren't the only ones who passed here. The Palliser expedition came by, as did Henry Youle Hind's group in 1857–58, sizing up the country for the government back in Ottawa. James Carnegie, Earl of Southesk, also traveled through on his hunting trip in 1859.

Bethune No Relation to Bethune
Highway 11, 27 miles (46 km) northwest of Regina

Sorry, no relation. This town was not named after Norman Bethune, the famous Canadian doctor who served in both the Spanish Civil War and the Chinese Revolution during the late 1930s. Although Bethune the doctor is idolized in China and is credited with forming the world's first mobile blood transfusion service, this Bethune is named for one C.B. Bethune, the locomotive engineer on the first train to travel this line and no doubt a worthy man in his own right. The railway Bethune goes back a bit further than the medical Bethune, too. The inaugural journey that left this name on the map was made back in 1887.

Lake Vessel Joins Age of Steam on Last Mountain Lake
Highway 20, 4 miles (7 km) northwest of Craven

The age of steam on prairie waters was already dissipating when the Pearson Land Company commissioned a small stern-wheeler to billow its way up and down Last Mountain Lake in 1905.

The first paddle-wheeler in the West had huffed and chugged its way up the Red River from the United States to Fort Garry 46 years earlier. About six stern-wheelers eventually navigated the shallow, sandbar-blocked waters between Fort Garry and Cumberland House all the way to Fort Edmonton.

The big boats were a much more efficient and pleasant way to travel than cart train or York boat. *The Princess,* launched in Winnipeg in 1881, could carry 600 passengers and boasted two bridal suites and a $5,000 piano. Steamboat passage from Fort Garry to Fort Edmonton cost about $70 for a cabin and $35 on the deck. Freight rates were $6.25 cents a pound (.5 kg). A good speed was about 16 miles (26 km) an hour. Here, the *Lady of the Lake*—later the *Qu'Appelle*—was used to haul grain, supplies and the household effects of homesteaders up and down the lake, where settlements were becoming established.

But just as were her river-going sisters, the *Lady* was eventually replaced by railways. She spent the last two years of her life as an excursion vessel and was eventually beached in 1913. There she rested until 1918, when crowds rejoicing over the end of World War I set her old timbers aflame and celebrated around the bonfire.

Trader's First Posting Short but Adventurous at Last Mountain House
Highway 20, 30 miles (50 km) north of Regina

Isaac Cowie was only 21 back in 1869, but it had already been two years since he had left his native Scotland to join the Hudson's Bay Company. Last Mountain House was his first major assignment.

The post was built for a couple of reasons. Independent traders west of Fort Qu'Appelle were cutting into business. The thinning buffalo herds were moving west, too, and a hunting base was needed. The idea was to operate Last Mountain House as a winter outpost of Fort Qu'Appelle. Using local logs, stones and clay, the Hudson's Bay Company built a master's house, store, barn, ice cellar, outhouse and spring shelter. In the men's house dwelled the post's eight employees, at least four of whom had wives and children living with them in 5.5 x 4-yard (5 x 3.6-m) apartments.

Cowie's tenure here was short, but he probably remembered it the rest of his life. On November 6, 1869, Cowie rode alone to the post from Fort Qu'Appelle. The 50-mile (80-km) trail grew faint, and he decided to camp for the night, only to find he had somehow lost his fire-making kit of flint, steel and tinder. Wrapped only in a blanket, he awoke the next morning to a raging blizzard and 6" (15 cm) of snow. Lost, cold and hungry, he was lucky enough to stumble into an Indian lodge, where he found shelter and directions home. Later that winter, he was again returning to the post when he fell through the ice on Last Mountain Lake and got soaked to his knees. Then his dogs ran off with his sled, and he had to crawl to the post on his knees. Cowie later recalled the quick action of his partner, Joseph McKay:

> *Joe was at home and he at once tore off my shoes and exclaimed that my feet were frozen solid. He then got a tub of ice water and put my feet in it till the ice formed over the skin, as it does when meat is thawed in water. After they were properly thawed, I dried them and bathing legs as far as affected and the feet with laudanum, I went to bed, slept soundly, and next morning, to Joe's astonishment, got up without any sign of what Joe predicted would be a very bad case, of which the whole skin, at least, would be shed.*

Nor were those mishaps Cowie's only problems. The region was home to the Young Dogs, a native band who were part-Cree, part-Assiniboine and had been banned by both. They attempted to impose a fine on visitors for every buffalo killed, but killing buffalo was the whole idea of Last Mountain.

If the Young Dogs were making an attempt at conservation, it was too late. While the 1869 hunt was good at Last Mountain, the next year's was a failure. By 1871, the post was abandoned and Cowie went on to further adventures in the southwest at Chimney Coulee.

Reeve of Tiny Municipality Pioneers Medicare
Highway 20, 31 miles (50 km) north of junction at highways 11 and 20, Bulyea

The idea of state-sponsored, universal health insurance had to come from somewhere. Before the provincial government finally instituted medicare in 1962, several municipalities had been doing something similar for a generation.

Matt Anderson had come to Bulyea from his native Norway, which already had a state health insurance program. He felt his new country should have the same thing and began campaigning for one back in the mid-1920s. Finally, in 1938, he became Reeve of the Rural Municipality of McKillop and introduced a municipal health care plan. It provided unlimited access to a doctor, 21 days in hospital and prescription drugs for an annual fee of $5. Anderson had to get permission from the province to charge the fee, and the so-called Matt Anderson Bill allowed many other communities to set up their own plans. In 1946, Swift Current, for example, set up a regional medicare scheme in which doctors worked for a salary from the municipality.

Most of these plans lasted right until they were replaced by the provincial plan.

Name of Nokomis Betrays Literary Imagination
Highway 20, 12 miles (20 km) south of Lanigan

Never let it be said that Saskatchewan's pioneers were without learning or devoid of romantic imagination. There wasn't much here before the building of a branch of the Grand Trunk Railway, which took from 1907 to 1914. But there was Mrs. Thomas Halstead, the wife of a local homesteader who applied to open a post office in her sod house near here, where the Grand Trunk tracks would cross those of the Canadian Pacific Railway.

She took the name Nokomis from a place in Henry Longfellow's poem "Hiawatha." To Mrs. Halstead, newly arrived from England, the name rang with the romance of the frontier, a romance she must have found in the new country around her.

Grand Trunk officials wanted to call the place Blakemore and the Canadian Pacific Railway had chosen Blaikie. But when the settlement at the junction started to grow, the post office was moved into a local store. Mrs. Halstead carried on as post-mistress and brought the name Nokomis right along with her. It's been Nokomis ever since.

Nor is this the only prairie town whose name betrays a literary bent. About 56 miles (90 km) southeast of here is Southey, named for the English poet Robert Southey.

Chapter 7

The Kelsey Region

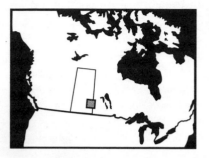

Kelsey Country
Heart of Old
Fur Trade

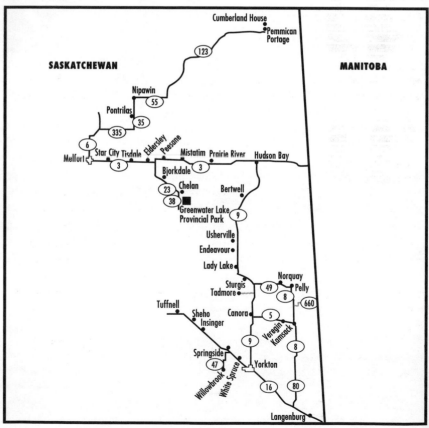

THROUGH HERE, where four rivers flow on their way to Hudson Bay and the Atlantic, is the heart of the old fur trade on the prairies. The first European to pass this way was Henry Kelsey, a fur trader who set out in 1690 on a two-year mission, not to explore, but to convince Indians who lived inland to trade at York Factory, the Hudson's Bay Company post on Hudson Bay.

By 1753, bold traders and explorers from what was still New France had paddled through here up the Saskatchewan River and founded posts to the west. Within a generation, the independent traders from Montreal who were to form the North West Company made this river the cutting edge of the fur trade, with the Assiniboine River to the south that blade's other edge. Along the Assiniboine elbow south of present-day Norquay, one historian counted no fewer than 14 posts as the 1700s drew to a close, including some of the Hudson's Bay Company's earliest incursions inland from their base at York Factory. So important was this area that after the two companies merged in 1821, the post at Fort Pelly became the administrative center for the entire district.

Historical tales of traders competing for market share, profits and a certain kind of glory echo today's business headlines. But several of these early merchants recorded in their journals more personal glimpses of the fur trade—the image of Cree families waiting at Nipawin for the men to return from the bay, the rituals of trade, the shifting relationships between European men and native women.

There are other stories here, too. The paradox of the Doukhobors—a pacifist, agrarian Christian community that nevertheless harbored a small group of near-anarchist extremists—is one of the strangest tales of Saskatchewan's settlement days. While the vast majority of the Doukhobors worked hard to build their tidy villages and communal farms, a splinter group decided that life exploited both humans and animals. To express their views they burned buildings and marched naked through town and country.

But it's Kelsey, sometimes called North America's first traveling salesman, who gave his name to the area. And the echoes of his industry are still clear.

Short-Lived Fur Post at Isaac's House Pattern for the Future
Highway 6, south of Saskatchewan River

Isaac's House, also known as Fort aux Trembles after the trembling aspen of the area, was just the sort of fur post that gave the Hudson's Bay Company fits. While the Baymen huddled behind the stockade of York Factory on the shores of Hudson Bay and waited for trappers to bring furs to them, independent fur traders based in Montreal were brazenly heading upriver and inland to take their trade to the customers. Banding together in 1779 into the North West Company, these swashbuckling fur barons used a tenuous, overextended supply line of fast canoes and strong backs to nearly topple the monopoly of the mighty Hudson's Bay Company.

This post was funded by two of the original Nor'Westers, James McGill and Joseph Frobisher, as well as Maurice Blondeau. They sent out a party of French-Canadian voyageurs led by François le Blanc and Bartholomew Blondeau to this site well upstream of the Baymen. It was a classic Nor'Wester maneuver: moving upstream allowed them to intercept trappers heading east with furs to trade, and working together prevented the trappers from bargaining prices down. The Hudson's Bay Company's Matthew Cocking, in his journal entry for August 29, 1774, watched this bold business stroke with dismay and a sniff of disapproval:

> *I have been informed by me Leader that he heard of forty-five Canoes of Pedlers [the Hudson's Bay Company's term for independent traders] that came from the Great Carrying Place [Grand Portage on Lake Superior]. . . . My Leader also informed me that Franceway [François] & the rest of the Pedlers that were up Saskatchewan River Traded as always was done there at a dear rate, But that all Below traded everything as reasonable as at the Companys Forts.*

Once the Hudson's Bay Company realized it had been out-flanked and that trappers would pay more for goods they didn't have to travel so far to buy, it changed its hundred-year-old policy of sticking close to the bay. In 1774, the company sent out Samuel Hearne to scout a spot for its first inland post, which became Cumberland House. Although Isaac's House lasted only four years before the area was trapped out, it and forts like it had set the pattern for the fur trade's next 50 years until the rival companies merged in 1821.

By then, some of the original Nor'Westers had done very well indeed, accumulating large fortunes and building mansions in Montreal, some of which still stand. James McGill's name remains particularly prominent on the university that his fur trade fortune founded.

Fur Traders Blaze Early Trail Between Fort La Corne and Cumberland House
Highway 35, 3 miles (5 km) south of Nipawin

An Indian packer loaded up for the portage.

One of the earliest of the old fur trade trails, this path dates back to 1753, when Fort St. Louis was built by explorers from New France, then a vigorous colony a decade away from defeat at the hands of the English.

The French, under Chevalier de la Corne, abandoned the site after four years. But its location was too good to remain untenanted for long. Here, the two forks of the Saskatchewan River gave access to both the northern woods, source of the best furs, and the southern plains, where buffalo herds made a plentiful food supply. After the Hudson's Bay Company built Cumberland House in 1774, it wasn't long before the Hudson's Bay Company and the North West Company had small posts on or near the site of la Corne's original fort. By 1795, the two companies and various independents staffed no fewer than five posts along that stretch of river.

In summer, the Baymen supplied their outposts by river. But in winter especially, an overland route was needed, too, and the sledges and carts that kept the fur trade running passed along here back to Cumberland House. Business, and traffic, was heavy enough that by 1846 the Hudson's Bay Company built a new post on the Saskatchewan River. In honor of the old French explorer, they called it Fort La Corne and kept it open until 1932.

Like the other early trails, the traffic of traders was eventually replaced by the footsteps and cartwheels of policemen, loggers and settlers. Trappers and native bands at Red Earth Lake also used it.

Orphan Boy Becomes First Aboriginal Priest
Junction of highways 35 and 55, Nipawin

The Church of England could hardly have been luckier in its first aboriginal minister. Henry Budd, ordained an Anglican priest in 1853 and posted here right after, was a large, handsome man, eloquent in Cree and English, and a methodical and patient administrator.

Budd was set on his path early. In 1819, he was a young orphan at Norway House in what is now Manitoba when he came under the wing of John West, the Hudson's Bay Company chaplain, and George Harbridge, a teacher. He was baptized Henry Budd three years later; by then, at about the age of 10, he could read the New Testament and knew the Church of England catechism.

Young Henry followed Harbridge to the Red River settlement, where he continued his studies. After a brief clerkship with the Hudson's Bay Company in the Columbia River country, he returned to Red River to farm. In 1837, he was asked to teach at a parish school, and was so good at it that he was soon asked to head northwest to Cumberland House area to start a school for Indian people. Under the sponsorship of the Church Missionary Society, he set up at The Pas in modern-day Manitoba and his little mission soon bore fruit. In 1842, a church official visited The Pas to baptize 39 adults, 27 babies and 22 schoolchildren, all swayed by Budd's teaching.

By 1850, Budd was taken back to Red River to be coached in theology. Three years later, he was ordained at The Pas. His first posting was here, at what was then called Nepowewin. He stayed until 1867, earning the deep affection of his people and a reputation for tidiness that showed in his immaculate gardens and livestock.

Budd returned to The Pas, where he died in 1875. After his death, one of Budd's flock remarked that he knew now what it was like to lose a father.

Name of Nipawin Recalls Fur Trade's Earliest Days
Junction of highways 35 and 55, Nipawin

The name of this town dates back to the earliest times of the fur trade in the North-West. When trappers used to paddle furs up the Saskatchewan River to Cumberland House or even farther to York Factory on the shores of Hudson Bay, they took the arduous trip without their families. The name *Nipawin* derives from a Cree word meaning "a standing place," and on a high bluff about 4 miles (7 km) upstream from the present town was the place where families watched for the trappers' return. This standing place also was useful to Indians looking to conduct a little business of their own.

That's what was happening in 1794, when the North West Company's Duncan McGillivray passed by and reported three traders busily transacting with "a few Tents of Cree and Saulteaux." Traders were often spotted from the bluff and invited ashore for some deal-making.

By that time, Nipawin was well known to almost two generations of fur traders.

As early as 1748, Chevalier de la Verendrye, son of New France's great naval hero la Verendrye, paddled past here on his way to the forks of the Saskatchewan in an effort to convince trappers there to trade with the French instead of the English. Another Frenchman, Chevalier de la Corne, canoed through in 1753 to build a fort at the forks.

And although the Hudson's Bay Company didn't actually build an inland fort until 1774, it regularly sent parties upstream to talk up trade with the company. Between Anthony Henday's 1754 journey and the construction of Cumberland House, the Hudson's Bay Company sent 60 of its employees down the Saskatchewan past Nipawin.

None was ever likely to forget the trip, either. Once past Nipawin, the river's current became too strong to paddle against. McGillivray's journal describes a laborious portage:

This part of the River is an object of terror. . . . The usual mode of navigation is here rendered useless by the Strength of the Current, which makes it necessary to haul the Canoes up along the Shore with a line, for that purpose, for the space of 6 days on an exceeding bad Road.

That current, of course, is now gentled by the François-Finlay dam, built in 1985 and named after François le Blanc and James Finlay, two traders from Montreal who built a post here in 1768. During that first season alone, Finlay made enough money to retire and return east, where his lavish haul of furs made him the toast of Montreal. Le Blanc remained, shutting the trapped-out post in 1773 and heading upstream to build Isaac's House, or Fort aux Trembles.

Oldest Community in Saskatchewan Begins as Fur Post
End of Highway 123, 100 miles (163 km) northeast of Nipawin

Cumberland House, the oldest still-occupied community in Saskatchewan, got its start for a good, solid reason: money. For a century the Hudson's Bay Company kept to its fort at York Factory along the shores of Hudson Bay, waiting for trappers to come there to trade. But by the 1770s, independent traders from Montreal were pushing west, paddling incredible distances into the interior every year and taking their trade directly to the Cree and Chipewyan of the Saskatchewan country. The Baymen knew the best furs were paddling right past them, and by 1774, they decided to do something. They tapped Samuel Hearne to head upriver and set up the Hudson's Bay Company's first inland post.

Described as a handsome, red-faced man who raced moose to stay in shape, Hearne had already had a distinguished Hudson's Bay Company career when he got the offer for this job. A few years earlier, the company had asked him to check out reports they'd heard of a great, navigable route north with valuable copper deposits at its mouth. After two false starts Hearne attached himself to the band of a leading Chipewyan named Matonabbee, and they headed out. Hearne had chosen his guide well. Matonabbee was not only familiar with Europeans, he had great prestige among the northern Indians and had negotiated peace settlements among them. Moreover, Matonabbee insisted that Hearne travel in the aboriginal style, with women and children, following the caribou. Hearne became one of the first European explorers to adapt to aboriginal life. He got so used to eating Indian food that later, while dining in London restaurants, he would order trout and salmon "not warm to the bone." Hearne's openness to native culture allowed him and Matonabbee to develop mutual respect and a warm friendship. Still, the 19-month trip was brutally hard. The party suffered days without food and blizzards in July, hauling huge packs on foot across the tundra. Frostbite cost Hearne his toenails. He concluded that the Coppermine River was unnavigable and the namesake deposits at its mouth were too small to mine. Nevertheless on July 17, 1771, Hearne became the first European to reach the Arctic Ocean overland.

The bush savvy that Hearne gained on that voyage made him a natural choice to found an inland post, which must have seemed easy in comparison to his northern trip. On June 23, 1774, he took a few provisions, eight Baymen and two Cree, and selected a spot on Cumberland Lake after a 40-day paddle from York Factory. It was a great spot. Here the canoe routes back to York Factory and Montreal converged. The area was connected to the great fur regions of Athabasca and Churchill as well as the buffalo-rich plains to the south. The location was so great, in fact, that about 150 independent traders were already well established here, and the riverbanks were lined with their posts.

Still, Hearne and his men went about building their own post, a log shack about 28 x 14' (8.5 x 4.25 m), caulked with moss and thatched with grass. It was a tough, hungry winter with few furs collected because the men were busy hunting, fishing and cutting timber. But Cumberland House was established. When not engaged in survival, Hearne fed the birds (as well as pet foxes, squirrels and beavers) and read Voltaire.

The next summer, Hearne handed the post off to Matthew Cocking. Cocking had originally been hired as a writer, someone who could chronicle trade and exploration a bit more coherently than some of the Hudson's Bay Company's regular staff. Although he didn't know how to steer a canoe on his first trip to the interior in 1772, by the time he traveled with trappers as far west as the Eagle Hills south of Battleford, he had seasoned well. Cocking stayed at Cumberland House until 1777, when he moved to Fort Severn along Hudson Bay. Throughout, Cocking kept writing. His transcriptions of fur trade letters and journals, flowing out in his elegant handwriting, are a major source of information for today's historians.

Cumberland House became even more important, emerging as the jumping-off point for a series of fur posts up the Saskatchewan River. Eventually, Cumberland House became the Hudson's Bay Company's headquarters for the whole inland trade in the Churchill and Athabasca regions. Still, the leaky, drafty building was not in great shape. A doctor who visited Cumberland House in the winter of 1808–09 (after the post was rebuilt in the 1790s) called it "the most miserable hovel that imagination can conceive. . . . Such temporary shelter, infinitely below what an Ourang-Outan would have contented himself with, can only bespeak the glimmering dying lights of an expiring Commerce, not the residence of Britons, not the Settlements of the Adventurers of England."

Nor was its sales force particularly impressive. The 26 Baymen stationed at Cumberland House around 1780 were facing competition from 300 independents ensconced in a nearby fort in relative comfort. Even by 1811, the Hudson's Bay Company had only 320 men inland compared with 1,200 Nor'Westers.

Despite its problems, Cumberland House remained a vital link in the Hudson's Bay Company fur chain until 1821, when the North West Company's increasingly long and tenuous supply line forced it to merge with the Hudson's Bay Company in 1821.

Norway House at the northeast end of Lake Winnipeg became the inland headquarters, and the post was downgraded to a regional distribution center. Cumberland House remained a shipping and distribution point for the Hudson's Bay Company until the mid-1920s.

Small-Town Quebec Girl Undaunted by Western Frontier
Highway 123, 100 miles (163 km) northeast of Nipawin at Cumberland House, Cumberland House Provincial Historic Park

---

Cumberland House's position at the headwaters of the inland fur trade made the post a busy way station for travelers heading into fur country. One of the most interesting visitors was Marie-Ann Lagimodiere, a determined, fiery Quebecois who became the first European woman to live on the North-West frontier.

In 1805, Marie-Ann Gaboury was 25 years old, the house-keeper for a priest in Maskinonge near Trois Rivières, when Jean-Baptiste Lagimodiere returned to town from one of the fur brigades after a five-year absence. The two fell in love and were married the following winter. But the next spring, the lure of the West overtook Jean-Baptiste and he announced he was going to rejoin the fur trade. He expected to head west alone, but Marie-Ann was not about to bid adieu to her husband for another five years. She declared she would accompany Jean Baptiste. Her will must have been formidable; no European woman had ever traveled with a fur brigade, yet Jean-Baptiste agreed to take his bride.

The traveling was hard. They paddled from dawn to dusk. Before they even reached Lake Superior, the party had been through 36 portages, during which everything had to be unloaded and carried to the next river or lake. Marie-Ann was responsible not only for her own 80 pounds (36 kg) of luggage; she also mended clothes and cooked food, mostly dried peas, salt pork and biscuits.

By the summer, the couple had reached a Métis encampment in what is now North Dakota. They had to move upriver, however, when a common-law Indian wife whom Jean-Baptiste had left behind threatened Marie-Ann's life. Eventually, Jean-Baptiste settled into his old living as a buffalo hunter for the

North West Company. The couple's first child was born in May 1807. The little girl, who was wrapped in a bag of moss and christened Reine, became the first legitimate European baby born in the old North-West.

It was the next spring when the Lagimodieres came through Cumberland House. The local Indians were holding a great feast at the time, and the family was a big hit at the party. Marie-Ann and little Reine were the first European woman and child the aboriginals had ever seen. Marie-Ann must have been pregnant at the time, for her second child was born that summer, under somewhat hair-raising circumstances.

The family was riding across the plains one day when a buffalo crossed their path. Marie-Ann's horse was an old buffalo-runner and immediately shot after it. As Reine dangled in a moss bag off the saddle and her mother hung on for dear life, Jean-Baptiste chased the runaway, finally cut in front of it and got the horse under control. A few hours later, the couple's second child, a boy, was born. They named him Laprairie, after his birthplace.

The Lagimodieres had more adventures after that, including the time in 1815 when Jean-Baptiste hotfooted it to Montreal to warn authorities of the trouble that was to explode into the Seven Oaks Massacre, while Marie-Ann waited in fear for him for nearly a year. There were more children, too—eight in total. The Saulteaux called her Ningah, meaning "mother." Marie-Ann's life on the frontier must have agreed with her, for she lived to be 95. She died in 1875 in St. Boniface, now part of Winnipeg, surrounded by children, grandchildren and great-grandchildren.

But the Lagimodiere clan wasn't through with history yet. The second-last of those children, Julie, had married a man named Jean-Louis Riel. Their son Louis had already led one resistance on behalf of the Métis; in 10 years, he was to lead another.

Historic Steamboat Molders on Riverbank
Highway 123, 100 miles (163 km) northeast of Nipawin at Cumberland House, Cumberland House Provincial Historic Park

It may seem odd to write about naval history in landlocked Saskatchewan, but the saga of the *Northcote*, whose remains molder here on the riverbank, demands telling. The first steamboat huffed and chugged its way into the old North-West in 1859, up the Red River from the United States to Fort Garry. By the 1870s, a good half-dozen stern-wheelers were taking prairie rivers from Fort Garry to Fort Edmonton into the Age of Steam.

The *Northcote*, launched in 1874 from Grand Rapids at the mouth of the Saskatchewan on Lake Winnipeg, was the first to ply the Saskatchewan River. On August 26, it reached The Pas. According to Henry Budd, the Anglican minister at the station:

They blew the whistle so loud they made the very cattle rear up their heels, and took to full gallop with their tails up in the air at full speed into the woods. But not only the cattle but the people of all ages and sexes were no less excited at the sight of the boat, the first boat of its kind to be seen by them all their life; in fact, the first steam boat going in this river since the Creation.

The Hudson's Bay Company used the *Northcote* to move supplies to Cumberland House, where they were transferred to York boats and canoes going to more remote posts. Navigation was hard on the shallow Saskatchewan. Although the *Northcote* drew only about 3' (1 m) of water fully loaded, sandbars were a problem. A steamer could push over the little ones just by taking a run at them. For bigger ones, the pilot had to turn the boat around and thrash the water with the boat's paddle, hoping to wash the bar away. The final resort was "grasshoppering"—jamming a pair of sturdy spars into the sand and using the engine's power to lever the boat along a few yards at a time.

By the middle 1880s, steamboats were dying out. But the *Northcote* had yet to play its most famous role as the only warship ever to sail the Canadian plains. On May 9, 1885, the North-West Rebellion had reached its turning point at Batoche, a small town on the South Saskatchewan River that Louis Riel had made his headquarters. Major-General Frederick Middleton and the Canadian army planned to attack the 175 dug-in Métis and Cree from the south with 800 men, four cannons and a Gatling gun. The *Northcote*, attacking from the north, was to provide a diversion.

The now famous steamer, reinforced against rifle fire, duly chugged in from Prince Albert. But the rebels were ready for her: they had stretched a ferry cable across the river, which tore off the boat's smokestacks, mast spars and pilot house. Its crew pinned down under heavy fire, the unsteered steamer ran into a sandbar, where it harmlessly remained. For three days, the crew and about 30 soldiers remained on board, tending to the wounded, firing on the rebels and listening to enemy gunfire constantly pinging off the steamer's boilers. A reporter from the *Manitoba Free Press* divided his time between passing ammunition and telling stories to keep up morale. "We had a charming time for three days," recalled one man pinned down in the steamer. "I expected the old *Northcote* to go up in chariot of fire at any moment."

The old *Northcote* was never the same after that. In 1886, the Hudson's Bay Company beached it permanently at Cumberland House, where it remains to this day.

ALONG HIGHWAY 3

Henry Kelsey Passes Through on Two-Year Voyage of Discovery
Highway 3, 36 miles (60 km) east of Melfort, then 24 miles (40 km) southeast on Highway 38 to Greenwater Provincial Park

---

Although the Hudson's Bay Company sent Henry Kelsey out in 1690 on a mission of trade, not exploration, discovering new travel routes was something he could hardly help. Kelsey was the first European to head inland on the Saskatchewan River; consequently, he was the first European to venture into what is now Saskatchewan, the first to spend a winter here, the first to see the Great Plains, the first to hunt buffalo. For two years every step he took uncovered new territory.

He was the first through here, too. In the fall of 1691, he was taken by his aboriginal guides up the Red Deer River to Nut Lake and passed near what has become Greenwater Park.

At least, that's what historians think. Kelsey was a trader, not a map maker, and with a canoe-load of attractive merchandise (such as beads, hatchets, kettles and 20 pounds / 9 kg of Brazilian tobacco), he was to glad-hand the local natives and convince them to shop at the Bay. He was also to broker peace between warring bands to make it easier and safer for everyone to head to York Factory and trade, although few of his treaties lasted long. His journal entries, not terribly concerned with precise landmarks or sextant readings, make it difficult to retrace his path. In fact, Kelsey's journal is often written in verse:

Because I was alone and no friend could find,
And once in my travels was left behind,
Which struck fear and terror into me,
But still I was resolved this same Country for to see....

Perhaps Kelsey was eccentric. Or perhaps the spectacle of so much utterly new and wondrous country moved him to attempt poetry.

Whatever his motives, Kelsey soon felt the disdain of his employers at York Factory. It would be another 60 years before the Hudson's Bay Company got serious about trade missions up the Saskatchewan River. In all, Kelsey served the company nearly 40 years, all but three of them at York Factory. Eventually, he became chief trader at Albany and governor of all the fur posts. Still, he died poor and alone in East Greenwich, England, in 1724. His unique journal was lost until 1926, when it turned up in Northern Ireland.

Red Deer Lake Trail Links Early Fur Trade Hunting Grounds
Highway 9, 14 miles (22 km) south of Hudson Bay in picnic site

This northeast section of the province was rich trapping ground in the days of the fur trade and was one of the earliest parts of the province to be opened up. Members of the North West Company built Fort Rivière a la Biche just north of here in 1787, one of several posts constructed in this area because of its abundant beaver. This point is on the old trail halfway between Nut Lake in the southwest and Red Deer Lake to the west. It was traveled by many a trapper and trader long into the next century.

In 1888 and 1889, Joseph Burr Tyrrell led a geological survey party through here. Tyrrell filled in many blank spots on the maps of western and northern Canada during his 17 years with the Geological Survey of Canada. He also edited the diaries of some of the men who first explored parts of the country he later came to map, including the journals of David Thompson and Samuel Hearne. A lake and a mountain bear Tyrrell's name, but he's probably best remembered for discovering the astonishing dinosaur bone beds of southern Alberta. The Royal Tyrrell Museum of Palaeontology in Drumheller, Alberta, is named after him.

Eventually, before it was replaced by roads and rail, this trail was used by settlers and loggers heading into bush country.

Fort Rivière a la Biche Part of Once-Bustling Fur Trade Grounds

Highway 9, 2 miles (3.2 km) south of Hudson Bay, in regional park

One of a proliferation of fur trade forts built in this area as the 1700s drew to a close, Fort Rivière a la Biche was opened in 1787 by the North West Company. Back then, trading was more than an exchange of goods. It was a ritual that helped establish the relationship between Indians and European traders as well as rank within a band. It was a ceremonious break in the routine, a chance to renew friendships, share news of the country and if circumstances allowed, it was an excuse for a feast and party. The ritual varied little from post to post, and here's how Nor'Wester Duncan McGillivray described it:

> *When a Band of Indians approach near the Fort it is customary for the Chiefs to send a few young men before them to announce their arrival, and to procure a few articles which they are accustomed to receive on these occasions—such as Powder, and piece of Tobacco and a little paint to besmear their faces. . . . At a few yards distance from the gate they salute us with several discharges of their guns, which is answered by hoisting a flag and firing a few guns. On entering the house they are disarmed, treated with a few drams and a bit of tobacco, and after the pipe has plyed about for some time they relate the news with great deliberation and ceremony. . . . When their lodges are erected by the women they receive a present of Rum proportioned to the Nation and quality of their Chiefs and the whole Band drink during 24 hours and sometimes much longer for nothing. . . . When the drinking match has subsided they begin to trade.*

However, such events were not as frequent at this fort as the North West Company would have liked. Traders stuck it out here for 13 years, but business was disappointing and the post was abandoned in 1800.

ALONG HIGHWAY 9

Fort Qu'Appelle–Fort Pelly Trail Links Hinterland with Headquarters
Highway 47, 4 miles (6.1 km) south of Willowbrook

Back in the middle 1800s, this trail was the only land link between Fort Qu'Appelle and its administrative headquarters of Fort Pelly. Most of Pelly's business was in furs, but Qu'Appelle's main activity was to help supply pemmican for the Hudson's Bay Company's sprawling fur trade empire. Consequently, most of the traffic along this trail for about 50 years consisted of noisy brigades of squealing Red River carts and shouting Métis freighters.

Like so many other trade routes, the North-West Mounted Police began to patrol along here during the 1870s. By the next decade they were joined by the first settlers coming to the region. The Fort Qu'Appelle–Fort Pelly Trail was used until the first roads in the region were built.

Assiniboine River Becomes Focus of Fur Trade Battle
Highway 9, 3.5 miles (5.5 km) southeast of Tadmore exit at crossing of Assiniboine River

As the 1700s drew to a close, this stretch of the Assiniboine River was the cutting edge of the fur trade's westward creep. Here, the North West Company's Pierre Falcon built Fort Alexandria along the south bank of the river in 1795, upstream from both the Hudson's Bay Company's Albany House and a post of its own. Fairly long-lived for a fur post, Fort Alexandria operated from 1795 to 1805, then again from 1807 until 1821, the year the Nor'Westers and Baymen amalgamated.

From 1800 to 1805, Fort Alexandria was staffed by Daniel Harmon, a godly New Englander whose diaries constantly decry the boozing and loose morals of fur trade society. During his time here, Harmon resolutely refused to have anything to do with Métis or aboriginal women, despite the fact that it was common among fur traders to do so. Called *marriage a la façon du pays,* it was a well-established custom with its own formalities and even a certain amount of legal standing. Although both the Hudson's Bay and North West companies tried from time to time to discourage such alliances, anyone who wintered in the North-West was aware of their benefits. Not only did an aboriginal or Métis wife soften a trader's harsh, lonely life, but she had much to teach him about frontier survival. She also could help forge useful alliances. Many traders left their so-called "country wives" back in the country when it was time to return to civilization, often making provision for their support. But many such unions lasted a lifetime.

Eventually, Harmon could no longer hold off loneliness. Shortly after he left here, he found his own frontier love, a young Métis named Elizabeth Duval, who followed him from post to post until his retirement in 1819. When it came time to return east, Harmon found he couldn't leave without Elizabeth. His diary reads

> *The union which has been formed between us in the providence of God has not only been cemented by a long and mutual performance of kind offices, but, also, by a more sacred consideration. We have wept together over the early departure of several children, and especially, over the death of a beloved son. We have children still living, who are equally dear to us both. How could I spend my days in the civilized world, and leave my beloved children in the wilderness? How could I tear them from a mother's love, and leave her to mourn over their absence, to the day of her death? Possessing only the common feeling of humanity, how could I think of her in such circumstances without anguish?*

Harmon took Elizabeth to Vermont, where they were married as their many children looked on. They later moved near Montreal, where Harmon died.

ALONG HIGHWAY 8

Chief Gabriel Coté Straddles Old World and New with Difficulty
Highway 8, 5 miles (8 km) south of Kamsack

Although many in the old North-West were able to straddle the worlds of the Indians and Europeans, it was not an easy life.

Gabriel Coté could have told you that. At least, Gabriel was what his Métis father called him. His Saulteaux mother called him Meemay, and those were the two poles between which his life was played out.

Coté was a successful hunter who, by 1850, was leading a small band of English-speaking Métis and Saulteaux around the Swan River area just northeast of here. They moved between the woodlands and the plains and traded at Fort Pelly. Coté was often at the fort, and his good relationship with the local Hudson's Bay Company traders and government officials gave him a reputation as one of the principal Saulteaux chiefs. Acting on that assumption, the commissioners who came west in 1874 to negotiate Treaty No 4 concluded that Coté could speak on behalf of all the Saulteaux. In fact the Saulteaux around the Qu'Appelle River and Quill Lakes distrusted Coté. They called him a "company chief," a leader whose position came from his cosy relationship with the whites rather than the support of his people. As the negotiations opened some of his supposed followers confined Coté to his tent and even allegedly threatened his life.

These Saulteaux were upset that the Hudson's Bay Company had sold its land to Canada. They claimed the land was theirs, not the company's, and that proceeds from its sale should go to them. The commissioners explained that the government was trying to be fair to both Indians and the company. The Saulteaux must have been satisfied because they released Coté and allowed him to sign Treaty No 4 but only on behalf of his own band.

Coté still wasn't free from controversy. The woodland hunters in his band weren't happy with the reserve he chose, north of present-day Kamsack. About one-third of Coté's band left, leaving behind approximately 270 followers. Although Coté had been a hunter, he left the traditional life and took up farming. He tilled his land there until his death in 1884, an event widely mourned by all who knew him.

Doukhobors Attempt to Create Earthly Paradise
Highway 5, Veregin

Saskatchewan has been no stranger to groups of immigrants from the same area or religion who settled together in colonies. Such groups have arrived here from nearly every faith and nation

A Doukhobor couple in Kamsack.

in Europe. But surely one of the strangest of all such sagas was the arrival around the turn of the century of the Doukhobors.

The Doukhobors were a radically pacifist sect that broke from the Russian Orthodox Church in the early 1700s. They spurned the trappings of most organized religion and worshiped in prayer houses, not churches, with no ritual sacraments. Their

Doukhobor women pulling plow.

holy book was an oral heritage of psalms, songs and prayers shared at their services. They were pacifists, puritanical, vegetarian and held all property in common. They were popular with neither the tsars nor the church, and in 1887, their leader Peter Veregin, was exiled to Siberia.

Finally, in 1898, the tsars gave the Doukhobors permission to leave. Cyprus, Texas, Hawaii and Brazil were all considered, but someone had read an article by anarchist Peter Kropotkin that said Russian Mennonites on the Canadian prairies were thriving on good land in blocks that enabled them to live together. The Canadian government, pleased to welcome such hardworking, experienced farmers, promised them exemption from military service and set aside large tracts of land around what is now Kamsack and Yorkton. And the great Russian novelist Leo Tolstoy, who admired the Doukhobors, donated the proceeds of his novel *Resurrection* to their emigration. So Canada it was.

On January 24, 1899, the first group of Doukhobors sailed into Halifax Harbour singing a prayer "like that of a mighty choir chanting a solemn Te Deum," according to the *Halifax Morning Chronicle*.

They moved onto their land near present-day Veregin and built 57 villages of about 130 people each. Although they initially lived in sod shacks, tents or dugouts in hillsides, their villages were self-sufficient and tidy, with whitewashed walls, fenced

A naked Doukhobor woman watches a home burn.

yards and well-tended gardens. What farming equipment they had was shared; bread was baked in large communal ovens. While the men hired out for the summer on other farms or on the railway to earn capital, the women broke land by hitching themselves 24 at a time to the plows, singing as they furrowed.

In 1902, Veregin was released from exile. The status of his people had much improved thanks to their hard work and some financial support from the American Quakers. Perhaps inspired by the progress, Veregin penned some musings on an earthly paradise that was humble, pious and nonexploitive. Using farm animals would be immoral. Metal tools should also be rejected because in mines "people are tortured to obtain ore." The trouble began.

A sect called the Sons of God sprang up. Taking Veregin literally, they drove their hard-won farm animals into the woods and hitched themselves to their wagons. They burned their books and their warm sheepskins and gave their money to the nearest official.

They felt God had instructed them to find land nearer the sun, and in October 1902, a group of 1,100 marched south toward Yorkton to demand new lands, singing all the way and living off grasses, rosebuds and donated bread. At Yorkton, the North-West Mounted Police took the women and children. But the men continued south, littering the roads with their scattered boots, socks and shirts, huddling together at night in the snow. Finally, at Minnedosa, Manitoba, they were rounded up and returned to their farms.

Alarmed, Veregin arrived in December to explain that such extremism was unnecessary and that horses and men worked together for mutual benefit. Things calmed down, and Veregin, nicknamed Peter the Lordly, bought land for the town that now bears his name. But the following spring, the radical spirit reappeared in a new sect called the Sons of Freedom. Although they never numbered more than 600 in Saskatchewan, this sect became the brush with which all Doukhobors were painted. That May, in an attempt to convert more moderate Doukhobors, some Sons of Freedom marched naked through several villages.

"We went in the manner of the first man Adam and Eve, to show nature to humanity, how man should return to his fatherland and return the ripened fruit and its seed," recalled marcher Alex Makharov.

They were not always welcome. One village beat the 52 marchers off with willow twigs. The Sons kept marching, eating grass and leaves, until they were stopped outside Yorkton and forcibly dressed. Most of them returned to their farms, but 10 did not. Preaching having failed to move people to renounce their possessions, the Sons turned to sabotage, rolling flat a wheat field and burning a binder.

Most Doukhobors, however, were peaceful and thrived. By 1907, there were 8,700 living on Doukhobor reserves. But by then, some of the same old conflicts that had driven them from Russia were coming to a head. Veregin wanted no part of civil society. He refused to collect vital statistics and wouldn't enter names on homestead records. Villagers wouldn't give their names to census takers. They also balked at paying taxes, although they eventually did, and they didn't see the need for schools, although they did build a few. Nor would the Doukhobors swear allegiance to their new country, thinking it was a first step toward military service.

Finally, in 1906, the government ruled that all Doukhobor lands were to be treated as regular homesteads. That meant each Doukhobor family had to live on its quarter section (65 square ha), which effectively destroyed the communal villages. In the spring of 1907, the Doukhobors lost about half their land to other settlers.

The Sons of Freedom began marching again, this time wearing long blue robes, and once again the Doukhobors discussed moving. British Columbia was the new promised land, and by 1912 about 5,000 had moved. By this time the old Doukhobor ways were beginning to disappear. By 1910, most of the Doukhobors who had settled near Prince Albert had abandoned the communes and were living on their own land. They were, however, allowed to register as conscientious objectors in World War I.

In 1924, Peter Veregin was killed in a railway car explosion that some suspect was deliberately set. His son, the hard-drinking and financially irresponsible Peter Jr., took over. Although prairie membership was shrinking drastically, a few Sons of Freedom remained active, burning buildings they saw as too worldly or as intrusions of the state. Between 1929 and 1931, 25 schools around Kamsack and Canora were burned. At one point they burned Peter the Lordly's home, threw their clothes into the fire and stood around it singing hymns.

By 1939, the Doukhobor central organization was bankrupt and its remaining land was transferred to the Land Settlement Board. That year, Peter Jr. died of liver and stomach cancer. All Doukhobors in Canada had abandoned communal living by 1950, although the Sons of Freedom in British Columbia committed occasional arson attacks until 1962.

There are more than 30,000 descendants of Doukhobor settlers throughout western Canada, a large number still holding to the faith of their fathers. The Orthodox Doukhobors, or the Union of Spiritual Communities of Christ, is the largest denomination.

Fort Pelly Trail Connected Trading Post with Rich Fur Country
Highway 5, 6 miles (10 km) east of Kamsack, turn northeast at junction of highways 5 and 57, and drive 3 miles (5 km) to Duck Mountain Provincial Park

Blazed by native trappers, the Fort Pelly Trail connected the fur trade center of Fort Pelly with the rich fur country of the Upper Shell River to the west and Madge Lake in what is now Duck Mountain Provincial Park. Fort Pelly Chief Trader William Todd wrote in 1832 that in one trip alone a skilled Saulteaux trapper came out of Shell River with furs worth 60 MB (made beaver), the standard Hudson's Bay Company unit of exchange based on the value of one beaver pelt.

Later, this trail came to serve loggers, surveyors and the area's first settlers.

Assiniboine Elbow Strategic Fur Trade Spot
Municipal Road 637, 9 miles (15 km) south from Norquay

This northerly jog of the Assiniboine River brings it within 12 miles (20 km) of the Swan River. The proximity of these river systems helped make this spot a native gathering spot long before Europeans came. When they did arrive, the Assiniboine elbow, with its beaver-rich bushlands and marshes, became a strategic point in the fur trade almost immediately.

The first fort in this area was the Hudson's Bay Company's Marlboro House, built in the fall of 1793 along the east bank of the elbow near a shallow crossing place. Mere weeks later, on December 5, the North West Company arrived and built within a stone's throw of its rival. The Hudson's Bay Company rebuilt in 1795, just upstream of the original post; not to be outdone, so did the Nor'Westers. Independent traders, banded together under the name XY Company, also built in the vicinity. Competition grew so intense that one Hudson's Bay Company trader complained of threats and intimidation from the Nor'Westers after trappers stole into his post at night to pay off their trade debts.

The Hudson's Bay Company moved upstream again in 1798 but returned to the elbow in 1807. Finally, the Baymen and Nor'Westers amalgamated in 1821 and together built Fort Pelly in 1824. The journal of Fort Pelly Chief Trader William Todd tells of traders from the Red Deer River in the west to the Red River in the east coming here to the elbow. Fort Pelly became the headquarters for the entire district and stayed open until 1912.

But fur traders weren't the only people who congregated hereabouts. Bands of Cree, Stoney, Saulteaux and Mandan also came through. Trails from Fort Qu'Appelle and Fort Ellice crossed the river near here. And occasionally, the Hudson's Bay Company steamer *Marquette* chugged this far up the Assiniboine River from Fort Garry.

Assiniboine Elbow Longtime Fur Trade Headquarters at Fort Pelly

Highway 49, 6 miles (10 km) south and 1.5 miles (2.4 km) west of Pelly

---

Two hundred years ago, the area near the elbow of the Assiniboine River must have seemed like the fur trade equivalent of a shopping mall for local trappers. One historian has counted no fewer than 14 fur posts in the region over the years, so local Cree or Saulteaux had plenty of choice about where to trade their beaver and otter pelts, produced in abundance in this bushy, swampy parkland. Competition got so stiff that one Hudson's Bay trader reported he had been insulted and threatened by the neighboring Nor'Westers.

That competitive era ended when the two companies merged in 1821. Three years later, they built a new fort here and named it after the Hudson's Bay Company's governor, Sir John Pelly. From the start, it was an important post, serving as the administrative center for posts as far-flung as Fort Qu'Appelle and Moose Mountain. Fort Pelly did brisk business on its own, too. The 1832, journal of Chief Trader William Todd reports constant visits from local traders, sometimes coming to trade, sometimes asking for advances of supplies. Other entries hint at what life was like at the post:

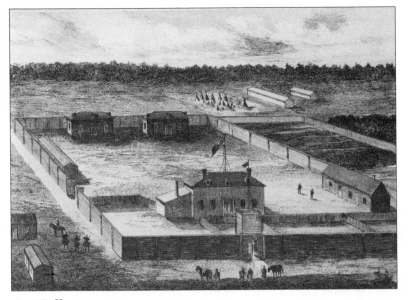

Fort Pelly.

Saturday [October] 20th. fine Weather as a few Rats are reported to be about the Blacksmith has been employed some days Making Rat Spears. People repairing and Plastering the Houses.

Sunday 28th. enveloped in darkness by smoke from the Plains which still continues to Burn

Friday [November] 2. Constant snow which no doubt will extinguish the fire that has been raging for the Last ten days An Indian called two heads arrived having lost his wife from sickness. he was nearly naked and destitute of everything having given all away as is customary on such occasions.

In 1856, the Hudson's Bay Company built a new, more imposing post a short distance away, eventually complete with a 10' (3-m) -high stockade and heavy gate. The factor's house was similarly grand. James Carnegie, the Earl of Southesk, traveled through here in 1859 and said it had the best accommodations of any post west of the Red River.

By the 1870s, Fort Pelly ceased to be the district headquarters, but it remained a prosperous trading post that operated until June 1912.

First North-West Mounted Police Headquarters Abandoned After One Winter

Highway 49, 3 miles (5 km) north and 1 mile (1.6 km) northwest of Pelly

Few forts made a grander debut, but today only a cairn marks the site of Fort Livingstone, the first western headquarters of the North-West Mounted Police and the original seat of government for the Northwest Territories. The fort was originally built in 1874, alongside a shack that served as a repeater station for the telegraph line between Winnipeg and Edmonton. It was supposed to have been the barracks for the North-West Mounted Police as they marched west, but the fort wasn't ready when Commissioner George French arrived in mid-October with the first troops. It was, by all accounts, a miserable winter. The fort had been built with green lumber and warped immediately, leaving large gaps between the logs. As one Mountie described it,

> *Between these logs you can see the beautiful snow coming down in flakes and thro' these chinks and crannies you can hear the wind howling and whistling. We have 6 stoves and a large log fire going all the time and yet many a blue face can be seen. . . . I might add here that we burn 4 cords of wood a day.*

The policemen had to buy winter gear from the Baymen at nearby Fort Pelly to replace their worn-out clothes. By the following summer, the Fort Livingstone Mounties were more likely to be seen in deerskin and foxtail hats than the ragged remains of their red serge.

Nevertheless, the Mounties carried on, fighting cold and boredom by printing the *Swan River Daily Police News* and forming a cricket club and band. In 1876, when the Northwest Territories Act was proclaimed, Lieutenant-Governor David Laird moved here to hold the first session of government before the capital was moved to Battleford.

That was also the year that Sitting Bull and the Sioux fled from the United States to Wood Mountain after wiping out the Seventh Cavalry at the Battle of the Little Bighorn. Because of the volatile situation their flight to Canada created, the North-West Mounted Police moved their headquarters south to Fort Walsh. Fort Livingstone was abandoned in 1878 and burned down six years later.

But one thing all those Swan River Mounties probably remembered about Fort Livingstone was the garter snakes. The area literally crawled with them. One summer, the officers celebrated Victoria Day with a snake-killing contest. The winner dispatched 110 in half an hour. Explorer and geographer John Macoun visited the fort and described the local wildlife:

Coiled on every bush and forming cables from the size of a hawser up to writhing masses three feet in diameter were snakes from one to five feet in length. Around the hollow, but more particularly on the sunny side, they lay in great heaps, so closely packed together that nothing but heads could be seen. It was terrible to look upon the glittering eyes that were fixed upon us by thousands, and see the forked tongues thrust out and withdrawn as the perpetual hiss unceasingly fell on our ears. After a few minutes . . . we saw beauty in every fold. The rays of the western sun falling on their bodies at every angle caused a mingling of color that none but a master pen could depict.

Chapter 8

The North-West Calling Region

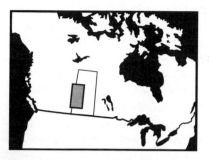

Fur Trade Draws Colorful Characters to North-West

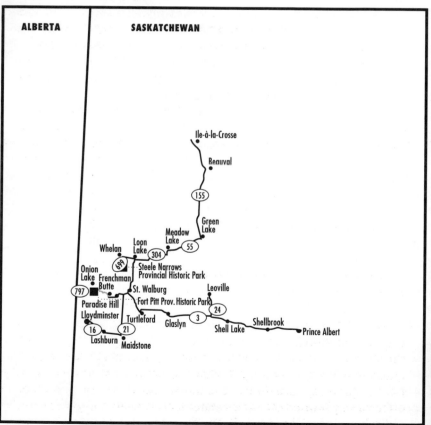

ALBERTA

SASKATCHEWAN

Ile-à-la-Crosse

Beauval

155

Green Lake

Meadow Lake   55

Loon Lake   304

Whelan

699

Steele Narrows Provincial Historic Park

Onion Lake   Frenchman Butte

797

Paradise Hill

Lloydminster

St. Walburg

Fort Pitt Prov. Historic Park

Leoville

24

16

21

Turtleford   Glaslyn   3   Shell Lake   Shellbrook

Lashburn   Maidstone   Prince Albert

A LTHOUGH FUR TRADERS were active all over the old North-West, it was the North that provided the real bonanza. In the Athabasca and Mackenzie districts, drained by rivers such as the Churchill, the furs were the richest and most plentiful. And this region of Saskatchewan was the gateway to that vast area. They are tiny communities now, but in their time Green Lake and Ile-à-la-Crosse were both major jumping-off points for both Nor'Westers and Baymen; Green Lake was the Hudson's Bay Company's supply depot for the entire North.

Throughout its history, this region has remained on the frontier of the frontier. It was the site of the last battles of the North-West Rebellion and took longer than most areas to be settled. Perhaps because of that status, the region has attracted more than its share of colorful and dynamic personalities. Here, the malevolent, violent fur trader Samuel Black had a post. Here was where the Cree leader Big Bear brought his people and where his journeys ended. The bumbling Royal Canadian Mounted Police Inspector Francis Dickens (third son of the novelist Charles Dickens) was stationed here. And here was where the Reverend Isaac Barr (part visionary, part con man) brought hundreds of naïve, inexperienced colonists.

The main flow of trade to the North no longer moves through here; the green-as-grass homesteaders have founded prosperous cities, and the area has long been peaceful. But the old stories and characters still hold fascination, and the echoes of those busy turbulent days of the old North-West can still be heard.

ALONG HIGHWAYS 16 AND 23

First Commercial Oil Well Drilled
Highway 16, 45 Avenue, Lloydminster

Geologists and drillers had been already been poking holes in the earth around here for seven years on Good Friday 1934, when the Discovery well blew in about .6 miles (1 km) northeast of here, gushing in at 16.75 million cubic feet (.47 million cubic meters) of natural gas a day. Gas didn't have much value back then and was often simply burned off out the flare stack. However, Lloydminster didn't have to wait long for oil. The first indications came in 1935.

By 1945, the area's first commercial producing well had been drilled about 4 miles (6 km) south of here, the first tapping of a significant pool that continues to be profitable. The oilpatch—both servicing and drilling wells—is still a big part of the area's economy, and a heavy oil upgrader was built here specifically to handle the local crude's high sulfur content.

The Blairmore Formation oil and gas around Lloydminster is just part of the energy industry's history in Saskatchewan. Oilmen were punching holes through the sod near Belle Plain as far back as 1888 and around Saskatoon in 1906. But they had to wait until January 4, 1952, for the big-time gusher, when Fosterton No. 1 blew in west of Swift Current. That well produced continually from February 1952 to November 1996. Over that time, it yielded 4,839,602 barrels of oil. The field is still producing.

Fosterton No. 1 touched off an oil boom. Within 20 years, that corner of the province had 1,029 oil wells and 373 gas wells.

Hunters, Traders, Settlers Wear Meadow Lake–Battleford Trail
Highway 4, .3 miles (.6 km) north of Glaslyn

Long before highways and railways laced the prairies, settlements and gathering places were linked by trails worn through the bush by Indians hunters, then Métis cart trains and finally settlers' buckboards. The Meadow Lake–Battleford Trail, pioneered by hunters and fur traders, linked the bustling settlement of Battleford with Meadow Lake. The Mounties patrolled here, and homesteaders got first sight of their quarter sections (65 square ha) from these tracks. As late as the 1930s, farmers whose southern fields had dried up and blown away in the drought came through here seeking lusher land. Eventually, surveyed roads replaced the trail that once passed this spot and the old path was plowed up and planted.

Doomed Explorer Follows Fort Carlton–Green Lake Trail
Highway 24, 6 miles (10 km) south of Leoville, just north of Creek River

---

Pioneered and developed by fur traders, the Green Lake–Fort Carlton Trail was the fastest link between the Saskatchewan and the Churchill river systems and it was followed by anyone who wanted to get into the North. Of course, fast is relative. This trail was 93 miles (150 km) of rough corduroy road at its best and soggy, mosquito-filled muskeg and beaver meadow at its worst. It took at least six days to travel it one way. Still, it was the gateway to the North and one of the best-known explorers to travel it was Sir John Franklin.

Before his doomed 1845 quest for the Northwest Passage, Franklin spent from 1819 to 1821 mapping the Arctic coast, traveling overland up the Coppermine River to its mouth on the Beaufort Sea. On his way he passed through here from Fort Carlton in mid-February 1820.

This part of his journey seems to have been pleasant enough. He recorded the good habitat for beaver, otter and muskrat, and noted that the great depth of Green Lake kept the ice off it until December, making it a good source of late-season fish. The weather was very cold, but the trail was well-packed and his party made good progress on their snowshoes, stomping as much as 15 miles (24 km) a day. Franklin seems to have found his travel legs over this trail. After arriving in Green Lake, he wrote with pride, "Mr. Back and I did not need the rest, having completely surmounted the pain which the walking in snowshoes had occasioned."

Cree Chief Earns Government Gratitude
Highway 3, in Shell Lake Regional Park, Shell Lake

Mistawasis, a Cree leader, was also the uncle of Poundmaker, another influential leader. But while they may have been family, they found themselves at serious odds during the negotiation of Treaty No 6, signed in 1876.

Poundmaker, although he ultimately signed the document, was deeply suspicious of it and bargained hard for improvements. Mistawasis, or Big Child, was satisfied with the treaty's original guarantees—much to the government's relief, for Mistawasis was an important chief. His signature was important at a time when dissident chiefs such as Big Bear were trying to unite opposition to the treaties to force more concessions.

Mistawasis earned even more government gratitude during the North-West Rebellion, when he helped convince his people not to ally themselves too closely with the rebel Métis, despite the pleas of Métis leader Louis Riel. A combined Indian–Métis rebellion was Ottawa's greatest fear. Together they would have vastly outnumbered and outgunned the whites, and could have greatly disrupted the settlement of the North-West.

Mistawasis remained an influential chief until his death in 1895.

Whites Like "Grasshoppers that Cloud the Sky," Says Chief
Highway 3, in Shell Lake Regional Park, Shell Lake

Star Blanket (or Ahtahkakoup, also spelled Ahchacoosacoot-acoopits) was a Cree chief willing from the start to sign Treaty No 6, which delivered the middle third of what was to become Saskatchewan to the Canadian government in 1876.

"Can we stop the power of the white man from spreading out over the land like the grasshoppers that cloud the sky?" Star Blanket asked. But hard-liners, including chiefs Poundmaker and Badger, wanted guarantees the government would see them through the difficult transition from hunting to farming. They wanted training, tools, stock, seed and, most of all, food. Eventually, Poundmaker and his allies negotiated more help to start farms, as well as a "medicine chest" and a clause promising aid during "pestilence, or . . . general famine."

Star Blanket took his people to a reserve at Sandy Lake. Reverend J. Hines had opened an Anglican mission there two years earlier and came to know Star Blanket well. "I have no hesitation in saying a better Indian never roamed the plains," said Hines. Star Blanket died in 1896 at more than 80 years of age.

ALONG HIGHWAY 26

Green-As-Grass Colonists Lay Foundation for Prosperous City
Highway 16 and 45 Avenue, Weaver Park, Lloydminster

Talk about no previous experience. The immigrants who founded St. John's Minster and the now-prosperous city that surrounds it had no idea what they were in for when they sailed

Barr colonist homestead near Lloydminster.

from England in March 1903. Lured by the word-and-paper cas-
tles of Reverend Isaac Barr, the Barr colonists have become a
prairie watchword for naïveté triumphing over trouble.

When he arrived in England in 1902 with a scheme for an all-
British colony on the plains, Barr was an Ontario clergymen with
a spotty record of service in his native province, the North-West
and the United States. Exaggerating his knowledge of both farming and the climate, he wrote such stretchers as "Agriculture on
the prairies is simple, the work not very hard." Joined in his
noble endeavor by fellow cleric Reverend George Exton Lloyd,
he soon had hundreds of Britons eager to escape the island's
overcrowded, industrial-revolution cities. Barr moved fast, and
by the end of 1902, he had been to Canada, reserved every second homestead in eight townships of land west of Battleford and
returned to England. When the overcrowded vessel *Lake
Manitoba* sailed from Liverpool the next spring, she carried
1,960 hopeful homesteaders who were soon to call themselves
Barr's Lambs.

Many Canadians feared the West was being overrun with
East Europeans, so a boatload of British settlers was politically
popular and the Canadian government wanted to see the colony
succeed. It had, however, growing doubts about Barr. His
advance agents had appeared in Winnipeg and Battleford
charged with lining up supplies for the coming homesteaders,

but none had any money. Minister of the Interior Clifford Sifton sensed disaster. He told his officials to have a supply of tents awaiting the colonists at Saskatoon and to make sure food and firewood were cached along the route from that city to Battleford and beyond.

And a good thing he did. When the colonists arrived at Saskatoon on a sweltering April 17, 1903, Barr's tents were still a day behind. When their baggage did arrive, it was unceremoniously dumped on the train platform. The colonists had begun to doubt Barr on the sea crossing, and now their anger flared up again. The promised stagecoaches to Battleford for the women and children were nowhere to be found; the North-West plains were far from the green and pleasant land they had been led to expect; Saskatoon was, as one colonist described it, a heap of "large boxes rushed up without regard to architecture or comfort." The crew that was supposed to ready the colony site got lost, mired their cattle in muskeg and returned to Saskatoon after wandering the plains for three days. Local merchants gouged the colonists for supplies, for which Barr was demanding a 10 percent commission, and Barr seemed to be nickel-and-diming everyone to death, coming up with a new surcharge every day. As well, it was immediately clear to immigration officials that few of the supposed homesteaders had enough money to set themselves up and fewer still knew how to farm even if they could afford to. An employment bureau was set up, and farming classes were hurriedly convened.

Finally, on April 24, the colonists began to move out. The plan to move in one guided wagon train had fallen apart, so the settlers were on their own. Fewer than one in 20 knew how to hitch a team. Some referred to charts; others drew chalk diagrams directly on their animals. The hugely overloaded wagons—baggage at Saskatoon had included at least six pianos, books, bathtubs, bicycles, formal wear and more than 100 dogs—got mired in one spring bog after another. When the early heat failed, the colonists fought through blizzards, then prairie fires. Their inexperience caused them to overwork and underfeed their horses. One freighter counted 18 dead horses on the way to Battleford. Some gave up and pitched tents along the trail, hoping to sell their possessions for enough money to sail home.

When they finally made it to the colony in early May, there was nothing: no lumber, no buildings and supplies only at prohibitive prices. It was the last straw. In a meeting at Battleford on May 16, the colonists removed Barr as their leader and installed Lloyd.

The two had made an odd couple from the start. Barr was stocky, verbose and mustachioed; Lloyd was tall, gaunt and side-burned. Barr was mercurial, thin-skinned and not entirely trust-worthy; Lloyd inspired loyalty, was upright to a fault and a good organizer. Now Barr was out and Lloyd was in. Barr refunded money to anyone who felt he had been cheated, turned over anything of value to the colony and left for the United States.

Still, the colony got off to a slow start. Because Lloyd at first insisted that no non-British homesteaders be allowed to settle in the colony, the green colonists had few experienced neighbors to learn from. Many became preoccupied with building the St. John's Minster, establishing committees on municipal govern-ment, even forming musical societies and tennis clubs than with breaking land. But finally, after a few tough winters, things got rolling. By 1907, the local immigration agent reported that Lloydminster had surpassed all expectations. The community was on its way to becoming today's city.

E.J. Ashton, a Norfolk bank teller and Boer War veteran before he became a Barr colonist, later wrote, "Strangely enough, as the years rolled by, it was apparent that several among the most suc-cessful farmers were men who had no previous experience."

Long and Winding Road for Fur Trader's Final Rest
Grid 797, 13.7 miles (22 km) west and south of Frenchman Butte

---

Fort Pitt shipped innumerable pieces of cargo over its 60-year history, but the bones of John Rowand may have been the most unusual. Rowand was the chief factor at Fort Edmonton, which made him a big man in the fur trade back then because that was both the terminus of the Carlton Trail and one of the best sources of both furs and pemmican in the Hudson's Bay Company's far-flung empire. Rowand was a big man for other reasons, too, nicknamed Big Mountain for both his proportions and his forceful, volcanic temperament.

In the spring of 1854, Rowand was in Fort Pitt on his way east. Two of his Métis paddlers got into a fight, and, flushed and angry, Rowand stepped between the voyageurs. Suddenly, Rowand suffered a massive heart attack and died on the spot. So the odyssey began.

Rowand's will stipulated he be buried in Montreal, and his great friend George Simpson, the governor of the Hudson's Bay Company, had the desire and the means to see his old comrade's wish granted. The next spring, Rowand was disinterred and the flesh boiled off his old bones, which were then sealed in a keg filled with rum as a preservative. Simpson dispatched his own canoe and voyageurs to bring the keg to Red River. But the superstitious paddlers, attributing a storm that blew up while crossing Lake Winnipeg to their cargo, threw the keg overboard. Simpson was furious and ordered his men back to find the keg. Amazingly, they did. Simpson had the keg stored until fear of the jinx passed, then had it shipped north to York Factory on the shores of Hudson Bay.

Because there was no link between that post and Montreal, the keg went on a circuitous route to London, England, where Hudson's Bay Company officials greeted it with solemn ceremony, complete with muffled drums and flags. The keg was lost for a while in a Liverpool warehouse but was eventually shipped out to Montreal. Almost exactly four years after he died, John Rowand was buried in Mount Royal cemetery. When the wandering keg was opened, out poured not rum, but water.

Fort Pitt Falls in Rebellion
Grid 797, 13.7 miles (22 km) west and south of Frenchman Butte

Fort Pitt was originally built by the Hudson's Bay Company to help handle the burgeoning trade along the Carlton Trail. But it is best remembered for its role in the North-West Rebellion—and for its commanding officer, the inept Inspector Francis Dickens. The fort was originally built in 1829 as a way station for fur brigades traveling between Fort Edmonton and Fort Garry. The post's first buildings were transferred to the site from another Hudson's Bay Company post at a location then known as Dog Rump Creek.

Life at Fort Pitt followed much the same seasonal rotation as other posts. Fall was spent organizing the trade goods that had arrived by York boat or Red River cart over the summer. Wood for the coming winter was cut, and snowshoes and dog

The Fort Pitt North-West Mounted Police detachment in 1884, just before the outbreak of the rebellion. Commanding Officer Francis Dickens, son of the novelist Charles Dickens, is the bearded man standing alongside the third row.

harnesses were repaired. The winter was spent hunkered down in the fort, hunting and fishing as necessary. This was also the time when local trappers came to trade, settling their accounts with the company with furs or provisions such as pemmican or dried buffalo tongues. Trading finished up in the spring and the company's proceeds were packed up and shipped east. Summers were spent hunting, making pemmican and tending gardens.

And so it continued until April 3, 1885, when a settler named Henry Quinn brought news of the Frog Lake Massacre. The fort residents and area settlers found themselves in a bad spot, unable to escape because the fort's wagons had all been captured at Frog Lake, and the commander of the local North-West Mounted Police detachment found himself in way over his head. Francis Dickens, the third son of novelist Charles Dickens, had already failed at medicine, business and journalism when his famous father pulled some strings to get him a North-West Mounted Police commission. Deaf, alcoholic and tactless, Dickens Jr.'s superior officers called him "totally unfit to be an officer in the Mounted Police"; his father had given him the truly Dickensian nickname of Chickenstalker.

After 10 days of trying to shore up the fort's defenses with such measures as stacking bags of flour against the inside of the palisade, Dickens sent out three scouts on April 13. Three hours later, about 250 Cree appeared on the hill overlooking the fort. War chief Wandering Spirit gave the fort his terms: his men had no quarrel with the Hudson's Bay Company or settlers, but the Mounties were representatives of the government, so Wandering Spirit wanted them dead.

"We will make short work of them and kill them as if they were young ducks, but we want you to get your wife and children out of danger," Wandering Spirit said.

Dickens didn't know what to do. His small force, already reduced by the three scouts, could hardly hold off Wandering Spirit. Retreat seemed the best solution, but that would have meant abandoning the civilians to warriors fresh from the events of Frog Lake. All night he thought while the Cree drove the fort's cattle into their camp and the settlers cut gun slits in the fort's walls.

The next morning the two sides were parleying in the Cree camp when Dickens' returning scouts stumbled in. The Cree, thinking they were under attack, opened fire, killing one man and wounding another so badly he barely made it to the fort's walls. Finally, the fort's head trader and Chief Big Bear, whom Wandering Spirit had replaced, convinced the warriors to let the police retreat.

It was an ignominious retreat, but Big Bear hinted strongly to Dickens he'd better take the offer. "The young men are all wild and hard to keep in hand," he said.

On April 14, the traders and settlers became prisoners of the Cree, while the humbled police escaped the surrendered fort downriver in a scow.

The fort was then looted. Two days later some of the settlers were allowed back to salvage what they could of their possessions. One family got their Bible. Another played a last tune on the family organ, which frightened the Cree so badly they immediately chopped it up. The next day the fort was burned to the ground.

After the rebellion, the Hudson's Bay Company rebuilt the fort under Chief Trader Angus McKay, known to the local trappers as Kas-pa-pe-wazee-samp-okee-sah, or "one and sixpence a yard," the price McKay continually quoted for bolts of colored Hudson's Bay Company cotton. McKay was also the fort's last trader. It was shut in 1889 and moved to Onion Lake.

McKay eventually moved to Prince Albert, where he became a well-known local old-timer, often hailed in the street with his old nickname by area Cree.

Rebellion Disrupts Peaceful Settlement at Onion Lake
On gravel road about .6 miles (1 km) east of entrance to town of Onion Lake

---

After chiefs Seekaskootch and Makaoo chose their reserve in 1879, it didn't take long for a bustling community to develop on the busy trail between Battleford and Fort Edmonton. But all that was disrupted during the North-West Rebellion of 1885. Onion Lake was close to Frog Lake, and the violence of the Frog Lake Massacre was to spill over to this peaceful community. One of Onion Lake's ministers, Reverend Felix Marchand, visiting Frog Lake that April 2, numbered among the dead.

Meanwhile some of the Onion Lake Cree had gathered at the home of George Mann, the reserve's farming instructor. At about nine o'clock that night, some Cree friends of Mann's came to tell him what had happened that day and to warn him that he could be next. Mann and his family were shown a secluded trail to Fort Pitt and set off that night. One of Mann's children described what happened next:

After driving around for some time and through a large swamp of snow and water, Father found he was driving in a circle, decided to stop until the moon rose, to get the direction of Fort Pitt. While waiting we could hear the shrill war whoops of the Indians, and firing of guns. They were plundering our home and the warehouses. We were afraid that at any moment our horse might [whinny] or the dog, which had followed us, would bark and reveal our whereabouts.

Mann and his family reached Fort Pitt at about 1:00 A.M.

Eventually, peace returned to Onion Lake and the small settlement picked up where it left off. After the rebellion, it got a Hudson's Bay Company post and a police detachment. Within a few years it also had religious boarding schools and a telegraph office. It had to happen without one of the reserve's founder's, however. Chief Seekaskootch was killed in a surprise attack at Steele Narrows during the rebellion.

Desperate Times Drive Settlers to Desperate Politics
Highway 26, Loon Lake

By the late 1930s, most Canadians were looking across the Atlantic with mounting horror as Hitler's Nazi Party tightened its grip on Germany. But in Loon Lake, a picture of Hitler held an honored place in the front window of the local store. Desperate times had driven local German settlers to the desperate radical politics of the Deutscher Bund, Canada's homegrown Nazis.

In 1929, a group of 20 German families came to Loon Lake. The mixed group of small farmers, small businessmen and artisans had it tough right from the start. Heavy bush had to be cleared. Rough sod houses were all they had to live in on their remote homesteads. And to make matters worse, the Depression caused crop failures and destroyed markets for farm produce just as they were getting started. The immigrants were forced to work off their farms, shoot game, garden and accept relief. Their dreams crushed, many began to look back fondly on the Old Country: "If I had worked so hard and been as thrifty in Germany, I would have gotten ahead," one wrote.

Some began to embrace the Deutscher Bund, founded in Waterloo, Ontario, in 1934. The Bund called itself a social organization, but it combined evenings of German culture, songs and language with national socialist politics. It celebrated January 20, the date Hitler became chancellor of Germany, as well as Hitler's April 20 birthday. By 1939, the Bund had 2,000 members in 71 chapters across Canada. About half were in Saskatchewan, where most recent German immigrants lived, although they comprised less than one percent of the province's German population.

Loon Lake's Bundists were active by 1934, meeting regularly to hear lectures on the heroes of Hitler's 1923 *putsch*. Within a few years, they were well indoctrinated, demanding separate schools for German children, and criticizing Canada's "Jewish dominated government." In 1939, nineteen of the original immigrant families pulled up stakes and returned to Hitler's Germany. Most ended up working in munitions factories. Their homesteads were sold to farmers from the annexed Sudentenland, immigrants fleeing the same regime the Bundists were rushing home to embrace.

Regina members of Deutscher Bund on their way to Saskatchewan Tag, 1934.

Stubborn, Independent Big Bear Defeated in the End
Highway 3, next to RCMP station in Loon Lake

One of the greatest Cree chiefs from the time before the treaties sent natives to reserves, Big Bear (Mistahimaskwa) roamed the plains from the Cypress Hills and the upper Missouri River to the parklands and lakes of what is now central Saskatchewan. But even that vast territory was not enough to protect him from changing days, and it was here that Big Bear's journeys came to an end.

Stubborn and independent, Big Bear was the last major chief to sign Treaty No 6. Although it had been negotiated in 1876, Big Bear didn't make his mark until 1882, forced into it by the failure of the hunt. Even then, he refused to select a reserve and settle down.

Big Bear's goal was to unite all Indians so they could speak to Ottawa with one voice. He also wanted a series of adjoining reserves in the south to form, in effect, an Indian territory. He failed in both attempts, done in by government maneuvering and old intertribal suspicions. By the end of 1884, he was losing influence in favor of the Cree warrior societies. When news came next spring that Louis Riel's Métis had thumped the Mounties at Duck Lake, the warriors under Wandering Spirit took over. It was

Cree Chief Big Bear.

Wandering Spirit who took charge at the Frog Lake Massacre, although Big Bear was to carry much of the blame.

Wandering Spirit led the Cree successfully against Fort Pitt. But they began to retreat after the skirmish at Frenchman Butte and were badly stung at Steele Narrows. Although Big Bear did not take an active part in that battle, the story is told that during the shooting, Big Bear walked between the lines with a bear's claw hanging around his neck. He believed nothing could harm him as long as he wore the claw of his animal spirit protector, and his presence formed an invisible shield for his people.

Nevertheless, Steele Narrows was their last battle. The Cree retreated farther east to this area, where they scattered. The warrior leaders still surviving either fled or surrendered. Big Bear slipped past the soldiers looking for him and gave himself up later at Fort Carlton. In court, he was sentenced to three years in prison.

Big Bear, at 5'5" (165 cm), was short, stocky and strong. He was a powerful orator and owed his influence solely to the quality of his leadership and force of his personality. Deeply religious, he wore at appropriate times a power bundle given him by the Bear Spirit, the Cree's most powerful spirit. After less than two years in jail, the prison doctor reported that "Convict No. 103 . . . is getting worse. He is showing signs of great debility by fainting spells which are growing more frequent." He was released early on March 4, 1887, and went to live on Poundmaker's reserve. He died there within a year.

Last Battle an Inconclusive Skirmish
Grid 699, 6.2 miles (10 km) west of Loon Lake

The last battle of the North-West Rebellion, Steele Narrows was an inconclusive skirmish between rebels on the run and a hastily organized party of cowboys and policemen who fought weeks after the fate of the revolt had been decided. Louis Riel and his rebel Métis fought hard to preserve their lands and way of life, but their main stronghold at Batoche had fallen on May 12, 1885, and by the end of that month, the Canadian government was mopping up. The Cree, once led by Big Bear and now commanded by War Chief Wandering Spirit, were the government's main concern, and after the battle at Frenchman's Butte failed to subdue them, Steele's scouts were given the job.

The scouts were commanded by Sam Steele, already a legend in the North-West Mounted Police. He had been pulled away from keeping order on the Canadian Pacific Railway construction crews to help put down the rebellion with the Alberta Field Force. Steele's force of about 40 plainsmen—mostly southern Alberta cowboys—took off in pursuit. They caught up with the Cree at Steele Narrows on June 3.

It had been tough traveling for Wandering Spirit and his people. The terrain was hilly and swampy, the weather wet, and their party included not only women and children but a number of hostages from Fort Pitt. Most had camped along Makwa Lake, but some pitched their tepees on the narrows into Sanderson Bay. It was this smaller camp the scouts attacked. Three Cree were reportedly shot as they left their tepees.

Hearing gunfire, Cree from the main camp rushed over and fired on the scouts from high ground. The scouts backed off to their own hill and returned fire. At one point, the Cree sent out a hostage to negotiate a surrender but the troops, misunderstanding, fired on him and drove him away. After three hours Steele decided there was no way to advance, especially with his men running low on ammunition. Three scouts were wounded, and Steele ordered a retreat to seek medical attention for them.

The Cree dead totaled four, including Seekaskootch (Chief Cut Arm), whose intervention had saved the life of an Anglican missionary at the start of the rebellion. Disheartened, the Cree split in two parties. Big Bear took his Plains Cree south, eventually surrendering on July 2 at Fort Carlton. The Woods Cree and 27 hostages kept heading north, where the hostages were finally released at Lac des Isles. The Woods Cree surrendered in late June at Fort Pitt; Wandering Spirit, who had remained with them, was eventually hanged for his part in the rebellion on November 27, 1885.

Small Community Once Key to Fur Trade
Highway 55, 32 miles(53 km) northeast of Meadow Lake at north end of Green Lake

---

It's a small community now, but Green Lake was once one of the fur trade's key distribution points. Through Green Lake passed all goods flowing to and from the rich fur grounds of the Athabasca and Mackenzie districts. The North West Company had a post here as long ago as 1782, seventeen years before the Hudson's Bay Company arrived. As at so many other posts in the lawless North-West, there was open conflict between the two posts until the rival companies merged in 1821.

In April 1885, more than 220,460 pounds (100,000 kg) of supplies sat waiting here ready to be shipped to posts north after spring breakup. Among those supplies were 200 rifles and plenty of ammunition, which caused no little concern for Chief Trader James Sinclair, who feared their seizure by rebellious Métis or Cree. He cached them along the riverbank and was later able to convince a party of Cree that he had no weapons in stock.

Because this post was on such an important route to the North, anyone with business there usually passed through here.

The great explorer and map maker David Thompson visited Green Lake shortly after he defected from the Baymen to join the Nor'Westers. So did Sir John Franklin during his exploration of the northern interior from 1819 to 1821. His travels took him to the mouth of the Coppermine River. Franklin later commanded an ill-fated voyage that was lost with all hands trying to find the Northwest Passage. His loss in 1845 sparked one of the greatest searches of Victorian times. Between 1848 and 1852, the Royal Navy sent no fewer than six expeditions into the Arctic to find Franklin and his men. The Hudson's Bay Company and an American group also sent searchers. Finally, in 1854 explorer John Rae found evidence of the expedition's loss with all hands.

Business Rivalry Gets Ugly at Fort Black
Across from Ile-à-la-Crosse, on peninsula (with no public access)

The rivalry for furs between the Hudson's Bay Company and the independent traders wasn't pretty anywhere in the old North-West. But rarely was it taken farther than by Samuel Black, a man described by a contemporary as "ghastly, raw boned and lanthorn jawed, yet strong vigorous and active . . . equal to the cutting of a throat with perfect deliberation." In 1810, Ile-à-la-Crosse was an important gateway to the Athabasca fur region and both the Hudson's Bay Company and the XY Company (later absorbed by the Nor'Westers) had posts here. But the local Bayman, a worthy, skilled explorer and trader named Peter Fidler, was utterly outclassed by Black in guile and ruthlessness.

The two weren't strangers. A few years before, by Lake Chipewyan, Black had raided Chipewyan camps that had traded with Fidler, slashed his fishing nets, torched his woodpile, tore up his garden and physically blocked trappers from entering his post. Black had howled all night outside the Hudson's Bay Company post, tossed rocks at its walls and once covered its chimney top with bark, nearly asphyxiating the occupants. He had even killed and eaten the post's dog.

Here, Black and a companion named Peter Skene Ogden got up to the same tricks. The two invaded the Hudson's Bay Company post and beat one of its clerks. The outnumbered Baymen were forbidden to leave the post, and Fidler's son was shot at, though not injured. Fidler eventually abandoned the post in 1811.

When the North West and Hudson's Bay companies merged in 1821, the Hudson's Bay Company's Governor George Simpson described Black as

The strangest man I ever knew. So wary and suspicious that it is scarcely possible to get a direct answer from him on any point, and when he does speak or write on any subject so prolix that it is quite fatiguing to attempt following him. A perfectly honest man and his generosity might be considered indicative of a warmth of heart if he was not known to be a cold blooded fellow who could be guilty of any Cruelty and would be a perfect Tyrant had he had power.

Such men, apparently, were useful in the fur trade. Black was eventually promoted to be the Hudson's Bay Company's chief factor of the Kamloops district, where he was killed by an Indian in 1841.

First Catholic Mission in Saskatchewan Established at St. John the Baptist Mission

Highway 155, 83 miles (155 km) north of Green Lake, then south on Municipal Road 908 for 12 miles (21 km) to Ile-à-la-Crosse, at churchgrounds on south shore of Ile-à-la-Crosse

The yard here is considered the site of the first Roman Catholic mission built in what is now Saskatchewan. Founded on September 10, 1846, it was followed in 1860 by a school and a convent-run dispensary for the sick. The buildings were burned down and flooded out several times over the years, but the work of caring for the sick carried on. In 1927, the provincial government built a hospital for this community, which came to be run by the same nuns who had already served it for three generations.

If 1846 seems late for priests to become a fixture in a land that had seen traders for nearly 75 years, it may be because the fur trade was not that encouraging to clergy. The missionaries considered hunting and trapping heathen activities and tried to turn native hunters into farmers. But out on the land, catching furs to bring to the posts was exactly where the traders wanted the people. As well, churchmen were prone to raising a fuss and causing trouble over long-standing fur trade practices such as country marriages. Evangelizing, in short, was seen as both a threat to and a distraction from the business of turning furry animals into pelts. Hudson's Bay Company Governor George Simpson once wrote that preaching Christ in the wilderness had little more effect than "filling the pockets and bellies of some hungry missionaries and rearing the Indians in habits of indolence."

So while priests and ministers were occasional visitors in fur country, there was no permanent church anywhere in the Hudson's Bay Company's domain until 1818, when Father Joseph Provencher established a Catholic mission in the Red River country. Two years later John West of the Church of England joined him.

Chapter 9

The Northern Shores Region

Deceptive
Wilderness

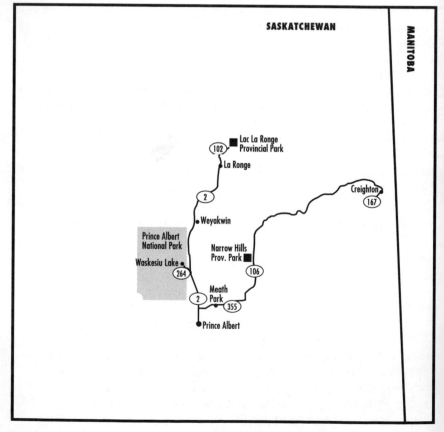

D RIVING THROUGH the vast forests and deep, blue lakes of this region, you might think that it is a classic example of the old saw about Canada having too much geography and not enough history. That's understandable. Much of this landscape does look untouched by humanity—and in its more remote corners, it is.

But there are some great stories here, some of the best-known stories in the whole country. Here, for example, was the home of Grey Owl, the world-famous Indian conservationist who turned out to have been born in England under the name Archie Belaney. Some of Canada's best-known figures have left their marks here. Here's where former Prime Minister John Diefenbaker got his start. And here's where a second former prime minister, William Lyon Mackenzie King, came when he needed a sure seat in parliament. Prince Albert National Park is the legacy of that bit of politicking. There are, of course, fur trade stories. Peter Pond, a Nor'Wester infamous for his violent ways, was briefly a resident here—not so briefly, however, that he didn't leave under suspicion of murder.

So don't let the apparent wilderness fool you. Plenty has happened here. And while the main attraction of this beautiful part of the province is its wilderness, don't miss the stories for the trees.

ALONG HIGHWAY 2

John Diefenbaker Goes from Home-Built Office to Prime Minister's Office
246–19th Street West, Prince Albert

John Diefenbaker was a well-known figure in Canadian life by the time he came to live in this house. But when he first came to Prince Albert in 1924, he was still an ambitious young lawyer, looking to make his mark.

By then, he had already been practicing law for five years in Wakaw, population 350, farther south on Highway 2. He had started from nothing. He built his office himself, a 12 x 16' (3.7 x 4.9 m)space with a desk, waiting room heated with a wood stove, no secretary and no plumbing. Before his law career, he'd been a teacher, a traveling Bible literature salesman and an army officer, so he was quite willing to do what was needed to make a living. Until his law practice took off, selling insurance and arranging mortgages paid the Wakaw bills, which, given his abstemious nondrinking and nonsmoking life, were modest enough.

At 24, Diefenbaker's court career began, quite literally, with a bang. His first case was the defense of a farmer charged with shooting his neighbor's son. Diefenbaker, with a little help from a former classmate and future Supreme Court Justice Emmett Hall, won the case. The serious, ambitious young lawyer was soon a fixture in Wakaw, helping run local sports clubs and sitting on town council.

Diefenbaker became a successful defense lawyer when he moved to Prince Albert, but politics were never far from his mind. Success with the electorate, however, proved a lot tougher than success with a jury. He ran for the Conservatives in the 1925 federal election, even though he had supported the provincial Liberal candidate a few weeks earlier. He lost that fight and lost again in the by-election the following year against a parachuted William Lyon Mackenzie King. "The Liberal Party is noted for its bulldog determination," Dief fulminated during the campaign. "Well, a bulldog is noted for its determination to hang on, but not for its intelligence." Diefenbaker was no slouch in the bull-doggedness department himself, for he lost provincially in 1929 and again in 1933, when he ran for mayor of Prince Albert. He was elected provincial Conservative leader in 1936, but his party failed to win a single seat in the 1938 election. Finally, in 1940, he won election to the House of Commons. His parliamentary career was off, culminating in two terms as prime minister from 1957 to 1963.

Diefenbaker dreamed of a national unity forged from Canadians putting aside their past allegiances to build something new and uniquely their own. He worked all his career for this, but hinted at it first in Prince Albert on June 19, 1925, when he told local Conservatives, "The word 'New Canadian' has got to be eliminated and a united nationality developed, instead of the hybrid variety as it exists today."

Beloved Natural Playground a Political Payoff
North on Highway 263, or west on Highway 264, Prince Albert National Park

The lakes in this area have been popular spots for many centuries. Indians used the narrows on Lake Waskesiu as long ago as 5,000 years, and when the settlers came, they found these wooded, productive lakes just right for fishing and camping. But it took a blatant piece of political favor-trading to make them a national park.

The 1925 federal election was a squeaker for the Liberals. They had won the most seats, but they could form a majority in the House of Commons only with the support of the Progressive Party. As well, party leader William Lyon Mackenzie King had lost his seat. He needed a safe Liberal riding to put him back in the House, and Prince Albert was judged to be one.

That was fine with the local Liberals—a prime minister as your Member of Parliament could come in handy. And they did have one small request, which they outlined in a meeting in King's railway car. The forestry reserve northwest of town, already subject to some cottage development, would make a lovely national park and help boost the local tourism industry. Could King see his way to making it so? King thought he could.

The votes were duly delivered. King won the February 15, 1926, by-election (clobbering a political neophyte named John Diefenbaker) and the park was declared on March 24, 1927.

On August 10, 1928, Prince Albert National Park was officially opened. King gave a speech as flags fluttered around him, then took a swim in the lake to cool off from the summer heat. To thank King for his role in founding the park, citizens paid for and gave him a new log cabin overlooking Waskesiu Lake. King slept there that night after spending the day in the park. He seemed to have had a good time, but that was to be his only visit. He never spent another night in his cabin, and ever after pretty much ignored the national park he was largely responsible for creating. The cabin still stands.

Like those at other national parks, the facilities here were soon to benefit from the Great Depression. By the fall of 1930, the park was home to five relief camps, full of young, rootless unemployed men. For a little cash plus room and board, they filled in muskeg; helped build highways 263 and 240; installed drainage

Early swimmers at Prince Albert National Park.

in the campgrounds, built a breakwater; constructed the first nine holes of the golf course and laid out the next nine; erected kitchen shelters, tennis courts, the park's administration building and community hall; and put in its sidewalks. In January 1933, there were 1,000 relief camp workers here, with "subversives" sent to outlying camps to isolate them. By most accounts, the park was a popular posting: the camps offered healthy, useful, outdoor work with regular meals, all of which must have sounded pretty good back then.

The relief camps closed in 1935, but similar ones reopened six years later for conscientious objectors to World War II, most of them pacifist Mennonites. They filled four 50-man camps around the park, clearing new trails and widening old ones, pitching horseshoes and singing hymns when not at work.

Grey Owl Both Con and Conservationist
Beaver Lodge, Prince Albert National Park, access by canoe across Kingsmere Lake or by 12-mile (20-km) hiking trail from south end of Kingsmere Lake

---

The lights came down in the crowded lecture hall. Excited whispers rose and fell with the rustle of leaves in a gust of wind. Then, like a full moon in a dark sky, a spotlight picked out a solitary figure on the stage. As a gramophone played the haunting arpeggios of Beethoven's "Moonlight Sonata," he moved gracefully to center stage. He wore buckskins. An eagle feather rose from his shoulder-length braided hair. Shadows from the harsh spotlight exaggerated his angular features: the powerful shoulders on the lean frame, the hawklike profile, the gaunt, seamed face and deepset blue eyes.

"I speak with a straight tongue," the man said. "I will tell you only what is true. I have come from very far to speak to you and because you have come to hear me the sky is very bright."

The scene was any one of dozens of British lecture halls in the mid-1930s. The speaker was a man whom the whole world believed was of Scottish and Apache parentage, a man who grew up with the Ojibwa, who lived in Prince Albert National Park with his friends the beavers. He called himself Grey Owl.

Now, of course, we know that Grey Owl's tongue was far from straight. We know his real name was Archibald Stansfeld Belaney and that he was an Englishman with not a drop of Scottish or Apache blood. But his pose, together with his books on the untouched northern woods, made him one of the most widely known and admired Canadians of his day. And today he is remembered as much for his pioneering writing on conservation as for his extraordinary fraud.

Grey Owl had been trying to bury Archie Belaney for years. He preferred to forget his past as an English boy with an alcoholic father, missing mother and two strict maiden aunts as caregivers. As far back as 1907, when he came to the Temagami region of northern Ontario as a young man of 19, he began telling people he'd spent his boyhood in the American southwest. He worked on losing his accent, befriended local Ojibwa and studied their language and customs. A local man nicknamed him kohom-see, or Little Owl, after his wide-eyed observance of aboriginal life. He became an expert canoeist and found work as a trapper, fire ranger and guide. He wore moccasins and buckskins and grew his hair. He married an Ojibwa woman, Angele Egwuna. Flight from reality became a habit. He left Angele after the birth of their daughter, then left another girl friend pregnant when he enlisted in the army for World War II. Before he returned to northern Ontario, he married yet a third woman in England, whom he never saw again.

By this time he had begun to write, filling page after page

with notes. He'd have a pack full of them by the end of a ranger season. He'd also begun to drink, making his own moonshine when prohibition cut off a regular supply of booze. Falling deeper into his Indian myth, he began to dye his hair black and darken his skin with henna.

In 1925, he moved to the Abitibi region of northern Quebec with a half-Iroquois woman named Gertrude Bernhard, whom he renamed Anahareo. Here, his feelings about hunting and trapping beaver began to change. The animals weren't as plentiful as they had been in the past, and killing them began to bother him. In 1928, he killed a mother beaver and was just about to shoot the two kits when Anahareo stopped him. The couple began raising the kits, and that was it for Archie's trapping days. For money, he turned to writing and began to sell articles to a British magazine called *Country Life*. In 1930, for the first time, he signed an article "Grey Owl." The next year, he called himself an "Indian writer who writes as an Indian."

Grey Owl's passionate, poetic evocations of the north woods and his pleadings on their behalf touched a nerve both at home and abroad. His articles and an address he gave in Montreal drew the attention of National Parks Commissioner James Harkin. Harkin decided to hire Grey Owl to live in a park as both a tourist attraction and a one-man conservation campaign. After a six-month stint in Riding Mountain Park in Manitoba, Grey Owl and Anahareo came here in 1931.

In a custom-built cabin on Lake Ajawaan, Grey Owl finished *The Men of the Last Frontier* and wrote *Pilgrims of the Wild, Sajo and the Beaver People* and *Tales of an Empty Cabin*. The books were wildly popular. *Last Frontier* alone sold 50,000 copies in England. But the cost to Grey Owl was Anahareo, who couldn't stand to be with him when he was writing. She left the couple's daughter, Dawn, with a woman in Prince Albert and went on long prospecting trips. Despite visits from tourists and his animal friends (his beavers had an underwater passage right into the cabin) Grey Owl was alone much of the time, drinking and brooding.

His books and films, however, made him an international celebrity. He toured England in 1936 and 1937, giving hundreds of lectures and speaking to hundreds of thousands of Britons with a message ahead of its time: Canada's forest and wildlife were not limitless. He met Canada's governor-general and prime minister. He gave a command performance to England's royal family.

And everywhere he went, his version of his origins was believed. The *Toronto Star*'s London correspondent Matthew Halton said Grey Owl

> *looks to good to be true to life. With his marvelous, sculptured faced; his great feather and fringed buckskin costume; his long, lean body and powerful shoulders. He moves with the grace of a cat; or sits motionless as a perched eagle; yet he is absolutely without pose.*

In reality, Grey Owl was nothing but pose, and more people were coming to know it. In 1935, his former wife, Angele, told a reporter from the *North Bay Nugget* of Grey Owl's true identity; city editor Ed Bunyan spiked the story out of sympathy for Grey Owl's cause. In 1936, the Justice of the Peace for the Temagami region, who had married Archie Belaney twenty years ago, realized what had become of that bridegroom. He chose to keep it to himself for the same reason. So did his mother and aunts in England, who met their little Archie when he was touring as Grey Owl. John Tootoosis, a Cree leader from Saskatchewan's Poundmaker reserve, who met Grey Owl in Ottawa, had serious doubts about his friend's Ojibwa roots. So must have any aboriginal who saw Grey Owl's awkward, invented dance steps and heard his war song, which contained no words, only Indian-sounding gibberish. But they knew Grey Owl was their ally in their continuing fights with Ottawa, so they didn't expose him either.

Grey Owl must have known the curtain was coming down. Perhaps that was why he worked so hard the last two years of his life—to get as much done as he could before the charade ended. Filmmaking, writing and lecturing consumed him in 1937. So did drinking, which was beginning to threaten his parks job.

But he didn't let up, and in January 1938, he left on a three-month tour of Canada and the United States where he gave 28 lectures and traveled 6,214 miles (10,000 km) by train. His new wife, Yvonne Perrier, whom he had married two years before, was hospitalized from exhaustion after the tour. Although Grey Owl made it to Beaver Lodge, he was hospitalized three days later. Then three days later, on April 13, he was dead, killed by pneumonia that his drink-ravaged and exhausted body was too weak to fight. The same day, the *Nugget* ran the story it had sat on for nearly three years, and by the end of the week, the whole story was world news. None of the eight

Canadian papers that editorialized on Grey Owl's death criticized him.

He was buried on a hill overlooking Beaver Lodge. His cabin lay untended for decades but was finally restored in the 1970s and can be visited today by hikers and canoeists. Grey Owl's reputation has been restored, too. The lie he lived lives still, but so do words such as these, from his first book *The Men of the Last Frontier:*

> *Too many regard the wilderness as only a place of wild animals and wilder men, and cluttered with a growth that must somehow be got rid of. Yet it is, to those who know its ways, a living, breathing, reality, and has a soul that may be understood, and it may yet occur to some, that part of the duty of those who destroy it for the general good is to preserve at least a memory of it and its inhabitants, and what they stood for.*

Stanley Mission One of Earliest Anglican Stations
End of Highway 915, Lac la Ronge Provincial Park

Although one of the conditions under which the Hudson's Bay Company received its royal charter was the spread of European-style settlement and civilization in Rupert's Land, the company was not notably warm to churchmen. Missionaries, it was felt, would only distract trappers from the serious business of gathering furs.

Still, by the middle of the 19th century, there were 42 missionary stations throughout fur country, most of them Anglican. Stanley Mission is one of the earliest ones. Its church, Holy Trinity Anglican Church, is the oldest building in Saskatchewan.

The church got permission from the Hudson's Bay Company to build a mission in Churchill River country in 1845. But because the church was keen to establish a farm at the mission, it took six years to find a site near Lac la Ronge's marshes, rocky outcrops and lakes that could support crops. This point of land was finally chosen in 1851, and Reverend Robert Hunt immediately got busy. He oversaw the construction of a parsonage, a schoolhouse, a warehouse, storeroom, barn, icehouse and carpenter's shop. In 1854, work began on Holy Trinity.

Stanley Mission.

The locks, window frames, hinges and glass for the church were brought from England. Local stone and timber supplied the footings, frame and siding. The structure was insulated with a mixture of moss and mud. When it was finished in 1860, it was quite an edifice for such a remote location: 82 x 33' (25 x 10 m) and ceilings arching 50' (15 m) above the floor. The steeple rose an impressive 89' (27 m) into the sky. Its windows contain over 10,000 pieces of stained glass, shipped from England and delivered by boat from Hudson Bay.

Two years after the church was finished, Hunt and his wife returned to England. They were replaced by an aboriginal minister, Reverend John MacKay, who increased the amount of land under cultivation and had a flour mill built. He also brought in a printing press to publish texts in Cree syllabics. By 1877, when MacKay left, several hundred people were living here. But by the turn of the century, the settlement at Lac la Ronge had become more important and Stanley Mission declined.

Today, Holy Trinity Church is the only remnant of the original settlement on the north shore of the river. It is open to visitors, but the only access is by boat.

Fight Over Furs Ends in Murder at Peter Pond's Post
Highway 102, Sucker River

The freebooting days of the early western fur trade, when the long arm of the law did not yet hold sway over the region, brought its share of violent, unpredictable men. Peter Pond, who wintered here in 1780–81, was one of them. Pond was born in relatively civilized Connecticut—too civilized by half, thought Pond, who fled his father's shoe shop at 16 to join the army. He rose to the rank of captain, then left the service to trade furs along the Mississippi. Pond came to the Canadian northwest after killing another trader in a duel: "We met the morning eairley and discharged pistels in which the pore fellowe was unfortenat," is his much-quoted summary.

In 1778, Pond's restless nature drove him to become the first trader to head west from the Saskatchewan River system up the Churchill, over the 656' (200-m) cliff at Methy Portage, into Athabasca country. When Pond and his paddlers returned the following spring to Cumberland House, they carried 140 packs of prime pelts, all they could carry without dumping their canoes. More pelts had been stashed along the way. For the newly formed North West Company, of which Pond was partner, it was El Dorado.

On his way back to Athabasca in 1780, Pond was caught by an early freeze-up and forced to overwinter here. He built a shack near the post of fellow Nor'Wester Jean-Etienne Waden. At this time, the North West partners were debating who should control Athabasca country. One faction favored Peter Pond; the other didn't. Unfortunately for Waden, he was among the latter. One night in March, there was a fight in which Waden died. Pond was never charged with the death, but he fled the country.

He returned to the Athabasca after five years. Again, there was an argument with a neighbor. Again, the neighbor died, although this time one of Pond's staff faced charges in the death. Pond spent his last season in the region that he helped open up working on a map that purported to show a great river leading to the Pacific just a few day's paddle from Great Slave Lake. The river didn't exist, but the map was persuasive enough to inspire a young 24-year-old trader named Alexander Mackenzie, who was second in command to Pond at Fort Chipewyan, on the southern shore of Lake Athabasca in what is now Alberta.

Pond left fur country forever in 1788 and died in poverty in New England. Mackenzie, who had spent many winter nights in the Athabasca talking to Pond about his river to the Pacific, went to Montreal to talk the fur barons into letting him try to find it. He tried twice. The first time, in 1789, he paddled to the mouth of the river that now bears his name, although Mackenzie himself called it the River of Disappointment because he hadn't reached the Pacific. On his second trip, in 1793, he became the first European ever to cross the continent by land.

ALONG THE HANSON LAKE ROAD (HIGHWAY 106)

Road Name Honors Old-Time Trapper and Prospector
Off Highway 55, the Hanson Lake Road leaves from Smeaton

Yes, there is a Hanson Lake near the end of this 224-mile (360-km) road, but that's not what gives this road its name. Olaf Hanson was a longtime trapper, prospector and outdoorsman who spent much of his life in this area. He knew the land like few did, and he was a great help to the government surveyors picking a path through the rocky outcrops, muskeg, lakes and rivers of this part of the Canadian Shield. It's for him this road is named, the first all-weather road between Prince Albert and Flin

Flon. It opened up the entire northwest corner of the province to fishing, hunting and mining.

Partnership Foreshadows Great Fur Company
West bank of Amisk Lake, north side of portage between Amisk Lake and Balsam Lake

By 1775, when this post was built, the fur trade was becoming well established in what is now northeast Saskatchewan. The year before, even the cautious Hudson's Bay Company had ventured west from York Factory to build Cumberland House a little to the south on the Saskatchewan River. Still, this was the first post built by way of a partnership between Alexander Henry the elder and the Frobisher brothers, Joseph and Thomas. All three were charter members of the hard-drinking, hard-paddling group of independents who relentlessly pushed their canoes and fur brigades farther and farther west in search of virgin fur territory.

The Hudson's Bay Company snootily referred to these bold businessmen as Pedlars, but for two generations after coming together in 1790 to form the North West Company they traded the Baymen to a standstill. After the first decade of the 19th century, they controlled 78 percent of fur sales in Canada. As well, it was they who opened up the continent. Nor'Westers Alexander Mackenzie and Simon Fraser voyaged to the mouths of the rivers that bear their names; Mackenzie was the first European to cross the continent by land. David Thompson, the first European to see the mouth of the Mississippi, left the Hudson's Bay Company to survey much of the interior for its rival.

The fierce and sometimes bloody rivalry between the two companies lasted until their merger in 1821. That violence was one reason for the merger. Stunned by the increasing loss of life in the North-West, the British ordered the Hudson's Bay and North West companies to make peace. As well, the Nor'Westers supply line, which stretched from Montreal to the Athabasca country, was becoming increasingly difficult to maintain.

Here, the Henry–Frobisher post lasted for about three seasons, although for the last two seasons it was run by a pair of employees. In true Nor'Wester style, Henry and the Frobishers had pushed on, farther northwest to the Churchill River district.

Dinosaurs and Coal Beds Make Young Explorer's Name
Along Hanson Lake Road, Tyrrell Lake

Joseph Burr Tyrrell, for whom this lake is named, was the kind of man who paved the way for the development of the Canadian West: bold, energetic and relentlessly curious, with a Victorian passion for taming the mystery of this sprawling new land through the rigor of scientific observation. Other map makers and explorers may be better known. But Tyrrell's achievements, which include two epic Arctic trips as well as the discovery of Alberta's oil sands and great fossil beds, rank with the best of them.

Tyrrell was an aspiring young lawyer, articling in 1881 with a Toronto firm, when his life changed forever. A bout with tuberculosis seriously threatened the 23-year-old's life, and his doctor told him that returning to his sedentary indoor life would likely kill him. "I didn't know much about farming, so I applied for a position to the Director of Canadian Geological Survey," Tyrrell recalled.

It probably wasn't as matter-of-fact as that. As a boy, Tyrrell had always had a keen interest in the natural world. He had roamed the banks of Toronto's Humber River, collecting interesting leaves and colored rocks, capturing crayfish and studying them in his mother's bathtub. Still, Tyrrell's first year with the survey was unpacking box after box as it moved from Montreal to Ottawa.

Finally, Tyrrell got his first field assignment: he was to be part of an 1883 expedition to map the Crowsnest and Kicking Horse passes, as well at the Kootenay River and the eastern foothills of the Rockies. That trip went well, and the next summer Tyrrell returned to the West for the expedition that was to make his name.

He headed an expedition charged with mapping the country between the Bow and Saskatchewan rivers in Alberta. As the party was rafting down the Red Deer River, Tyrrell noticed a coal outcrop along the bank. Coal had been mentioned by earlier explorers such as Peter Fidler, but Tyrrell was the first to give any idea of the precise location and extent. These coal beds would turn out to be the largest in Canada and give birth to the city of Drumheller.

Two days after that discovery, Tyrrell and his party found

vast numbers of fossil beds along the Red Deer River. The presence of dinosaur bones had been rumored there, but Tyrrell was again the first to conduct any study or collection of them. Bones from this area are now in museums around the world. The name of Drumheller's Royal Tyrrell Museum of Palaeontology honors the find of the then 25-year-old geologist.

Tyrrell spent the next two seasons mapping what is now Alberta, tracking down rumors of oil seepages north of Edmonton and becoming the first to give any idea of the extent of the Athabasca oil sands, now one of the largest energy reserves in the world. He then turned his attention to the north country of Manitoba and Saskatchewan, including this area.

By 1893, the mysterious Barren Lands of the North began to fascinate him. No explorer had been through since Samuel Hearne in the 1770s, and Tyrrell was determined to go. With his brother James and six other men, they set out from Lake Athabasca, headed for Hudson Bay. Nearly half of the 3,293 miles (5,300 km) they traveled by canoe and foot had never before been seen by Europeans. The expedition went well until the party reached Chesterfield Inlet along the western coast of the bay. Although Tyrrell was a crack shot who could snuff out a candle flame from 20 paces, food was scarce and the weather was deteriorating. Gales and blizzards beset them; hunger and frostbite got so bad the men could hardly walk. Then a polar bear got close enough for them to shoot. Fueled by the rich bear meat, the party made the remaining 311 miles (500 km) to Fort Churchill. From there, they snowshoed the remaining 932 miles (1,500 km) to Winnipeg.

The party was three months overdue, and newspapers had been full of speculation regarding their fate. But their concern had been nothing compared to that of Edith Carey, the young woman Tyrrell had been courting back in Ottawa. Her relief at seeing the young explorer again was great. Tyrrell made light of his ordeal, telling Edith that he had never missed a meal, although he had sometimes been two or three days late for one. The two married in February 1894.

The next summer Tyrrell was heading north again. The 2,983-mile (4,800-km) route was similar, but this time the traveling was much easier.

Tyrrell continued to roam, exploring the areas that later yielded the uranium mines of northern Saskatchewan and rich metal deposits around Flin Flon and Thompson, Manitoba. He went to the Klondike for the gold rush of 1897 and became the first to discover how the gold got into the creeks flowing into the Klondike River. He also became a successful mining executive and consultant.

Even after he retired from active exploration, Tyrrell was indefatigable. He wrote about 300 papers. He edited and had published the first editions of the journals of the great explorers David Thompson and Samuel Hearne. He built a farm near Toronto that became famous for its apples. At the age of 65, he became president and general manager of Kirkland Lake Mining and continued to attend board meetings until the age of 98. In his 80s, he became interested in flight and was annoyed to learn he was considered too old to earn a pilot's license.

Tyrrell died in 1957 at the age of 99. "I have always believed you can find the time to do the things you want to do," he once wrote. For Tyrrell, finding ways to spend his time was never a problem.

Directory of Saskatchewan Museums

HORSESHOE REGION

Blumenfeld and District Heritage Site
10 miles (16 km) west of Prelate
Prelate SK S0N 2B0
June 1–September 30, or call
(306) 673-2200
Museum in church built in 1915.

Buffalo Bean Bygones
Central Street off Highway 1
Tompkins SK S0N 2S0
Open year-round
No phone
Antique farm machinery.

Cabri Museum
202–1st Street
Cabri SK S0N 0J0
Open year-round
(306) 587-2500 or (306) 587-2915
Early farm equipment; arrowheads, fossils.

Climax Community Museum
Climax school grounds
Climax SK S0N 0M0
July 1–August 23, or call

(306) 293-2963 or (306) 293-2051
Local history and early farming equipment.

Doc's Town
Exhibition grounds, 17th Avenue SE and S Railway
Box 146
Swift Current SK S9H 3V5
June 1–September 1
(306) 773-2944
Reconstruction of prairie village, c. 1900.

Eastend Museum
Downtown in former theater
Eastend SK S0N 0T0
May 16–September 1, or call
(306) 295-3375
Fossils, homestead artifacts, including genuine late-1800s log house.

Fort Walsh National Historic Site
34 miles (55 km) southwest of Maple Creek, Highway 271
Box 278
Maple Creek SK S0N 1N0
May 17–October 13

(306) 662-3590 or (306) 662-2645
Reconstruction of North-West Mounted Police fort.

Grand Coteau Heritage and Cultural Centre
440 Centre Street
Shaunavon SK S0N 2M0
Open year-round
(306) 297-3882 or (306) 297-3844
Natural and human history of area.

Great Sand Hills Museum
Highway 32
Sceptre SK S0N 2H0
Open year-round
(306) 623-4345 or (306) 623-4329
Natural and human history of Great Sand Hills.

Jasper Cultural and Historical Centre
311 Jasper Street
Maple Creek SK S0N 1N0
Open year-round
(306) 662-2434 or (306) 662-3602
Frontier history with emphasis on ranching.

Lancer Centennial Museum
Ballaclava (Main) Street
Lancer SK S0N 1G0
Open year-round
(306) 689-2925 or (306) 689-2922
Pioneer, Indian and wildlife exhibits.

Perreault's Museum and Guided Tour
210-1st Street N
Val Marie SK S0N 2T0
Open year-round
(306) 298-2241

Area artifacts; tour of Grasslands National Park.

Sod House
Central Avenue
Tompkins SK S0N 2S0
Open year-round
(306) 622-2020
Replica of pioneer sod house.

Southwest Saskatchewan Old-Timer's Museum
218 Jasper Street
Maple Creek SK S0N 1N0
Open year-round
(306) 662-2474 or (306) 662-4159
Many early photos and artifacts of North-West Mounted Police, ranching, Indians.

St. Angela's Museum
St. Angela's Convent
201–3rd Avenue
Prelate SK S0N 2B0
May 23–November 1, or call
(306) 673-2200
Displays of pioneer life of Ursuline Sisters.

Swift Current Museum
105 Chaplin Street E
Swift Current SK S9H 1H9
May 20–August 31
(306) 778-2775
Pioneer and natural history artifacts.

GREAT TRAILS REGION

Assiniboia and District Historical Museum
506, 3rd Avenue W
Assiniboia SK S0H 0B0

Open year-round
(306) 642-4216
*Reconstructed doctor's office,
coal mine, blacksmith's shop, and
so on, c. 1912.*

**Athol Murray College Archives
and Museum**
Athol Murray College, beside rink
Wilcox SK
Open year-round
(306) 732-2080
*Artifacts pertaining to the histo-
ry of Athol Murray College.*

**Avonlea and District Heritage
House**
Main Street, in CNR station
Avonlea SK S0H 0C0
June 15–August 31
(306) 868-2101 or (306) 868-2064
*Early medical tools, ranching
history, schoolhouse and rural
telephone system.*

Bengough Museum
1st Avenue W
Bengough SK S0C 0K0
May 15–September 30, or call
(306) 268-2909 or (306) 268-4404
Local history and artifacts.

Briercrest Museum
Main Street
Briercrest SK S0H 0K0
May 1–September 30
(306) 799-4406
Old country store setting.

Coronach District Museum
240–1st Street W
Coronach SK S0H 0Z0
May 1–September 30
(306) 267-5724 or (306) 267-2456

*Local history photos and arti-
facts.*

Deep South Pioneer Museum
West of Government Road
Ogema SK S0C 1Y0
May 15–September 30
(306) 459-2431 or (306) 459-2294
*Twenty buildings depicting
stores, offices, theater and so on.*

Glentworth Museum
Glentworth SK S0H 1V0
Open year-round, call first
(306) 266-4320
*Reconstructed old schoolhouse
and teacherage.*

Herbert CPR Station
625 Railway Avenue
Herbert SK S0H 2A0
June 28–September 1
(306) 784-3124 or (306) 784-2655
*Railway artifacts in restored
1910 CPR station.*

Homestead Museum
Former hospital building
Hodgeville SK S0H 2B0
Open year-round
(306) 677-2673 or (306) 677-2660
*Homestead-style museum
below floor of antique giftshop.*

Lafleche and District Museum
207 Main Street
Lafleche SK S0H 2K0
Open year-round
(306) 472-5276
*Variety of homestead displays;
archive.*

Mankota Museum
4th Street

Mankota SK S0H 2W0
Open year-round
(306) 478-2716
Old schoolhouse and machinery display.

McCord Museum
Main Street, CPR station
McCord SK S0H 2T0
May 1–October 31
(306) 478-2522 or (306) 478-2559
Refurbished CPR office, c. 1930.

Moose Jaw Art Museum
Athabasca and Crescent Park
in library
Moose Jaw SK S6H 0X6
Open year-round
(306) 692-4471
Early history of area, traveling exhibits.

Morse Museum
3 blocks west of Main Street
Morse SK S0H 3C0
Open year-round
(306) 629-3626 or (306) 629-3230
Local school, homestead history.

Mossbank and District Museum
115–3rd Street W
Mossbank SK S0H 3G0
July 1–September 30
(306) 354-2889
Displays of settler's shack, military uniforms.

Musee de Gravelbourg Museum
Legion Hall, 5th Avenue E
Gravelbourg SK S0H 1X0
July 1–August 31
(306) 648-3301 or (306) 648-3349
Early Francophone settlement artifacts.

Notukeu Heritage Museum
110 Railway Avenue
Ponteix SK S0N 1Z0
Open year-round
(306) 625-3340
Large collection of Indian artifacts

Rouleau and District Museum
Main Street
Rouleau SK S0G 4H0
July 1–August 31
(306) 776-2363
School and farm history, including old wheat pool house.

Sukanen Pioneer Ship and Museum
8 miles (13 km) south of Moose Jaw, Highway 2
Moose Jaw SK S6H 7T2
June 1–September 15
(306) 693-7315 or (306) 693-3506
Pioneer artifacts including cars, buildings and ship built by Tom Sukanen.

Tunnels of Little Chicago
Corner of Main Street and River Street
Moose Jaw SK
Open year-round
(306) 693-5261
Tours of tunnels used by rum runners and gamblers under streets of city.

Vanguard Centennial Library Museum
Main Street
Vanguard SK S0N 2V0
Open year-round
(306) 582-2244 or (306) 582-2214
Community history.

Western Development Museum
50 Diefenbaker Drive
Moose Jaw SK S6H 4N8
Open year-round
(306) 693-5989 or (306) 693-6556
  *Displays of transportation in
the West.*

Willow Bunch Museum
Old convent on 5th Street
Willow Bunch SK S0H 4K0
Open year-round
(306) 473-2806 or (306) 473-2245
  *Local history, including arti-
facts from Edouard Beaupre, the
Willow Bunch Giant.*

**Wood Mountain Rodeo and
Ranching Museum**
Wood Mountain Regional Park
Wood Mountain SK S0H 4L0
May 18–September 2
(306) 266-4953 or (306) 266-4539
  Local ranch and rodeo history.

REGINA

Alex Youck School Museum
1600–4th Avenue
Regina SK S4R 8C8
Open year-round
(306) 525-9688
  *A fully operational one-room
schoolhouse with artifacts dating
back to 1900.*

Diefenbaker Homestead
Lakeshore Dr,
west of Broad Street
Regina SK S4P 3S7
May 19–September 1
(306) 522-3661
  Restored boyhood home of for-

*mer Prime Minister John
Diefenbaker; moved from Borden.*

Government House
4607 Dewdney Avenue
Regina SK S4P 3V7
Open year-round
(306) 787-5773
  *Official residence of Lieutenant-
Governors, 1891–1945.*

Heritage Regina Tours
Box 581
Regina SK S4P 3A3
Open July 1–September 15
(306) 585-4214
  *Historic walking tours of
Regina, guided by local volunteers.*

RCMP Centennial Museum
RCMP Depot Division,
Dewdney Avenue W
P.O. Box 6500
Regina SK S4P 3J7
Open year-round
(306) 780-5838
  *History of RCMP, including
extensive display of artifacts.*

Regina Plains Museum
1801 Scarth Street
Regina SK S4P 2G9
Open year-round
(306) 780-9435 or (306) 780-9434
  *Cultural history of Regina
Plains area.*

Royal Saskatchewan Museum
2445 Albert Street
Regina SK S4P 3V7
Open year-round
(306) 787-2815 or (306) 787-2810
  *Natural, Indian and settlement
history.*

Saskatchewan Military Museum
Rm 112, The Armoury, 1600
Elphinstone Street
Regina SK S4T 3N1
Open year-round
(306) 347-9349
Prairie military history, 1885 to present.

Saskatchewan Sports Hall of Fame
2205 Victoria Avenue
Regina SK S4P 0S4
Open year-round
(306) 780-9232
Photos, artifacts and resource material on Saskatchewan sports.

HORIZON REGION

Abernethy Nature-Heritage Museum
Main Street
Abernethy SK S0A 0A0
Open May 18–October 12
(306) 333-4801
More than 300 mounted birds and other items from naturalist R.P. Stueck.

Arcola Museum
Railway Avenue
Arcola SK S0C 0G0
May 2–September 26
(306) 455-2462
Pioneer artifacts, including clothing.

Bienfait Coalfields Museum
Highway 18, in old CPR station
Bienfait SK S0C 0M0
May 19–September 30
(306) 388-2494 or (306) 388-2286

Artifacts and examples of coal mining from 1895 to present.

Broadview Museum
N 10th Avenue
Broadview SK S0G 0K0
June 1–August 31
(306) 696-2286 or (306) 696-2612
One-room school, pioneer artifacts.

Carlyle Rusty Relics Museum
3rd Street W and Carlyle Avenue, in old CNR station
Carlyle SK S0C 0R0
June 9–September 1
(306) 453-2232 or (306) 453-2235
Pioneer dentistry artifacts.

Esterhazy Community Museum
2nd Avenue
Esterhazy S0A 0X0
May 19–September 1
(306) 745-2988
Old country store, doctor's office, pioneer artifacts.

Estevan National Exhibition Centre
118–4th Street
Estevan SK S4A 0T4
Open year-round
(306) 634-7644
Pioneer artifacts, touring exhibits.

Fort Qu'Appelle Museum
Bay Avenue and 3rd Street
Fort Qu'Appelle SK S0G 1S0
July 1–September 2
(306) 332-6443 or (306) 332-5941
Joined to original Hudson's Bay post, c. 1864; fur trade, North-West Mounted Police artifacts.

Gervais Wheel Museum
4 miles (6.4 km) north of Alida,
Highway 601
Box 40
Alida SK S0C 0B0
Open year-round
(306) 443-2370 or (306) 443-2303
One hundred years of farm tools and implements.

Grenfell Museum
711 Wolsley Avenue
Grenfell SK S0G 2B0
June 27–August 1
(306) 697-2431 or (306) 697-2580
Large 1904 house; military and pioneer artifacts.

Indian Head Museum Society
Corner of Otterloo and Bell Street
Indian Head SK S0G 2K0
July 1–August 31
(306) 695-3800
Pioneer artifacts, including 1883 Bell farm cottage.

Kaposvar Historic Site Museum
3 miles (5 km) south of Esterhazy
Box 115
Esterhazy SK S0A 0X0
May 15–October 15
(306) 745-6761 or (306) 745-2692
Site of first Hungarian colony, with homestead buildings and restored church rectory.

Kipling and District Historical Society
4th Street E and Centennial
Kipling SK S0G 2S0
June 1–September 1
(306) 736-2488 or (306) 736-2605
Restored schoolhouse, service station, 1903 home.

Kisbey Museum
245 Ross Street
Kisbey SK S0C 1L0
July 1–August 31
(306) 462-2162
Story of Kisbey family, area's first settlers.

Melville Heritage Museum
Heritage Drive
Melville SK S0A 2P0
May 15–October 15
(306) 728-2370 or (306) 728-2070
First seniors home in province; large library; military and rail exhibits.

Melville Railway Museum
Melville Regional Park
Melville SK S0A 2P0
July 1–August 31
(306) 728-4177
CN steam engine, caboose; 1913 station being restored.

Ralph Allen Memorial Museum
Railway Avenue at McCall Street
Oxbow SK S0C 2B0
May 21–September 1
(306) 483-5065
Memorabilia pertaining to Ralph Allen, author and war correspondent.

Rocanville and District Museum
Qu'Appelle Avenue and St. Albert
Rocanville SK S0A 3L0
May 1–September 30
(306) 645-2113 or (306) 645-2605
Farm machinery, church, CPR station, restored carousel.

Soo Line Historical Museum
411 Industrial Lane
Weyburn SK S4H 2L2
Open year-round
(306) 842-2922
Pioneer artifacts in restored 1902 home.

Spy Hill Museum
Main Street
Spy Hill SK S0A 3W0
Open year-round
(306) 534-4534
Artifacts from prehistory to war years.

Stoughton Museum
327 Main Street
Stoughton SK S0G 4T0
June 1–August 31
(306) 457-2413
Local history displays.

The Red Barn
301 Sullivan Street
Stoughton SK S0G 4T0
Open year-round
(306) 457-3198
Collection of restored horse-drawn buggies.

Turner Curling Museum
532–5th Street
Weyburn SK S4H 0Z9
Open year-round
(306) 848-3217
Curling memorabilia from Canada and around the world.

Wawota and District Museum
101 Main Street
Wawota SK S0G 5A0
July 1–August 31
(306) 739-2110 or (306) 739-2216

Town's first firehall, built early 1900s.

Whitewood Historical Museum
607 N Railway
Whitewood SK S0G 5C0
July 1–August 31
(306) 735-2517 or (306) 735-4388
Pioneer and agricultural displays.

Windthorst and District Museum
19 miles (30 km) NW of Moose Mountain Provincial Park, Highway 48
Windthorst SK S0G 5G0
June 1–September 5
(306) 224-4633 or (306) 224-4323
Local settlement history.

Wolseley and District Museum
Blanchard Street
Wolseley SK S0G 5H0
July 1–August 31
(306) 698-2248
Early 1900s restored home, with doctor, news and insurance offices upstairs.

SCHOONER REGION

Biggar Museum and Gallery
107–3rd Avenue W
Biggar SK S0K 0M0
Open year-round
(306) 948-3451
Indian, railway and pioneer displays.

Central Butte District Museum
Main Street
Central Butte SK S0H 0T0
June 1–July 31
(306) 796-2146

*Set up as 1920s farmhouse, with
Masonic temple.*

Craik Oral History Room
Corner of 3rd Street and 1st
Avenue
Craik SK S0G 0V0
Open year-round
(306) 734-2737 or (306) 734-2252
*Local history archives including
about 600 tapes and 1,000 photos.*

Dodsland and District Museum
Main Street
Dodsland SK S0L 0V0
Open year-round
(306) 356-2178
Pioneer artifacts, Prairie Times
newspaper, 1917–43.

**Elbow Museum and Historical
Society**
Saskatchewan Street
Elbow SK S0H 1J0
July 1–August 31
(306) 854-2108 or (306) 854-2125
*Pioneer artifacts including fur-
nished sodhouse.*

Elrose Brick School Museum
110–4th Avenue E
Elrose SK S0L 0Z0
May 17–September 30
(306) 378-2201 or (306) 378-2213
*Antique clothes, photos, furni-
ture and archaeological displays.*

F.T. Hill Museum
Main Street
Riverhurst SK S0H 3P0
Open year-round
(306) 353-2271 or (306) 353-2112
*Indian artifacts, pioneer
clothes, tools, firearms.*

Harris Heritage Society Museum
Railway Avenue
Harris SK S0L 1K0
May 1–October 31
(306) 656-2172
*Historic water tower and
caboose.*

Herschel Interpretive Centre
West Street
Herschel SK S0L 1L0
Open year-round
(306) 377-2045 or (306) 377-2014
Indian displays and artifacts.

Homestead Museum
1 mile (1.6 km) west of Biggar,
Highway 51
Biggar SK S0K 0M0
May 20–October 31
(306) 948-3427
*Pioneer buildings including
furnished sodhouse.*

Kerrobert and District Museum
Mary Rodney School
Kerrobert SK S0L 1R0
May 15–September 30
(306) 834-5277
*Historical photos, pioneer
kitchen, law office, barber, dairy,
blacksmith displays.*

Kindersley Plains Museum
903–11 Avenue E
Kindersley SK S0L 1S0
May 1–September 30
(306) 463-6620
*Archaeological and pioneer
artifacts.*

Leonard Farm Museum
Highway 7 between Tessier and
Harris

Box 265
Harris SK S0L 1K0
June 1–September 28
(306) 656-4440 or (306) 373-3059
Large selection of horse and old farm equipment.

Lucky Lake Heritage Museum
Main Street
Lucky Lake SK S0L 1Z0
April 1–September 30
(306) 858-2005
Homesteader and Indian artifacts.

Luseland and District Museum
Main Street
Luseland SK S0L 2A0
June 1–October 31
(306) 372-4331 or (306) 372-4258
Local historical artifacts.

Macklin and District Museum
Herald Street
Macklin SK S0L 2C0
June 1–December 30
(306) 753-2610 or (306) 753-2078
Set in Macklin's first hospital, opened 1922.

Outlook and District Heritage Museum
100 Railway Avenue
Outlook SK S0L 2N0
July 1–August 31
(306) 867-8285 or (306) 867-9660
Settlement artifacts, including replica of 1910 Lutheran Church.

Plenty and District Museum
Grand Avenue
Plenty SK S0L 2R0
June 1–September 30
(306) 932-4727 or (306) 932-2101

Pioneer and military memorabilia.

Prairie Pioneer Museum
Park Street and old Highway 11
Craik SK S0G 0V0
May 15–September 30
(306) 734-2480 or (306) 734-2252
Local history displays.

Prairie West Historical Centre
946–2nd Street SE
Prairie West SK S0L 1A0
May 22–October 13
(306) 962-3772 or (306) 962-3346
Displays in restored 1910 farmhouse.

Rosetown Museum
5th Avenue E
Rosetown SK S0L 2V0
Open year-round
(306) 882-2686 or (306) 882-3197
Local and family histories.

Saskatchewan Railway Museum
2.5 miles (4 km) southwest of Saskatoon, highways 7 & 60
Saskatoon SK
May 17–September 30
(306) 382-9855
Six acres (2.4 ha) of railway displays, including engine, caboose, streetcar and buildings.

St. Joseph's Colony Museum
14 miles (22 km) north of Luseland, Grid Road 675
Luseland SK S0L 2A0
June 1–August 31
(306) 228-2020
Restored church, including 15 Imhoff oil paintings.

Unity and District Heritage Museum
Just north of town, Highway 21
Unity SK S0K 4L0
Summers only
(306) 228-4464
Pioneer and settlement artifacts.

Wilkie Museum
1st Street and 3rd Avenue
Wilkie SK S0K 4W0
July 1–August 31
(306) 843-2565 or (306) 843-2978
Six-building complex includes blacksmith shop, newspaper office, old store.

Wilson Museum
115 Government Road
Dundurn SK S0K 1K0
Open year-round
(306) 492-4729 or (306) 492-4731
Restored 1903 house with artifacts from 1884–1940s.

YesterYears Community Museum
Main Street
Dinsmore SK S0L 0T0
June 1–October 31
(306) 846-2156
Pioneer displays, including blacksmith shop.

OLD NORTH-WEST REGION

Blaine Lake Museum
Station grounds, north end of Blaine Lake
Blaine Lake SK S0J 0J0
Open year-round
(306) 497-2531 or (306) 497-2400
Local settlement history.

Borden and District Museum
200 Main Street
Borden SK S0K 0N0
June 15–September 30
(306) 997-2030 or (306) 997-2075
Local history, replica of Diefenbaker homestead, toy museum.

Chief Poundmaker Historical Centre
Poundmaker Cree Nation, 9 miles (14 km) south of Highway 16
Paynton SK S0M 2J0
Open year-round
(306) 664-2259 or (306) 398-2727
Displays and artifacts on history of Poundmaker Cree nation, including 1840 Cree–Sarcee battle.

Clayton McLain Memorial Museum
Tomahawk Park campground
Cut Knife SK S0M 0N0
June 1–September 1
(306) 398-2345 or (306) 398-2590
Indian and pioneer artifacts, working railway handcar.

Duck Lake Regional Interpretive Centre
5 Anderson Avenue
Duck Lake SK S0K 1J0
Open year-round
(306) 467-2057
Artifacts from 1885 North-West Rebellion and Indian, Métis and Pioneer life, 1870–1905.

Foster's Store
1st Avenue and Shepherd Street
Borden SK S0K 0N0
Open year-round

(306) 997-2030
Pioneer artifacts set in c. 1912 general store.

Fred Light Museum
20th Street and Central Avenue
Battleford SK S0M 0E0
May 23–September 1
(306) 937-7111 or (306) 937-6200
Antique firearms, military uniforms from the 1800s to World War II.

Hepburn Museum of Wheat
West end of Main Street
Hepburn SK S0K 1Z0
May 19–September 1
(306) 947 2170
Refurbished 1926 elevator, displays on history of agriculture.

Kinistino and District Museum
Main Street
Kinistino SK S0J 1H0
June 1–October 15
(306) 864-3106
Fur trade and early pioneer artifacts.

Langham and District Museum
232 Main Street
Langham SK S0K 2L0
Summers only
No phone
Pioneer and settlement artifacts.

Milden Community Museum
Centre Street
Milden SK S0L 2L0
Summers only
No phone
Pioneer and settlement artifacts.

Saskatchewan Baseball Hall of Fame and Museum
121–20th Street
Battleford SK S0M 0E0
May 1–September 6
(306) 445-8485
Photos and artifacts on the history of baseball in Saskatchewan.

Saskatchewan River Valley Museum
Main Street
Hague SK S0K 1X0
May 17–October 13
(306) 225-2112 or (306) 225-4542
Pioneer artifacts, including 1850s grand piano.

Shell Lake Museum
At entrance to town of Shell Lake, in CNR station
Shell Lake SK S0J 2G0
June 28–September 1
(306) 427-2272 or (306) 427-2280
CNR station, c. 1930, with caboose.

Shellbrook Museum
South end of Main Street
Shellbrook SK S0J 2E0
July 1–September 1
(306) 747-2898 or (306) 747-3524
Local history displays and artifacts.

Wakaw Historical Museum
3rd Avenue NW
Wakaw SK S0K 4P0
July 1–August 31
(306) 233-5282 or (306) 233-4223
Pioneer artifacts, including one-room shack, replica of John Diefenbaker's first law office.

Washbrook Museum
2nd Avenue
Edam SK S0M 0V0
May 1–September 30
(306) 397-2260
  Old CNR motor car, pioneer artifacts.

Western Development Museum
Junction of highways 16 and 20
North Battleford SK S9A 2Y1
April 28–September 19
(306) 445-8033
  History of agriculture.

SASKATOON

Little Stone School
Off College Drive, east of St. Andrew's College on university campus
Saskatoon SK
May 15–September 1
(306) 996-8384
  Saskatoon's first school, restored to 1904.

Marr Residence
326–11 Street E
Saskatoon SK S7N 0E7
Call ahead
(306) 665-6888
  The oldest residence in Saskatoon, used as a field hospital during the North-West Rebellion.

Musee Ukraina Museum
202 Avenue M South
Saskatoon SK S7M 2K4
Open year-round
(306) 244-4212 or (306) 384-3012
  Ukrainian culture and history.

Museum of Antiquities
Rm 237, Murray Building
University of Saskatchewan
Saskatoon SK S7N 5A4
Open year-round
(306) 966-7818
  Ancient Greek and Roman artifacts.

Saskatoon Sports Hall of Fame
Field House, 2020 College Drive
Saskatoon SK S7N 2W4
Open year-round
(306) 975-3354
  Local sports memorabilia.

Ukrainian Museum of Canada
910 Spadina Crescent E
Saskatoon SK S7K 3H5
Open year-round
(306) 244-3800
  Ukrainian history in Canada.

Western Development Museum
2610 Lorne Avenue S
Saskatoon SK S7J 0S6
Open year-round
(306) 931-1910
  Re-creates boomtown era.

LIVING SKY REGION

Cupar and District Heritage Museum
c/o Wes Bailey
Cupar SK S0G 0Y0
Summers only
No phone
  Pioneer and settlement artifacts and displays.

Dysart and District Museum
Qu'Appelle Avenue
Dysart SK S0G 1H0
June 1–September 30
(306) 432-2227
Pioneer and ethnic artifacts.

Foam Lake Museum Association
113 Bray Avenue, Highway 16
Foam Lake SK S0A 1A0
May 1–September 30
(306) 272-4292 or (306) 272-3519
Pioneer displays and artifacts.

Frank Cameron Museum
Highway 16 and 1st Street W
Wynyard SK S0A 4T0
May 12–September 8
(306) 554-3661
Sports, agricultural and medical artifacts and photos.

Humboldt and District Museum
Main Street and 6th Avenue
Humboldt SK S0K 2A0
April 1–December 10
(306) 682-5226 or (306) 682-2525
Schoolhouse replica, medical offices, general store.

Lanigan and District Heritage Centre
Main Street and Highway 16, in old CPR station
Lanigan SK S0K 2M0
June 1–September 14
(306) 365-2569
Potash display and pioneer artifacts.

LeRoy and District Heritage Museum
117 1st Avenue
LeRoy SK S0K 2P0

July 1–August 31
(306) 286-3464 or (306) 286-3600
Replica of control tower used in bombing and gunnery school at Dafoe during World War II.

Lumsden Heritage Museum
Qu'Appelle Drive
Lumsden SK S0G 3C0
June 9–September 20
(306) 731-2905 or (306) 731-2596
Features history of Qu'Appelle Valley.

Naicam Museum
210–3rd Avenue
Naicam SK S0K 2Z0
June 26–September 1
(306) 874-5518 or (306) 874-2125
Local artifacts and antiques.

Nokomis and District Museum
3rd Avenue and Highway 20
Nokomis SK S0G 3R0
June 1–September 1
(306) 528-2080 or (306) 528-2979
Junction City 1907 display includes old store, school, post office, hospital and various businesses.

Prud'homme Multicultural Providence Museum
77 Government Road
Prud'homme SK S0K 3K0
July 1–August 31
(306) 654-2177
Artifacts and memorabilia of Jeanne Sauvé, first female governor-general.

Quill Lakes Interpretive Centre
7 miles (11 km) south of Quill Lake on Grid Road 640

Quill Lake SK S0A 3E0
May 1–September 30
(306) 383-2616
Local history of Quill Lakes area.

Raymore Pioneer Museum
1st Avenue, across from post office
Raymore SK S0A 3J0
May 1–September 26
(306) 746-2180 or (306) 746-5707
Features Indian and settlement history.

Reynold Rapp Museum
200 1st Street S
Spalding SK S0K 4C0
May 1–October 31
(306) 872-2164 or (306) 872-2076
Displays of local history in historic home.

Rose Valley and District Heritage Museum
116 Centre Street
Rose Valley SK S0E 1M0
July 1–September 1
(306) 322-2034 or (306) 322-4642
Household articles, agricultural implements of early area settlers.

Rudy's Museum
Main Street and Assiniboia Avenue
Earl Grey SK S0G 1J0
Open year-round
(306) 939-2210 or (306) 939-2139
Antique autos 1917–32.

Semans and District Museum
Main Street
Semans SK S0A 3S0
Summers only

No phone
Pioneer and settlement artifacts

Southey and District Museum
Sports grounds, 1 block east of Highway 6
Southey SK S0G 4P0
May 1–October 1
(306) 726-2080 or (306) 726-2992
Indian and homesteading artifacts in 1900s setting.

St. Brieux Museum
300 Barbier Drive
St. Brieux SK S0K 3V0
May 1–August 31
(306) 275-2123
Displays of Quebecois, French and Hungarian settlers.

Strasbourg and District Museum
Main Street
Strasbourg SK S0G 4V0
Open year-round
(306) 725-3293
Homesteading and Indian artifacts.

Wadena and District Museum
South of Wadena along Highway 35
Wadena SK S0A 4J0
June 1–August 31
(306) 338-2145 or (306) 338-3454
Old 1914 homestead, railway buildings and machinery from 1900s.

Watson and District Heritage Museum
201 Main Street
Watson SK S0K 4V0
June 14–August 30
(306) 287-3263 or (306) 287-3396

Displays of early days of Watson district.

KELSEY REGION

Al Mazur Memorial Heritage Park
Junction of highways 9 N and 3 W
Hudson Bay SK S0E 0Y0
May 15–September 15
(306) 865-2180 or (306) 865-2555
Various museums on site include displays from antique tractors to 960 cups and saucers.

Dunwell and Community Museum, Living Sky
Main Street
Weekes SK S0E 1V0
Summers only
No phone
Pioneer and settlement artifacts.

Fort Pelly Livingstone Museum
1st Avenue S
Pelly SK S0A 2Z0
May 17–September 1
(306) 595-4743 or (306) 595-2056
Indian and pioneer artifacts; models of forts Pelly and Livingstone.

Hudson Bay Museum
Churchill and 4th Avenue
Hudson Bay SK S0E 0Y0
May 15–August 31
(306) 865-3116 or (306) 865-3030
Pioneer home and drugstore, toys and dolls, antique machinery.

Kamsack and District Museum
Near Centennial Park
Kamsack SK S0A 1S0
May 18–September 1
(306) 542-4415 or (306) 542-2758
Local settlement history; strong ethnic collection.

Kelliher and District Heritage Museum
Kelliher SK S0A 1V0
Summers only
No phone
Pioneer and settlement artifacts.

Melfort and District Museum
401 Melfort Street, adjacent to old schoolhouse
Melfort SK S0E 1A0
May 17–September 1
(306) 752-5086 or (306) 752-5870
Pioneer artifacts, blacksmith's shop, general store, replica log house.

National Doukhobor Heritage Village
Off Highway 5, near Verigin
Verigin SK S0A 4H0
Open year-round
(306) 542-4441 or (306) 542-4370
Eleven buildings re-create lives of early Doukhobor pioneers.

Nipawin and District Living Forestry Museum
Across from Home Ready Mix store, old Highway 35
Nipawin SK S0E 1E0
May 1–August 31
(306) 862-9299 or (306) 862-5231
Old working logging equipment, pioneer displays.

Parkland Heritage Centre
7 miles (10 km) SE of Yorkton,
Highway 16
Yorkton SK S3N 3L4
May 17–October 1
(306) 782-2657
Displays of pioneer life.

Pasquia Palaeontololgical Site
Near Pasquia Park, 3 miles (4.8
km) north of Arborfield
Arborfield SK S0E 0A0
May 1–September 30
(306) 769-8896 or (306) 769-8944
*Self-guided trail leads along
Carrot River to fossil site.*

**Porcupine Plain and District
Museum**
151 Windsor Avenue, in old hospital building
Porcupine Plain SK S0E 1H0
Open year-round
(306) 278-2317 or (306) 278-2794
*Pioneer artifacts, including lace
display.*

Prairie River Museum
CN Station
Prairie River SK S0E 1J0
May 1–October 31
(306) 889-4248 or (306) 889-4220
*Pioneer and Indian aritfacts;
logging and railway items.*

Saltcoats Museum
105 Allan Avenue
Saltcoats SK S0A 3R0
Open year-round
(306) 744-2206 or (306) 744-2977
Local history displays.

Star City Heritage Museum
5th Street and 3rd Avenue

Star City SK S0E 1P0
May 21–September 1
(306) 863-2309 or (306) 863-2231
*Pioneer machinery and tools,
telephone switchboards, radios,
gramophones.*

Sturgis Station House Museum
306 Railway Avenue SE
Sturgis SK S0A 4A0
June 1–August 31
(306) 548-5565 or (306) 548-2108
*Local history displays in 1900
CNR station.*

Tisdale and District Museum
South of town, Highway 35
Tisadale SK S0E 1T0
Summers only
No phone
*Pioneer and settlement
archives.*

Western Development Museum
Just west of Yorkton, Highway 16
Box 98
Yorkton SK S3N 2V6
Open year-round
(306) 783-8361
*Features ethnic immigration in
Saskatchewan.*

**NORTH-WEST CALLING
REGION**

**Barr Colony Heritage Cultural
Centre**
Highway 16 E and 45th Avenue
Lloydminster SK S9V 1T5
Open year-round
(306) 825-6184
*Barr Colonist displays; other
artifacts and exhibits.*

Big Bear's Trail Museum
1st Street S and Highway 26
Loon Lake SK S0M 1L0
July 1–August 31
(306) 837-2070
*Artifacts from Battle of Steele
Narrows; other Indian displays.*

Canwood Museum
3rd Avenue NE
Canwood SK S0J 0K0
May 17–September 30
(306) 468-2088 or (306) 468-2655
Town's first schoolhouse.

**Frenchman Butte Museum
Society**
In old railway station
Frenchman Butte SK S0M 0W0
May 17–September 7
(306) 344-4478 or (306) 344-4451
Blacksmith shop and log cabin.

Glaslyn and District Museum
Main Street
Glaslyn SK S0M 0Y0
July 1–September 1
(306) 230-2039 or (306) 298-4502
*Pioneer artifacts include trap-
per's shack, hospital displays.*

Imhoff Museum
5 miles (8 km) south of St.
Walburg
St. Walburg SK S0M 2T0
May 19–September 1
(306) 248-3812 or (306) 248-7536
*Restored home of Berthold von
Imhoff, painter.*

Lashburn Centennial Museum
1st Avenue W
Lashburn SK S0M 1H0
July 1–August 31

(306) 285-3860 or (306) 285-3257
*Pioneer artifacts, including
many from Barr Colonists.*

Maidstone and District Museum
Del Frari–Victoria Park
Maidstone SK S0M 1M0
May 17–September 26
(306) 893-4483 or (306) 893-2890
*Local artifacts housed in old
CNR station.*

Meadow Lake Museum
Entrance to town, Highway 4
Meadow Lake SK S0M 1V0
May 19–September 1
(306) 236-3622 or (306) 236-4447
Local history artifacts.

**St. Walburg and District
Historical Museum**
Old Church of the Assumption,
Main Street and 2nd Avenue
St. Walburg SK S0M 2J0
May 15–September 1, or call
(306) 248-3373 or (306) 248-3359
*Local history artifacts, includ-
ing Imhoff paintings, antique
clothing, magazines, photo studio.*

Turtleford Museum
Old CN station on west side of
Highway 26
Turtleford SK S0M 2Y0
June 30–September 1
(306) 845-2433
Area pioneer artifacts.

NORTHERN SHORES REGION

Buckland Heritage Museum
12 miles (19 km) north of Prince
Albert on Highway 2

Prince Albert SK
June 28–September 1
(306) 764-8470 or (306) 764-8394
   Photos, artifacts on local farm and forestry history.

Diefenbaker House
246 19th Street W
Prince Albert SK S6V 4C6
May 11–August 31
(306) 764-1394 or (306) 764-2992
   Last home of John Diefenbaker, furnished with personal belongings.

Mistasinihk Place Interpretive Centre
La Ronge Avenue
La Ronge SK S0J 1L0
Open year-round
(306) 425-4350 or (306) 425-4354
   Depicts northern lifestyles and culture.

Northern Gateway Museum
Moody Drive
Denare Beach SK S0P 0B0
July 2–August 31
(306) 362-2054
   Indian artifacts.

Prince Albert Historical Museum
River Street and Central Avenue
Prince Albert SK S6V 8A9
May 18–August 31
(306) 764-1394 or (306) 961-9682
   Displays on history of Prince Albert and area.

Rotary Museum of Police and Corrections
3700 2nd Avenue W
Prince Albert SK S6W 1A2
May 17–September 1, or call
(306) 922-3313 or (306) 953-4385
   Located in 1887 North-West Mounted Police guardroom; history of police and corrections in northern Saskatchewan.

Evolution of Education Museum
3700 2nd Avenue W
Prince Albert SK S6W 1A2
May 17–September 1
(306) 763-3506 or (306) 763-4171
   Educational artifacts 1900–40.

Bibliography

The following is a list of the volumes consulted in preparing this book. In addition to these sources, several general references were constant companions, including the *McClelland and Stewart Canadian Encyclopedia* and the *Dictionary of Canadian Biography*. *Saskatchewan History Magazine*, published by the Saskatchewan Archives Board, was also referred to repeatedly. Two major archival resources were used: the Provincial Archives of Saskatchewan at the University of Saskatchewan in Saskatoon, and the University of Saskatchewan Archives, particularly the Arthur Silver Morton collection. A large selection of brochures and pamphlets prepared by various federal, provincial and municipal agencies were also consulted.

Alias Will James. Dir. Jacques Godbout. Montreal: National Film Board, 1988.

Archer, John Hall. *Saskatchewan: A History*. Saskatoon: Western Producer Prairie Books, 1980.

Beal, Bob and Rod Macleod. *Prairie Fire: The 1885 North-West Rebellion*. Edmonton: Hurtig, 1984.

Berton, Pierre. *The Promised Land: Settling the West, 1896–1914*. Toronto: McClelland and Stewart, 1984.

Berton, Pierre. *The Last Spike: The Great Railway 1881–1885*. Toronto: McClelland and Stewart, 1971.

Bocking, D.H., ed. *Pages From the Past: Essays on Saskatchewan History*. Saskatoon: Western Producer Prairie Books, 1979.

Broadfoot, Barry. *Next-Year Country: Voices of Prairie People*. Toronto: McClelland and Stewart, 1988.

Broadfoot, Barry. *The Pioneer Years: 1895–1914*. Markham: PaperJacks, 1978.

Bryan, Liz. *The Buffalo People: Prehistoric Archaeology on the Canadian Plains*. Edmonton: University of Alberta Press, 1991.

Butala, Sharon. "The Last Horse Drive." *Western People*. Ed. Mary Gilchrist. Saskatoon: Western Producer Prairie Books, 1988 (item condensed from original 2,000-word essay).

Byers, A.R. *The Canadian Book of the Road*. Montreal: Reader's Digest Association, 1979.

Careless, J.M.H. *Canada: A Story of Challenge*. Toronto: Macmillan, 1970.

Charlebois, Peter. *Sternwheelers and Sidewheelers: The Romance of Steam-Driven Paddle Boats in Canada*. Toronto: NC Press, 1978.

Cheadle, Walter B. *Cheadle's Journal of a Trip Across Canada: 1862–1863*. Rutland, Vt.: Chartles E. Tuttle Co. Inc., 1971.

Christensen, Deana and Menno Fieguth. *Historic Saskatchewan*. Toronto: Oxford University Press, 1986.

Cruise, David and Alison Griffiths. *The Great Adventure: How the Mounties Conquered the West*. Toronto: Viking, 1996.

Dauk, Caroline. *My People*. Humboldt, Saskatchewan: Self-Published MSS, 1991.

Dempsey, Hugh. *Big Bear: The End of Freedom*. Vancouver: Douglas and MacIntyre, 1984.

Dickason, Olive P. *Canada's First Nations: A History of Founding Peoples from Earliest Times*. Toronto: McClelland and Stewart, 1992.

Douglas, T.C. and Lewis Thomas. *The Making of a Socialist: The Recollections of T.C. Douglas*. Edmonton: University of Alberta Press, 1982.

Daeger, Joseph, et. al., eds. *A Journey of Faith: St. Peter's Abbey 1921–1996*. Muenster, Saskatchewan: St. Peter's Press, 1996.

Francis, R.D. and H. Ganzevoort, eds. *The Dirty Thirties in Prairie Canada*. Vancouver: Tantalus Research Ltd., 1979.

Gorman, Jack. *Père Murray and the Hounds: The Story of Saskatchewan's Notre Dame College*. Red Deer, Alberta: Johnson Gorman Publishers, 1977.

Grant, Agnes. *No End of Grief: Indian Residential Schools in Canada*. Winnipeg: Pemmican Publications, 1996.

Gray, James H. *Booze: When Whiskey Ruled the West*. Saskatoon: Fifth House, 1995.

Gray, James H. *Men Against the Desert*. Saskatoon: Western Producer Prairie Books, 1967.

Gray, James H. *Red Lights on the Prairies*. Toronto: Macmillan, 1975.

Gruending, Dennis, ed. *The Middle of Nowhere: Rediscovering Saskatchewan*. Saskatoon: Fifth House, 1996.

Hanson, Stan. *The Estevan Strike and Riot*. Saskatoon: unpublished MA thesis, University of Saskatchewan, 1972.

Hatch, F.J. *The Aerodrome of Democracy: Canada and the British Commonwealth Air Training Plan 1939–1945*. Ottawa: Department of National Defence, 1983.

Herbert, J.D. *Guide to the Historic Sites of Saskatchewan*. Saskatoon: Saskatchewan Golden Jubilee Committee, 1955.

Humber, Charles. *Pathfinders: Canadian Tributes*. Mississauga, Ontario: Heirloom Publishers, 1994.

Jones, Laurence and George Lonn. *Pathfinders of the North*. Toronto: Pitt Publishers Co., 1970.

Lapointe, Richard and Lucille Tessier. *The Francophones of Saskatchewan: A History*. Regina: Campion College, 1988.

MacEwan, Grant. *And Mighty Women, Too: Stories of Notable Western Canadian Women*. Saskatoon: Western Producer Prairie Books, 1975.

MacEwan, Grant. *Sitting Bull: The Years in Canada*. Edmonton: Hurtig, 1973.

MacEwan, Grant. *Harvest of Bread*. Saskatoon: Western Producer Prairie Books, 1969.

MacSkimming, Roy. *Gordie: A Hockey Legend*. Vancouver: Douglas and McIntyre, 1994.

Massey, Vincent. *Great Canadians: A Century of Achievement*. Toronto: Canadian Centennial Publishing Co., 1965.

McCourt, Edward. *Saskatchewan*. Toronto: Macmillan, 1968.

McGowan, Don. *Grassland Settlers*. Victoria: Cactus Publications, 1975.

McGowan, Don. *The Green and Growing Years: Swift Current: 1907–1914*. Victoria: Cactus Publications, 1982.

McLeod, Thomas and Ian McLeod. *Tommy Douglas: The Road to Jerusalem*. Edmonton: Hurtig, 1987.

McMullen, Lorraine. *Sinclair Ross*. Boston: Twayne Publishers, 1979.

Miller, James Rodger. *Shingwauk's Vision: A History of Native Residential Schools*. Toronto: University of Toronto Press, 1996.

Mitchell, William Ormond. *Who Has Seen the Wind.* Toronto: Macmillan, 1947.

Newman, Peter C. *Caesars of the Wilderness.* Markham, Ontario: Viking, 1987.

Newman, Peter C. *Company of Adventurers.* Markham, Ontario: Viking, 1985.

Robin, Martin. *Shades of Right: Nativist and Fascist Politics in Canada: 1920–40.* Toronto: University of Toronto Press, 1992.

Ross, Morton. *Sinclair Ross and His Works.* Toronto: ECW Press Press, 1990.

Russell, E.T., ed. *What's in a Name?* Saskatoon: Western Producer Prairie Books, 1973.

Southesk, James Carnegie, Earl of. *Saskatchewan and the Rocky Mountains: A Diary and Narrative of Travel, Sport, and Adventure.* Edinburgh: Edmonston and Douglas, 1874.

Shillington, C. Howard. *Historic Land Trails of Saskatchewan.* West Vancouver: Evvard Publications, 1985.

Shipley, Nan. *Almighty Voice and the Redcoats.* Don Mills, Ontario: Burns and MacEachern, 1967.

Shury, Dave. *Wheat Province Diamonds.* unpublished MSS (no date).

Siggins, Maggie. *Revenge of the Land: A Century of Greed, Tragedy and Murder on a Saskatchewan Farm.* Toronto: McClelland and Stewart, 1991.

Siggins, Maggie. *Riel: A Life of Revolution.* Toronto: Harper Collins, 1994.

Smith, Donald. *From the Land of Shadows: The Making of Grey Owl.* Saskatoon: Western Producer Prairie Books, 1990.

Smith, Margot and Carol Pasternak. *Pioneer Women of Western Canada.* Toronto: Ontario Institute for Studies in Education, 1978.

Spry, Irene. *The Palliser Expedition: The Dramatic Story of Western Canadian Exploration: 1857–1860* Saskatoon: Fifth House, 1995.

Stegner, Wallace. *Wolf Willow.* New York: Penguin Books, 1990.

Vanderhaeghe, Guy. *The Englishman's Boy.* Toronto: McClelland and Stewart, 1996.

Van Kirk, Sylvia. *Many Tender Ties: Women in the Fur-Trade Society in Western Canada: 1670–1870.* Winnipeg: Watson and Dwyer Publications, 1980.

Waiser, W.A. *Saskatchewan's Playground: A History of Prince Albert National Park.* Saskatoon: Fifth House, 1989.

Wilson, Garrett. *Diefenbaker for the Defence.* Toronto: J. Lorimer, 1988.

Woodcock, George and Ivan Avakumovic. *The Doukhobors.* Toronto: Oxford University Press, 1968.

Wright, Richard T. *Overlanders.* Saskatoon: Western Producer Prairie Books, 1985.

Name Index

Subject Index

Calvary Baptist 109
Camp Rayner 146
Canada Temperance Act 117
Canadian Medical Association 202
Canadian Pacific Railway 141,
  217–218; arrival of, in
  Saskatchewan 86–87; grain
  monopoly and 102
Cannington Manor 120–122
Cariboo Gold Rush 208
Carlton House see Fort Carlton
cart trains 156
Catholic Settlement Society 212
cemeteries, Hirsch settlers 114;
  Maple Creek 16
Chaplin 41–42
Chesterfield House 131
Chicago Black Sox 169
Chimney Coulee 36–37
Chocolate Peak 32–33
City of Bridges see Saskatoon
Clark's Crossing 181–182, 191 see also
  river crossings
Claybank brick plant 78
Climax 37–38
Climax Cardinals 38
coal, discovery of 123–124, 285
coal miners 114
coal mining 114–116
colonization companies 149–150,
  175–176
combines, self-propelled 31
Commonwealth Air Training 73–74
Co-operative Commonwealth
  Federation 110
cooperatives 126
country wives see marriage a la
  façon du pays
Cowboys North and South (James) 57
credit unions 126
Cree, transition to farming 156–159
crested wheat grass 31
Cripple Camp 72
Cumberland House 226, 228,
  230–233
Cypress Hills Massacre 12, 17, 20–21
Deutscher Bund 264
Devil's Gulch 28
Dirty Thirties see Great Depression
Discovery well 253
Dominion Coke, Coal and
  Transportation Company 19

Dominion Experimental Farm 82
Doukhobors 225, 241–247
Drumheller 285
Duck Lake see North-West
  Rebellion
Dust Bowl 114 see also Great
  Depression
Eagle Creek 28
Eastend North-West Mounted
  Police post 35
Ellisboro Crossing 88
End of Track 86 see also Canadian
  Pacific Railway
Everitt Parsonage 181
farmers, Welsh 105–106
farming, dryland 29–31; industrial
  81
File Hills Colony 101
Fish Creek 191
forts 125, 260; Fort Alexandria 239;
  Fort aux Trembles 226; Fort
  Battleford 164–166; Fort Carlton
  23, 190, 193 see also North-West
  Rebellion; Fort Douglas 127; Fort
  Ellice 23; Fort Esperance 125; Fort
  Garry 45; Fort John 125, 127–128;
  Fort La Corne 197, 201, 228; Fort
  Livingstone 49, 72, 166, 250–251;
  Fort Pelly 225, 248, 249; Fort Pitt
  260, 266; Fort Rivière a la Biche
  237, 238; Fort St. Louis 200, 201,
  228; Fort Walsh 17–19, 49, 250
fossil beds 286
Fosterton No. 1 15–116, 254 see also
  oil, discovery of
François–Finlay dam 230
Frog Lake Massacre 261
fur trade 131–132, 170, 197, 220–221,
  225, 229–233, 236, 238, 248; routes
  55–56, 228
Gabriel's Crossing 183
gangs 68
Gardiner Dam 146, 148
gas industry 253, 254 see also oil
  industry
gentlemen hunters 207
German American Land Company
  212
Giant, Willow Bunch 64–66
gold miners 198–199
Goodwin House 27, 143
grain buyers 90–91, 102